To the water warriors of the world.

CONTENTS

ACKNOWLEDGMENTS

To travel and see what goes on with India's traditional water harvesting across the length and breadth of the country would have been impossible without help and guidance from a large number of people. I am extremely thankful to all those who took out time and spared no effort or expense to show me around their villages and towns and explain in painstaking detail how traditions had evolved, and where they were going.

The list is long, and I have given it in order I met my friends, philosophers and guides. It does not follow the order of the book

Niranjan Singh and Parshuram, Jhunjhunu in Shekhawati, Rajasthan
Karan Singh in Sawai Madhopur and Ram Bhajan Gujjar in Dausa, Rajasthan
Chaman Singh in Dausa
Brij Mohan Gujjar, Rajpur, Sawai Madhopur, Rajasthan
Sunetra Lala, Bhikampura, Rajasthan, and New Delhi; friend and guide who provided excellent inputs and encouragement right through the 3 year process
Ramesh Pahadi, his wife and daughter Ranjana in Gopeshwar, Chamoli, Uttarakhand
A Gurunathan, Dhan Foundation, Madurai, Tamil Nadu
J Elamurugu, Dhan Foundation, Madurai, Tamil Nadu
Suresh Kumar Raikwar, Tendura, Baandha, Uttar Pradesh
Bhagwan Singh Parmar, Nowgong, Chhatarpur, Madhya Pradesh
R K Rawat, Nowgong, Madhya Pradesh
Bhartendu Prakash, Tindwari, Baandha, Uttar Pradesh
A L Pathak, Dhubela, Chattarpur, Madhya Pradesh
Kumar Kalanand Mani, Peaceful Society, Cundalim, Goa
Sotter D'Souza, Panchayati Raj coordinator, Peaceful Society, Porvorim, Goa
Antonio Francisco Fernandes, Cortalim, Goa
Sushila Mendonca, Porvorim, Goa
Tilak Rai, Shillong, Meghalaya
June Lyngdoh, Jowai, Meghalaya
K D Pwawa, Jowai, Meghalaya
Suren Rai, Shillong, Meghalaya
Suresh Sharma, Shillong, Meghalaya
Samudragupta Kashyap, Guwahati, Assam
Prashant Dhar, Guwahati, Assam
Gyan Singh, Tughlakabad, New Delhi

O P Jain, INTACH, New Delhi
Rajendra Singh, Tarun Bharat Sangh, Rajasthan, who gave me the idea and
without whom I would not have been able to take the first step, nor the
last.
My wife Malvika, who stoically dealt with my long absences and visits to the
back of beyond
My son Aryaman, who also accepted the fact that his dad was half-crazy to
run off to strange places and talk only about water
My close friends who kept reminding of the importance of the book to my
life, and prodded me on.

1 PROLOGUE

It's late when my jeep pulls into Godia village, a dusty habitation about a 100 kilometres from the town of Jhunjhunu in Shekhawati. There is no electricity and the streetlights are dark – the only illumination is from cooking fires. The day's drive through hot dusty roads has left me fazed, the driver frazzled and my companions extremely thirsty. I had a bottle of water, but they had none.

We drive through the dark streets scattering dogs, chickens and pigs, and dodging cows. It seems we are hurtling through the village to some destination. A low wall appears out of the darkness in front and the driver veers left. A massive black buffalo looms out of the darkness there, and he stands on the brakes – we all grab whatever is in front to avoid going through the windscreen.

The buffalo moves, staring at the headlights truculently while chewing cud. The road opens into a wide space beyond the animal and as if on cue, the power comes on. A string of bulbs on a single wire come on lighting up the site of nocturnal construction. Hard manual labour is done from the evening late into the night because it's hot in the day and people tend to their lands in the daytime.

Three metal poles sunk in the ground form a tripod over a deep pit that a group of people – men and women – are digging at a point in the village where rainwater accumulates. The streets channel rainwater to this place and it forms a puddle that takes days to disappear, breeding mosquitoes in the process.

It's a recharge well. It will eventually be 60 metres deep, unlined at the bottom but brick-lined along the sides to prevent collapse and covered with a concrete slab. Around the top, two concentric concrete walls with holes will break the flow of water rushing into the well and stop large debris from getting into the well, and keep animals and children out. It costs Rs. 200,000 to make; the villagers are putting in 30 percent and a local NGO (non-profit organization), the rest.

This well is one manifestation of the profound link between man and water. Apart from the obvious – 80 percent of our bodies are made of water and without it we could not grow food or produce goods – water is the source of life. The quest for water is nothing short of a pilgrimage.

Over the millennia Indians evolved seemingly disparate systems to manage water. These are as varied as the country's climate and geography. They don't seem to have anything in common, on the face of it at least. But scratch below the surface – like still waters, traditions run deep. Each variety of local technology has evolved organically, been fostered locally and perfected through trial and error. "Stupid ignorant peasants" we educated city slickers call them, but their wealth of knowledge holds the promise of India's water security.

2 DESI DAWA FOR A BLUE CATASTROPHE

Water scarcity, a third world war over water – these are doing the rounds to stress just how critical India's water crisis is. For a country so well endowed with water, with the world's richest tradition of local community-level water management systems, it's strange to have come to this pass.

India gets the most rainfall per square unit of land area of any country in the world. If we walled the country and didn't let any rain escape into the sea, each year we would have water one metre deep on the ground. That's a lot of water. It's enough to comfortably meet every Indian's need for water – drinking, washing, bathing, manufacturing, farming and wasting. But we do not have that imaginary wall, and are not about to stop rivers in their tracks. So we do not have much water to play with.

It wasn't always like this. India believed in self-help, which is why we are such entrepreneurs and trend-setters abroad. At home, lethargy strikes, bringing the 'let the government do it' attitude. Amnesia strikes. The same Indians that pine for 'the good ole days' when abroad find nothing to cheer about once in their country. They forget 5,000 years of traditional water wisdom that stands behind them, which made India one of the richest countries in the world in not-to-distant past.

OK, I am not about to bemoan our long lost 'glorious' past. But I am about to make a case for respecting, learning from and incorporating our traditional knowledge, especially about water, the basic resource.

In these 6,000 kilometres of wandering, mostly by train, some by plane, and the rest by road, I've humbly learnt – that was what I set out to do without too much baggage – that our ancestors understood how to handle water, leaving the smallest ecological footprint. In simple words, they knew how to make the most of what nature provided.

We used local material, the topography, labour and money from our rulers to build an amazing variety of systems. These range from water harvesting and storage to distribution mechanisms. Every one of them evolved in situ and underwent organic modifications and improvements – more like farmers using selective breeding to improve their crops. In this, they were supported by the wealthy as well – 10 percent of profits made by businessmen and traders went towards community water works, and privatization was not on the agenda then.

Each region had a variety of mechanisms for different end-uses. It was never one-mechanism-suits-all-uses. So you had covered wells for drinking water in Rajasthan and open, deep *talaabs* for bathing, washing and watering animals, sheltered by trees from the sun to reduce evaporation. Agriculture was mostly rain-fed save for some places along rivers or where sub-soil water was easily available and could be lifted using Persian wheels or bullock-drawn systems. Social norms governed the use of water. These were not equitable, given our caste hierarchy, but still ensured that everybody had access to water. Groundwater was hard to get and scarcely exploited.

The local people – villagers and townspeople – helped to build most of these structures. It was contributory – labour from the people and money from the rich or wealthy. Cash never covered the whole cost of the work, usually accounting for between half and three-fourths of the total. This gave the locals a sense of ownership over the structures. They protected and repaired them as needed to the extent that money was not involved. If money was needed, to pour fresh mortar, for example, the headman would raise it from the ruler or other source.

This system worked fine for many centuries. Once the structure was built, its maintenance was assured. The ruler could get on with other business. It was impossible given the country's diversity and spread to attend to each and every well, tank and pond. If a structure was large, several communities shared the responsibility for its upkeep. Most structures carried edicts from the builders detailing the sharing of water and their preservation. People respected these and penalties existed for violators.

The village was the revenue unit. Its headman collected levies and gave them to the ruler. This collectiveness extended to land and natural resource ownership. While it wasn't perfect, it kept the bonds between people and their resources alive. Things changed when the British colonizers came.

They gradually changed the ownership pattern of land by the simple expedient of taxing farmers directly in villages and individuals in cities. The Crown also appropriated any resources that were not privately owned. These included water, land and forests. It was aimed to maximize the revenue from India and deprive it of natural resources. Wood was needed to feed Britain's industrial revolution, build its stupendous navy and the railway network in India – to fuel exploitation further. Water became a source of revenue – the government controlled the tanks and ponds and levied charges on farmers for using the water.

The colonial rulers initially recognized that they had to look after the water resources so they created the irrigation department. They had not bargained for the enormity of the task. A centralized, government-driven system could not satisfactorily maintain the multiplicity of water structures in India, from tanks, *tankas*, *kunds*, *baolis* and wells to canals and large dams. It needed people with various skills and in villages all over India. The department also had fixed procedures to maintain these structures that were not always in tune with how they had been built and cared for by villagers. The irrigation department engineers were corrupt and the work done by the department was almost always sub-standard; it never held up more than a year or so. The department took forever to respond to complaints with the result that structures started falling apart.

People in villages and towns also abdicated their responsibility, adopting a "government will provide" attitude – if the government owned them, it had to look after them. The system of labouring on water structures annually before the monsoons withered away. In its place came the engineers and contractors of the irrigation department.

Water resources management fell between their ineptitude and popular apathy. It took many decades for the rot to become noticeable but once it did, it became irreversible in many places. Rather than looking at the root of the problem, the government chose to look for mega-projects as solutions.

After Independence, 'our' government continued with the policies of British concerning natural resources management. The forest department has to generate revenue and does it in the only way it knows how – by auctioning trees or, in modern parlance, sustainable forest management. The irrigation department pretends to control water resources and to know how to look after them. Between them, there has been total chaos and engineers and their pet contractors have made it good. All at the expense of natural resource security in India. 'Our' government has further alienated villagers from the forests and water that kept them going since civilization began – if they enter forests for firewood, they are detained or worse. If they do not get water from the irrigation department ambitious projects, and agitate against the government, they get shot.

Instead of understanding where the causes lie, 'our' government has chosen to build 'temples of modern India' as our misguided western-oriented first prime minister chose to call dams. Dams, they said, would control floods and droughts and irrigate an 'additional' area. They ignored some facts in the headlong rush to build dams; dams do look good on the biodata of politicians and builders. J P Industries, for example, the builder of Tehri Dam, proudly claims to have built hydro-electric power projects with a total generation capacity of some 2000 mega watts (MW). I am not disputing the importance of power generation – we need power to move ahead. I am disputing the government's approach.

Tanks and wells were the main source of irrigation in India. Along with the monsoons, they allowed the country to grow food enough to feed itself. They maintained the groundwater levels. These were also the main source of water for other human needs.

There is enough evidence from around India that farmers and city folk had evolved systems to comfortably meet their requirements. The received wisdom was to build extra tanks, ponds or wells so that there was surplus water. These structures acted as flood and drought control mechanisms – when the rains were plentiful, they caught water that would otherwise flood villages or cause rivers to overflow. Water percolated into the soil and replenished the groundwater tables, nature's great reservoir, that sustained us in drought years.

The big drought in India's richest state Maharashtra is exacerbated by depleted groundwater. Last time there was a drought in 1971, people had no food to eat, but water to drink since tubewells had not proliferated; now they have neither. The state is punctured by several million tubewells that have sucked it dry of groundwater. The tragedy is, they have sucked out fossil water that take hundreds of years to replenish.

Against this, 'our' government wanted to create 'additional irrigated area' to let farmers grow more. There was little additional area to irrigate, because tanks and wells covered a large part of the country. Where there were no tanks or wells, people used other systems such as channeling streams from hills for irrigation. In fact, a major reason for the revival of tanks in recent years has been the lack of space to build new ones. Despite an expenditure of hundreds of billions of rupees over the past 20 years, the government has not added a single hectare of additional irrigated area.

What has happened was the Green Revolution. A potent mix of hybrid seeds, supposed to be higher yielding than traditional varieties, chemical fertilizers and pesticides, brought temporary prosperity and higher crop yields to parts of rural India. This was driven by a huge increase in the need for irrigation that was not met from the 'temples of modern India' but from groundwater sources. Farmers across the country discovered the magic of tubewells and an enormous industry sprang up, sinking tubewells wherever needed. Diesel was cheap, and kept that way to subsidize farmers, mainly the rich ones who could afford tubewells, pumps and diesel. Power was supplied free to these same farmers. They grew richer, those on the margins practicing sustenance agriculture, who could not afford modern agriculture on small plots of land, remained where they were or grew poorer.

With the tubewell revolution, the groundwater tables started falling. First the decline was slow, a few feet every few years and passed unnoticed. This accelerated as the population rose and the countryside industrialized. The demand was for water for agriculture and also industry. The fall in groundwater levels accelerated through the 1980s and 1990s so the extent that the Central Ground Water Board has rated the groundwater situation in a third of India as semi-critical to over-exploited; these are the mostly intensively cropped and industrialized parts. Where once groundwater available at 3-6 metres below surface, it has now dropped to several hundred feet. It is impossible to recharge such deep aquifers quickly and through simply digging more ponds. They need to be recharged through the same tubewells that were used to empty them or through deep-recharge wells. Both are expensive and slow options.

In other words, the Green Revolution, touted as the solution to India's food security, caused a Blue Catastrophe. It shook up the country's water security. It has been the single large cause of depletion of vital groundwater resources in India. Most of the people working to restore traditional water management systems in India say that India's cropping patterns, evolved over centuries, used crop varieties that were suited to the local climate and availability of water. It wasn't a one-size-fits-all approach, where water- and chemical-intensive agriculture was thrust upon the entire landscape.

The monoculture of the Green Revolution ensured that water was over-used where it was readily available, as in Punjab, causing water-logging and later, soil salinity. Where it wasn't easily available on the surface, farmers drew ground water and depleted this precious resource. From the deserts of Shekhawati to the rocky landscape of Bundelkhand, farmers blindly followed the Green Revolution. In the process, indigenous crop varieties disappeared, as did the ties that bound people to their natural resources.

The government became the sole provider of everything – water, chemical fertilizers and pesticides, seeds and advice on when to sow. Farmers who had accumulated this knowledge over millennia were reduced to passive recipients. Everything they knew or did was irrelevant. They were 'ignorant, illiterate peasants'.

But were they, really. At the village level, each region had evolved its systems to capture and manage water, the basic resource. Each monsoon, the villagers saw how the water flowed and where it accumulated. They either approached the local ruler or land owners (*zamindar*) to build a tank at that site, or built it themselves. If the spot was on village commons, it was fine. Otherwise, another spot was chosen so as not to deprive anyone of his land. The tank was designed to minimize flooding and submergence. Sometimes, they took amoebic shapes that no self-respecting engineer would allow. But this irregularity was deliberate, to maximize water storage while minimizing the loss of private or even common land.

Villagers could predict how much it would rain, and when. They had their own way to measure how much rain had fallen – no fancy rain gauges but household things like grinding stones. When the central hole was full, it was time to sow.

They appointed people to manage the water. These people, usually men from the lowest caste, were given the responsibility and authority to maintain the village tanks. They had to ensure the tanks and the approach channels were cleaned before the rains, the bunds were strengthened and the sluice gates were operational. During the rains, they had to patrol the bunds to check for weakness and possible breaches that would flood the village. After the rains, they had to release water to the fields so everybody could grow crops. They also had to ensure that people did not pollute the water by shitting or pissing on the bunds.

In return, these water keepers got a share of village produce. Their word was final in disputes over water. They were sought after as interlocutors in village disputes. These water keepers knew when it would rain, how much water each field needed and how much farming would be possible. They were illiterate, the skills they had were not learnt in any concrete classroom but through years of observing the rhythm of nature. They tuned in, and belted out the natural rhythm of life.

Why from the lowest caste? They had no land to till and no interest in inter-caste fights. Being below all this made them ideal interlocutors for water management. A fascinating example of how Indian society picked the weakest to manage the most vital part of its economy.

Where rulers built large water ponds and tanks, they laid down the rules to look after the tank and share water. The rulers never assumed to maintain the tanks and ponds, knowing it would be impossible to keep track of every structure they had built. They handed over maintenance to the *zamindar* or the village headman. Along with the charge, the ruler gave a gift of land, the revenue from which paid for the maintenance. The land and the water paid for themselves. Villagers contributed labour when repairs were needed. This was a self-contained maintenance unit that ran fairly well, save where a rapacious *zamindar* decided to appropriate common property for himself. This happened in many cases in Bundelkhand, for example.

Rather than map its strategy for increasing the irrigated area in India onto established social structures, the government decided to further colonial designs of centralized control. These had already failed to keep India's traditional water management systems going as they were aimed at extracting revenue, not perpetuating tradition. When these repeatedly failed, and floods and droughts became worse with every passing decade, the Indian government upped the ante.

The National Water Policy of 2002 set down a stupidly ambitious plan to link every major river in India together. The Inter Linking of Rivers (ILR) project, touted as the largest of its kind in the world, is an amalgam of old canal projects dating from the 1960s, and some new schemes. Where needed, water will be pumped up from a lower level to a higher one in order to achieve this end. In the process, the government will spend billions of dollars, submerge hundreds of thousands of acres of land and displace millions of people. Most of the submergence will happen in India's meagre forest areas. Most of the displaced will be poor or tribal people, already marginalized by our planners. The 2013 Water Policy continues this stupidity, compounded by orders from the Supreme Court to the government to act. Somewhere the government also recognizes the impossibility of the project and has dragged its feet for decades, hopefully forever.

This mega folly will supposedly generate a few hundred thousand hectares of more 'additional' irrigated area. It will be the final solution to India's droughts and floods by transferring 'surplus' water from one river to another through canals. And it will generate a few thousand megawatts of electricity. But it is unnecessary and wasteful.

The analysis of a few of the detailed project reports of the ILR shows that they have been hastily cobbled together. There has been no attempt to gather empirical data needed for a project of this magnitude. A lot of the data is based on much older reports that have been simply rehashed to present a rosy picture. For example, the link between the Ken and Betwa rivers in Bundelkhand proposes a canal to transfer 'surplus' water from the Ken to the Betwa. All the population and submergence figures are based on data from 1994-95, nearly two decades old, as are the costs. The project's proponents have simply not bothered to get up-to-date data and have assumed that the project becomes viable in the absence of this information. This is the case with most of the individual ILR projects.

It isn't just the data but the fundamentals that are also flawed. The canal will link two rivers flowing through the same agro-eco-climatic region. When one river is in spate, so is the other. When it rains in the catchment of one, it does in the other's as well. The canal will only aggravate problems of droughts and floods, not solve them.

This book captures a small sampling of India's traditional water management systems. It brings out the genius of our people in using local material, climate and techniques to build something that has endured so well for so long. I have written it like a travelogue with bits of history and legends thrown in to make the narrative interesting. I hope it will generate some small amount of debate over what is appropriate, and what is not, in India's quest for water and food security. It was in the works for a while because it took a while for me to cover 6,000 kilometres and visit around 300 villages, from Uttarakhand to Madurai and from Goa to Meghalaya. But I'm happy to say I managed it in a year and what I saw makes for happy reading, and sad.

3 FORGOTTEN HISTORY LESSONS: DELHI'S MISSED DATE WITH WATER

India's capital is one of the oldest cities of India, indeed of the world, if you believe mythology. It began as Indraprastha probably around 5,000 BC, grew through seven other cities into New Delhi. Among the metros, Delhi is certainly the only one old enough to have a tradition of water conservation and management that developed indigenously and wasn't imposed by the British.

Delhi lies at the tail-end of the Aravalli hills, where they merge with the Indo-Gangetic Plains. The Aravallis taper down from the southern to the northern end of Delhi, forming one watershed. Along the southern side, they run east-west forming another watershed. All the drains and seasonal streams flow north and east in Delhi, some making it to the river Yamuna, others terminating in depressions to form lakes and ponds. These artificial ponds helped recharge wells, that were the only source of water in the rocky Aravalli region, and the *baolis* that also tap into groundwater flows, in the rest of the city. The rocky Aravallis were ideal for bunding (low walls to hold water) and making more such depressions to store water that was used either by people or recharged the aquifers. In south Delhi and a little beyond, there are many artificial lakes and ponds created centuries ago for just this purpose. The western part of Delhi falls in the Najafgarh drain's watershed, which was originally the Sahibi River that rose in the Sirmaur Hills in Haryana.

The city first came up on the banks of the river Yamuna, once a holy river but now little better than a drain outside the monsoon months, that flows north-south along the city's eastern side – actually a quarter of the city is now in trans-Yamuna areas. The first city of Delhi probably existed between the ancient Aravalli hills, north India's oldest range of hills, and the river, in a sort of natural trough. Later rulers shifted the scene of action

10

south to the Aravallis, while the Mughals and British brought it back to the river. The river flows to the east and the Aravallis formed the western and southern borders of Delhi. Things have changed since 1947 when hundreds of thousands of people, displaced from Pakistan, made Delhi their second home. The city expanded rapidly over the Aravallis to the west and in the far south.

For over three decades after Independence, the city grew at a moderate pace. There appeared to be a modicum of planning and development of infrastructure that accommodated Delhi's slowly expanding population. Water shortages had surfaced in resettlement colonies like Chittaranjan Park and its surroundings but the abundance of groundwater, at just a few feet below the surface, helped tide over summer shortages. There were no farmhouses, only farms. Mehrauli near the Qutab still had its famed mango orchards and Gurgaon was just another halt en route Jaipur. Patel Nagar and Karol Bagh defined west Delhi and most industrial activity was across the river in Ghaziabad, or in Faridabad or along Rohtak road.

Then the Asiad came in 1982. An unprecedented Rs. 1,000 million was poured into developing new parts of the city. Houses sprang up in the south, far west, north and east – in the east particularly, multi-storeyed apartments sprouted, while farmlands disappeared under the 90-odd 'vihars'.

All these areas needed water and power and the manageable shortages exacerbated. Farms became farm houses with vast lawns and swimming pools. Borewells replaced wells, and quickly dried them up. Green areas and water bodies were cleared for settlement in the Delhi Development (sorry, Destruction) Authority's headlong rush to create housing.

By the turn of the century, Delhiites living outside the pampered New Delhi Municipal Corporation and Cantonment areas didn't know what assured water and power supply meant. Come summer and water pumps connected directly to the mains – strictly illegal, but permitted by the Delhi Jal Board after greasing the palms of engineers – ensured a steady trickle of water to their owners; those without these devices got nothing. Soon even those with online pumps got nothing because there was no water to be had. Officially, Delhi gets 75 percent of the water it needs. This does not account for the lack of piped water to slums and several 'authorised unauthorized colonies' (an euphuism for a bunch of people living on land they have forcibly occupied); it you take these into account, the shortfall will be much more.

The situation is all set to get worse. The Commonwealth Games has become another occasion for politicians, bureaucrats and builders to convert parts of what little green and blue cover it left into housing and sports facilities. They are especially keen to build on the Yamuna River's floodplain that feeds aquifers on which most of east Delhi depends. But being the capital city has its advantages – the Central and state governments bend over backwards to ensure water and power supply to its pampered citizenry. The Tehri dam, completed at enormous financial, social and environmental cost about 250 kilometres away in the Himalayas, is the latest in a series of projects to bring more water and electricity to Delhi.

Delhi wasn't always short of water – power was unknown in the past. All its rulers ensured that Delhi had enough water from the Yamuna, canals, wells and *baolis*. Delhi was the capital of north India for long periods in its history. Archeological evidence dates the city from 300 BC, the Maurya period, when a city existed under the Old Fort on the banks of the Yamuna. In 736 AD, the Tomar Rajputs founded their city of Delhi in Lal Kot, near Mehrauli on the Aravallis, and began a long tradition of harvesting and managing water for their needs. The Rajput bits of Lal Kot are all but gone save for a rubble dam across one of the gullies nearby. This is probably one of the rulers' irrigation schemes.

I drive off the Mehrauli-Mahipalpur road a little to the south and the curving road takes me to Lal Kot. It's more famous now for Sultan Ghari's tomb. Lal Kot was a sprawling city 1300 years ago but only the tomb and some ruins survive today. The octagonal tomb itself is a fine example of early Islamic architecture; the grave is in an underground chamber and there are verandahs on the surrounding plinth. The entrance, from the east, is richly covered with Quranic verses. To the south is a large well, about 10 metres across and 30 metres deep. I peer in – it is bone dry. It has been restored and covered to keep people from tumbling in. The ground water here is at least 30 metres below ground and the reasons aren't far to seek. I shall return to this later.

The Tomars' most famous contribution is Suraj Kund. It's across the southern border of Delhi in Haryana. The ancient complex of Suraj Kund, or the Pond of the Sun, was made in the 11th century by one of the Tomar Rajput Kings, Suraj Pal. Suraj Kund may be one of the earliest water harvesting structures in the Delhi region. Literally translating as Pond of the Sun, it has semi-circular stepped embankments made of large stones that impound rainwater flowing downhill. Legend has it that there was a temple to the Sun on the western side. The construction of Suraj Kund reminds me of other kunds made by the Bundela and Chandela Rajputs in Bundelkhand, a few hundred kilometres further south. Those tanks are of similar vintage and also have stepped embankments leading down to the water. At intervals there are stone arms reaching out, probably the remains of platforms for people to get to water from the kund. Strange that warring Rajput tribes thought alike when it came to water.

It's a pretty drive to Suraj Kund through a narrow winding road past a shooting range and the Jasola wildlife sanctuary. The complex is perpetually crowded with day-trippers. The lawns are clean enough because of the dustbins but the *kund* area isn't so lucky. I even see a mother holding her child over the miserable little puddle of water in the kund to pee. I give her a stare, which is lost on her, and turn away. The southern side of the kund is shaded by *keekar* (prosopis juliflora) so I sit there and watch the massive red ants go about their business.

To the north and east, Haryana Tourism has built a sprawling tourist complex – actually, its three complexes rolled into one. Between them, they have completely blocked water flow into the kund – whatever little water it has at the bottom is rainwater that's fallen directly into it. From 15 years ago, when I last visited it, the water level has dropped at least 6 metres, to the lowest possible level. Nearly all the steps in the kund are visible, like ribs on a malnourished human.

A short walk from the kund is the Peacock Lake, a medium sized water body formed in a natural depression in the Aravalli hills. A little gate regulates the outflow of water. I drive up the path, that was just a walking track earlier, and stop at what used to be boat jetty. There are a few hawkers lying on the low wall running along the depression. Because it's just a depression now – the water has dried up completely. I am stunned because many years ago, there was a lake that stretched away to the south and west on which people boated. It used to be full and quite an awesome site and in summer, sitting by its side, one could quite forget the 40°C plus temperatures.

"When did this dry up?" I ask one of the men sprawled on the wall.

"Last summer," he replies.

A lake that size could not have disappeared in a year. Why it's disappeared isn't hard to understand. It was shallow – around 6 metres deep at most. A spanking new Hill View hotel across the road from the Haryana Tourism complex, flats on the surrounding hills and widening the Suraj Kund – Faridabad road have combined to lower the water table and reduce water flows to the lake. The small drain that used to transport water from a depression to the north has also been blocked at places to accommodate the annual Suraj Kund Crafts Mela and the depression has turned into a giant parking lot.

Between the land sharks and Haryana Tourism, strike one water body.

I drive still further south along the rocky Aravallis. The road is wide and relatively empty till it meets another coming from Gurgaon. Then trucks takes over, carrying stone and rubble, mined illegally, for construction. In the early 1990s, the Supreme Court banned quarrying in these parts but work goes on, far from the main roads hidden by the hills. The road used to be deserted save for a few huts, but it's a highway now, a by-pass for people traveling from Delhi to Haryana. Then come the eye-sores.

There is a series of huge residential schools with fancy names and a massive temple painted in garish colours, with a traffic jam around it. The

Haryana Urban Destruction Authority has carved plots out of the hills. Land sharks have gone a step further and have made entire housing colonies here. All this is supposed to be forest land and these developments have happened without formal notifications for change in land use. Construction continues and the further I go from Suraj Kund, the more apartments I see. The Supreme Court did intervene in 2004 to stop the construction but evidently money talks louder than court orders. The Aravallis here were a watershed for south Delhi and the town of Faridabad but soon there will be neither shed nor water. There is already evidence of this, with the dry Suraj Kund Lake behind me.

I reach another lake called Badhkal, formed by the Anangpur dam that is actually a short distance as the crow flies from Suraj Kund, but a 20 kilometres drive. This was made by Anangpal, also of the Tomar dynasty, who also made Lal Kot, by building a dam between two hills; the other three sides of the lake have low hills. It is a massive lake, a favourite of bird watchers and Delhiites wanting a quick getaway. The Haryana Tourism Development Corporation has a restaurant and a hotel, sewage from which flows untreated into the lake. Badhkal's waters were used for irrigation and they recharged the aquifers in this extremely over-irrigated part of Haryana. Markings on the stone-faced dam indicate the water levels and there is a large sluice gate in the centre of the dam. The Tomars were big water harvesters, like their Rajput counterparts in Central India.

Badhkal Lake is also dry save for a puddle in the middle. Its bed is overgrown with *keekar* and grass. A woman washes her clothes in the puddle. The boats that used to take visitors around at Rs. 150 an hour lie abandoned, rotting on the side where the jetty used to be. On my last visit, in 2003, the lake was full. It's taken some effort empty this vast manmade lake, but Haryana's land sharks have succeeded here as well. The mind-numbing development of housing around the lake fed by groundwater has sucked the lake dry through lowering the water tables. Quarrying in the lake's catchment area has also impeded the flow of rain water, aiding its demise. And to cap it all, there is a water bottling plant right outside the Haryana Tourism complex that has been built up around the lake. Far be it for Haryana Tourism to protect the golden goose. A waiter in the restaurant informs me the lake dried up in the last one year because of quarrying and low rainfall but the trees on the lake bed could not have come up in year – this is several years' concerted effort.

I am struck by the sorry state of the Tomar's legacy, compared to what is left of their contemporary rulers' architecture in Bundelkhand. There are hardly any palaces, *talaabs* or *kunds* that have survived the 1300 years since they ruled here. It's also amazing that the descendants of those who built water conservation structures are hell-bent on doing everything they can to destroy them. Truly, as the Sufi saint said, only donkeys and Gujars will inhabit Delhi.

I take a leap forward in time, and northwards in space, to the village of Mehrauli. I drive the still-picturesque route back to Tughlakabad and then west along the Mehrauli-Badarpur road. You could call this the Tomar-Sultanate road as well – it connects the capital of the Tomars with those of the Sultanate dynasties. The road terminates at Mehrauli though, through a slight diversion, you get to Lal Kot.

Mehrauli is probably one of Delhi's oldest and best-known living villages – a misnomer really, it's now been swallowed up by the city and there is no farming anymore – is better known for the Qutab Minar than for water conservation. It's located on the southern Ridge, the tail-end of the Aravalli hills and has *hauzs* (large artificial ponds) and *baolis* (step wells) that form an ancient and intricate network of monuments around the village. *Hauzs* were the peculiar urban water structure that Muslims introduced when they entered India.

Mehrauli was famous for its mango orchards, where the Mughals spent many a languorous afternoon, as recently as 30 years ago, but they have gone the way of Suraj Kund, thanks to the Delhi Destruction Authority's decision to make the housing colony of Vasant Kunj nearby. A few trees in the erstwhile orchards still cling on but they are also disappearing under plant nurseries.

Hauz-i-Shamsi is the largest and oldest surviving tank in Mehrauli. It was built by Sultan Shamsuddin Iltutmish in 1230, one of the Slave Dynasty who ruled Delhi, and is named after him. It is said the Prophet came to Iltutmish in a dream and pointed out the spot where the *Hauz* of his dreams would be built – in the morning, the king saw the hoof-prints of a horse there and built the *Hauz* around it. He made a large platform in the centre of the *Hauz* where the hoof-print was and this could only be reached by boats. It was probably much larger than it is now because the platform is now accessible by a ramp from the western side. Iltutmish incidentally also completed the Qutab Minar, standing about 2 kilometres to the north-east.

The *Hauz* now covers about 2.3 hectares and is roughly rectangular in shape. Like the *talaabs* of Rajasthan, from where its builders seem to have drawn inspiration, it has stone-faced sloping walls that disappear into very murky, mucky, smelly green water. On the western side, the platform with a *chhatri* (carved stone canopy) extends into the waters and even on a hot day, the breeze from the *Hauz* acts as a natural air-conditioner. Its catchment, to the north, west and south, is almost completely encroached by locals with their houses. A road runs along the west, blocking water flow. To the south is a sewer that diverts sewage from the *Hauz*; presumably before it was built, the sewage comprised a fair percentage of the *hauz*'s 'holi waters'. The sewer stinks, as expected and the blood of slaughtered animals decorates its covers. To the north, houses barely 15 metres from the *hauz*'s wall discharge their filth into it through a little hole in the wall.

To the south is a small ground, presumably used for fairs and weekend markets. The local strongman – or thug, if you like – has built his palatial house next to this on land he has grabbed. This effectively blocks drainage and along with the sewer, prevents any clean water flowing into the *Hauz*.

The *Hauz* is quite full of water despite the locals' best attempts even though the water is filthy. It is all rainwater that falls into the *Hauz*, as natural flows into it are blocked. Standing on the platform, I see three men on the far side bathing in the water with apparent relish. It does not matter to them that the water reeks and is a bilious green; that the entire stretch along the walls on all sides is full of discarded bottles, chappals, plastic bags of household garbage; that from the far side, sewage trickles into the *Hauz*. But then, I ponder, such is faith that maketh pure the impure.

The Indian National Trust for Art and Cultural Heritage (INTACH) has restored the *Hauz* – I wonder what condition is it was in before. It has built a wall with a steel grill atop it to prevent people from using the *Hauz* as an open air toilet and garbage bin. It has worked to an extent though I can see water hyacinth creeping across the *Hauz* from the north. In a few weeks, it will have taken over the water completely. At the entrance to the platform, where people can access the *Hauz*, it is a rubbish dump. The locals have no respect for their natural resources, far less their history. It's also to do with the land mafia that seems to run India's cities – they encourage and participate in this desecration so that water bodies can be polluted, filled with garbage and ultimately, grabbed for building hotels, flats, restaurants, or whatever brings them money.

Our medieval rulers, who some of us now despise as 'conquering and plundering Muslims', felt more for the land and its people than those who jingoists who call who themselves sons of the soil. The 'invading Muslims' did more for water conservation and distribution than most local people of Delhi have done since. The Rajputs who ruled before the Muslim conquest realized the importance of water security and made an elaborate system of bunds across the gullies and ditches that criss-cross the Aravallis to provide water in this otherwise rocky landscape.

I walk around the *Hauz* along the road that runs to its west. At one point, there is a large parking area for trucks that extends into the *Hauz*. Another encroachment, this time by the owner of the transport company, whose office and godown abut the *Hauz* disguised as a temple. The road turns left, I turn right and enter a smelly swamp north of the *Hauz* that lies between the houses and the it's wall. My destination is the Jahaz Mahal to the north-east, somewhat tumbledown but still a testimonial to its splendid past. Sewage flows across the swampy ground and enters the *Hauz* through a gap in the wall where residents, full of concern for their environment, have removed a stone to let their filth into the sacred waters.

Jahaz Mahal does not show any signs of its colourful past, save for the handful of blue tiles set in the domes. It was probably a pleasure palace made by the Lodhis shortly after the *Hauz* was built when the place was greener and the water from the *Hauz* flowed past the Mahal into the forests to the east. The *chhatris* (ornate small domes) atop Jahaz Mahal still sport a few of the original blue-green glazed tiles, again reminiscent of its past. Most have fallen off during the centuries. It has a large central hall, with its roof now gone, surrounded by smaller rooms with *jharokas*, covered extended windows where you can sit and look out, sometimes with a stone lattice screen. The building was surrounded by a moat that is now dry. The *jharokas*, also all gone, extended over the moat. Presumably, it was shaped like a ship, once, with the moat giving the impression of a building floating on water.

The caretaker is an old Malyali, George. His mundu has been replaced by trousers, but the white shirt is in place. Sitting on a piece of cloth on the ground floor, he muses with his flask.

"Namaskar sir."

"Can I walk upstairs?" I ask. There are remains of a staircase behind him but they have broken from shoulder height down.

"Munni," George calls to a girl in a lime green frock, flitting in and out of the arches of the rooms flanking the main hall. She reminds me of the child guide for Jennifer Lopez in Tomb Raider II who flitted in and out of the ruined temple in Cambodia. "Show him the way to the roof."

Munni appears in an archway with the sun on her face. She darts in and reappears in another one, two arches down, dodging the sun. She is barefoot.

"Come," she says, and patters across the floor of a room to a narrow opening in the wall. It's barely two feet side, just wide enough for me to go through. Munni darts through and disappears to the left. I peer in and see typical high stone stairs leading to the roof. The staircase is also narrow. It turns at 90 degrees to the left and I emerge on the roof – no railings or parapets up here.

Munni escapes from the blazing sun under the largest *chhatri* that has little recesses, where the supporting pillars join it, for placing lamps. In each recess is a blue-painted tile. There are four other, smaller domes. This chhatris is directly the main entrance to the haveli and looks imposing from the street below.

There is a breath-taking view of the *Hauz* from up here. Before my greedy countrymen grabbed chunks of land beyond, to the west, to make their ugly mansions, forests or orchards would have extended to the *hauz's* margins on all sides, save this. The breeze coming off the *Hauz* is cool and strong, even in the late morning heat. It is tranquil, despite of the busy bazaar next door.

Munni has disappeared, presumably to flit in and out of arches. George appears and picks pieces of garbage from the corner of the roof, dumping them into the dry moat three floors below. Three men sit on the *hauz*'s wall under a tree below, talking about their masculine exploits.

I leave their scintillating conversation behind and go down the stairs. There is a large open space in front of the haveli, with a tumbledown mosque in a corner. An ugly fountain, with whitewashed steps, sits behind the mosque. The local Waqf board that owns all this land, decided to create a small park on the eastern side of the *Hauz* that encroaches on yet another part of the *Hauz*. It's pretty but further reduces the size of the *Hauz*. These grounds are from where the annual Phoolwalon Ki Sair ends in Mehrauli.

Phoolwalon Ki Sair is a deliciously colourful festival celebrated at the end of the monsoons at the shrine of the Sufi saint Khwaja Bakhtiyar Kaki, also known as Qutab Sahib. It begins from the Jog Maya temple in Mehrauli and goes through the village bazaars to the saint's shrine, that's across the road from the Jahaz Mahal. The only benefit for Hauz-i-Shamsi is an annual desultory cleanup.

Mumtaz Mahal, the wife of the Mughal ruler Bahadur Shah Zafar, started the festival in the 19th century and its story goes like this. The British chose Bahadur to succeed Akbar Shah II but Mumtaz made him change his mind, and put her son Mirza Jahangir on Delhi's throne. The British didn't agree and after an altercation, exiled Mirza to Allahabad. Mumtaz took a vow that if the boy was allowed to return to Delhi, she would offer a four-poster bed of flowers at Kaki's shrine. The British finally allowed the boy to return to Delhi on promise of good behaviour and his mother carried out her promise. Mirza didn't reform though, and was eventually sent back to die an alcoholic in Allahabad, but the festival continues to this day.

Across the road to the east of Jahaz Mahal is Jharna, literally meaning waterfall. It is a pretty little garden set in a rectangular area of about 1200 square metres. It was originally built by Iltutmish in the same year as the *Hauz*, proclaims a board by the Municipal Corporation of Delhi. Later rulers restored it, as did the MCD in 1988. Water from Shams-i-*Hauz* flowed through an underground channel into one end of this garden, cascaded down its side into a small covered area and flowed through shallow channels to cool the place. In the centre is a domed platform with a water channel running beneath, to keep it cool. From here, the water flowed to the end of Jharna and into the forests of Mehrauli.

Now, the only cascades in the garden in Jharna are of sewage and garbage. The sewer that skirts Hauz-i-Shamsi gurgles past the walls. No water cascades down the ancient waterfall set in the side of Jharna. To the south is a small slum of Bangladeshis. Plastic jerry cans to collect water from taps or tankers stand on a mud embankment next to the sewer. A small child plays on the embankment; the sewer is fast and deep enough to sweep him away. Inside Jharna, all the water receptacles and channels are full of garbage and shit, presumably from the Bangladeshis. The locals have certainly found use for the remains of our past. I shake my head in disgust and, suppressing the urge to spit, leave.

Goats are now the only occupants of an area where once the Mughal royalty chilled out in late summer. After the Sair, the king and nobility would retire here before moving to the nearby mango orchards, that Mehrauli was famous for. Standing there, I can picture Delhi's nobility gorging on mangoes in the summer heat, cooling their heels in the water channels. To the north of Jharna is Khwaja Bakhtiyar Kaki's tomb. A couple of children scurry about in the heat – all else is still.

The sojourn, if I can call it that, in Jharna has cooled me off. It was much needed after the walk around the *Hauz* in the heat. I ascend to the chaos of Mehrauli's main bazaar, immortalized in Lakdi Ki Kaathi, the song from the film Masoom. I remember coming here many years ago for a picnic, but in those memories, Jharna didn't have goats, garbage, goo or even Bangladeshis. It was reasonably pristine; a quarter century and a lifetime since, it is in a sorry state.

Water from Hauz-i-Shamsi flowed into Jharna and thence into a natural drain that carried it east to the Satpula dam about 4 kilometres away. There, impounded, it provides water to settlements and further, fed the lake outside Tughlakabad. This was one water system of ancient Delhi spanning a few centuries of early Muslim rule.

Manohar Singh runs a tiny street side shop selling hand-made garden tools. He looks younger than his 60 years; Manohar has been born and brought up in Mehrauli. He has seen it being swallowed by the city and change from a village to a multi-storeyed labyrinth.

"People didn't even own cycles when I was a boy. We had to reach Delhi on foot, a full day's journey or depend on the odd bus. There was a single narrow road and no traffic lights. We had to travel through forests and only in groups, during the day," he says.

And now, Mehrauli is on a main road to Gurgaon. What was a day-long journey now takes 30 minutes. The drive to Gurgaon is as fast.

"Land was 25 paise a square metre, and there were no takers," he continues. "It's priceless now. Where do you think you will find any *hauz*? Here? Only one survives, the rest have been swallowed up by the rich and powerful to make houses and malls. There were dozens of *hauz* here once, but now they are all gone."

Sure enough, like elsewhere in India, where cities have decimated their own water resources, localities have been named after the *talaab*, *baoli* or other water source that once existed there. Strange, human beings who cannot do without water for more than a few days find it hard to keep their sticky hands off the few sources of fresh water in India.

Hauz-i-Shamsi also drives home the interconnectedness of religion and water. Hindus, Muslims, Sikhs and Christians accord this simple liquid a holy place. No temple or mosque is complete without a water source. All gurudwaras have a *talaab*. All churches have at least one small receptacle of water for baptisms. Making a well was one of the most righteous things for Hindus and a shortcut to Nirvana; no temple was complete without an accompanying source of water and conversely, no large source of water exists in India without temples.

Kaki's shrine is a stone's throw from the *Hauz*. Water was needed for the faithful to cleanse themselves ere they appeared before the almighty. It was needed for weary pilgrims to refresh themselves. But increasingly, the connection is being lost and the reason is not far to seek – land grabbers along with our politicians and bureaucrats find water tanks easy to fill and convert into apartments, making a quick buck for all concerned.

Curiously enough the Qutab complex nearby does not have a water source, save for a single small well. It was once a thriving centre of learning and religion. There is a tank built by the irrigation department at the highest point in the complex – this is now a garbage dump. The well seems too small a source for the large number of people who must have lived there. But nearby, in Mehrauli, there were many other sources of water, now fallen into disuse. There is Gandhak Ki Baoli, or sulphur springs also built by Iltutmish, the Dargah Qutab Sahib Tank and Rajon Ki Bain made a few centuries later by Sikandar Lodhi. The whole area was enclosed by Qila Rai Pithora made earlier by Prithviraj Chauhan.

The Tughlakabad fort is some 8 kilometres east of Mehrauli, the next large settlement of ancient Delhi. I remember the imposing fort as an exotic picnic destination from decades ago. The Mehrauli-Badarpur road was a tenuous link and the remains of a vast lake lay to the south of the fort. It still remains as awe-inspiring as ever but the road has trebled in size and our defence forces, ever watchful of the country's culture and heritage, have built multi-storeyed flats opposite the fort. The ugly blue and yellow matchboxes – that's what they resemble from the fort's walls – stick out like sore, well, matchboxes, against the green of the surrounding countryside.

My car is the only one in the parking lot even though it's a holiday. There is another bike and the sundry staff you see loitering around all our monuments, in the name of taking care of them. The ticket is a pittance, Rs. 5, and the camera is free. The disinterested ticket guy, a tall, poncho-ed balding man with a pinched and long suffering expression, hands over two tiny blue tickets. Another short, extremely dark character materializes behind me.

"Is there a guide?" asks Malvika, my wife.

Mr. Disinterested nods at the dark character. "You can use him."

Mr. Dark isn't really a guide – Tughlakabad is poor pickings for any guide, what with a near total lack of tourists. This man, Gyan Singh, is a caretaker of sorts and has been posted by the Archeological Survey of India at Tughlakabad for the past decade. We settle for Rs. 50 as his fee and follow him up the fort's entry ramp. The doorway looms above us and voices pour forth.

It's a busy day here, with village men and women squatting and talking in the shade of the doorway. They give us the once-over as we pass, and I can almost hear their thoughts – no, these aren't lovers in search of a quiet getaway. Beyond the doorway, the fort suddenly opens up. Paths lead off left and right inside the walls while straight ahead is a large open area from where stones were extracted to make the fortress.

Gyan takes us up a flight of steep steps to what he calls the city area, where the rich lived. A girl and boy quickly separate from their embrace and the boy presses his mobile phone to his ear. Gyan Singh glares at them but they are oblivious. He pauses next to a large long stone lying on the ground.

"This was the top post of the city gate. To the right and left were guard rooms."

The one on the right still stands and is a toilet; the one on the left has collapsed. This section of the city was guarded, evident from the remains of the high walls with slits for archers to shoot from. Beyond, there are ruins of many houses, big and small, for the city's nobility.

"This is the VIP area. It was separated from the military part of the fort and the commoner's area by a wall. See the underground market," says Gyan, pausing in front of a tunnel. From beyond him emanates the stink of bat shit and the sounds of their conversation. We enter the tunnel – there are rooms on both sides which were shops, and openings in the roof to let in light and air. At intervals, there are large recesses in the walls were where candles and lanterns were kept.

We emerge at the far end, about 50 metres down and walk through an opening in the outer wall onto a ledge.

"Why did they build the fort here, where there is no water?" I ask.

"There was water. The entire area in front was a huge lake," says Gyan waving his arms. "It stretched from the wall to those hills and was as long as the fortress. This was the end of the road for water from Hauz-i-Shamsi in Mehrauli. Water was not a problem here at all. Then there are the lakes at Suraj Kund and Badhkal and the Yamuna."

Now there is no lake, just blue-and-white flats and some scrubland, playgrounds for the local village kids. The lake would have been huge indeed, about a kilometer across and a few in width but fairly shallow. It would have held enough water to keep groundwater levels high enough for wells or *baolis* inside the fort to have fresh water.

"There are seven *baolis* inside the fort for water. These were deep enough to be fed by underground water, whose level the lake maintained," says Gyan Singh. "This is a tunnel that connected this fort to the Adilabad fort." This outside a dark passage that leads into the fort's bowels.

We climb a tall square structure, the remains of an administrative palace in the centre of Tughlakabad's VIP area. I am horrified to see an entire housing colony in the middle of the fort. There are hundreds of multi-storeyed houses that belong to the city's new, elected rulers. Ramvir Bidhuri, Shish Pal and other local strongmen have happily encroached on a substantial part of the fort. Thereby hangs a tale.

Ghiyasud Din Tughlak, the fort's builder, on his rounds one day, saw a group of labourers sleeping on the job. He roused them saying, "Don't I pay you fare wages. Why are goofing off on the job?"

A man answered, "We work for you in the day and for Sheikh Nizamuddin at night."

Not wanting to anger a holy man by confronting him directly, Ghiyas-ud Din banned the sale of oil to that settlement so that no work could be done at night. Undaunted, Nizamuddin told his labourers to use the water of the *baoli* at Nizamuddin, and he blessed it so that it turned to oil. Sheikh Nizamuddin cursed the fort, saying henceforth only donkeys and Gujars will live there. He also prophesied that Ghiyas-ud Din, away on a military campaign, would never rule from there. Ghiyas-ud Din didn't – he died short of Tughlakabad while returning. His successors built Adilabad across the Mehrauli-Badarpur road. The owners of houses that now encroach inside the fort are supposed to have descended from the original inhabitants of the fort. They are mostly Gujars – Nizamuddin's prophecy has come true. Gujars are cowherds of yore but now have neither cows nor land; they have grown rich selling the land on which they grazed their cows to the Delhi Destruction Authority; the irony is they did not have formal title to the land they sold.

"Where are the *baolis*?" I ask Gyan.

He points to the west of the mound we are standing on. A high wall rises next to the *baoli* that supplied the elite area. I can see a depression next to the wall. It's about 12 metres by 20 metres. Walking through bushes and brambles, I get to the remains of the *baoli*. It's at about 25 metres deep, and was deeper still if it had to reach the water table. The walls have collapsed on three sides. The one remaining one is faced with large rectangular stones forming four very high vertical steps. There were steps leading down to the water but they have also disappeared.

The *baoli* only tapped underground water; surface runoff was limited as it was in the middle of a built-up area. It was a chore to climb nearly 25 metres down to bathe, wash and get drinking water. It's a small *baoli* but the elite population wasn't very large either.

Further west are the remains of the king's palace surrounded by the remains of his servants' quarters. Here is another *baoli*, in much better shape. It's about the same size but three walls still stand. All have large stone blocks – but where the ASI has 'restored' it, small irregular bits of stone embedded in mortar have taken over. There are remains of stairs leading to the bottom; the top of the staircase has disappeared and needs to be rebuilt. At the bottom of the *baoli* are two giant ledges, one above the other, that allowed people to use the water at different levels. These are the two surviving ledges of what must have been a series that started at the top.

"Where are the others?" I ask Gyan.

He points to the far walls of the fort that stretch away to the west and north. That's where the bulk of the people lived and the other five *baolis* were their source of water. *Baolis* were essentially stepped wells that led down to the water fed by underground streams. In Tughlakabad, their water was probably also used for drinking – maybe people used the lake outside for other purposes.

Going back in history, almost to mythology, I travel to Agrasen's Baoli in Connaught Place. This is one of the best preserved *baolis* in Delhi and looking at it, I wonder what state the others are in. Agrasen's Baoli reflects the ancient *baoli* building tradition in north and western India. From Gujarat, right across the Indo-Gangetic plains, *baolis* were one of the main sources of water for travelers. I recall the spectacular Chand Ki Baoli, about 200 kilometres south-west of here near Abhaneri in Rajasthan, where the magnificent architecture all around contrasts with the puddle of filthy water at the bottom. Or the derelict one near Mayur Dhwaj's ruined city near Dausa with its perfectly sweet water.

Whatever the size, the construction was such that travelers could rest in solitude inside the *baoli*.

An interesting aside, from O P Jain: *sarais* or stops on a route were 11 miles apart, this being the distance a horse could gallop at a stretch. Therefore, Ghaziabad is 11 miles from Shahjahanabad and Meerut 44 miles. This spacing made it possible for virtually overnight delivery of mail, from Delhi to Calcutta or Bombay and the Mughals, who devised the system, managed to rule their empire efficiently.

Agrasen is said to be the founder of the Agrawal clan, one of India's leading trading communities. The *baoli* named after him is tucked away between high-rise apartment and office blocks that have come up in place of old houses in the Connaught Place area. All the magnificent houses of the rich, famous and the royalty, abandoned by their Muslim owners after partition, were taken over by their latter day Hindu owners and over the past three decades, have given way to high-rises. These now peer into the tiny square that houses the 60 metres by 12 metres *baoli*, running roughly north-south. A road runs along three sides and the washermen or *dhobi* ghat makes up the fourth side.

It's extremely unimpressive from the outside. Stone and mortal walls tell me it's a monument. The outside walls of the *baoli* have archways that lift the wall to about 5 metres above road level. The entrance is at the southern end, through a barred gate. On either side are plaques explaining the *baoli*'s history. There is a masjid at the southern end, near the entrance. The gate is locked; its 5:30 PM.

I climb over the low iron railing that runs along the wall to get to a ladder propped inside one of the archways. That will take me to the top of the wall and into the *baoli*. A boy comes running from one of the houses next to the *baoli*, seeing me trying to 'break in'.

He fishes out a key from his back pocket and opens the lock. The gate opens silently, on well-oiled hinges. I walk through the arched entrance into the *baoli*. It's huge inside, deceptively small from the outside. The *baoli* stretches away in a north-south direction, and I am standing at the southern end. The stone sides reach down into the bowels of the earth, a pathway for people seeking water. Just behind me a small broken down mosque and a locked room. There is a bed and a mattress inside.

"I come here sometimes when the weather is good," Anil, my reluctant guide says. "Do you want to go down?"

I nod and he leads the way down to the bottom of the *baoli*. It's a steep climb, as with all ancient structures. Our ancestors were giants, given the height of the steps. There are five visible storeys to the *baoli* and Anil claims there is a sixth one hidden under the filth accumulated at the bottom of the structure. That is, the *baoli* is about 10 metres deep and there is filthy water at the bottom.

The *baoli*'s water was used for everything but drinking by humans; there is a well adjoining the *baoli* to the north for that. Men and women could bathe in seclusion in the *baoli*. Descending the steps, I enter a passage way that leads to an inner chamber that has five floors with a central opening for water. Small rooms surround the central opening and this is where people could bathe, pray or camp. Each floor has its own access from the surface so the *baoli*'s 'guest house' could accommodate several families at the same time; the rest could camp around the *baoli* in the archways.

I remember seeing water right up to the top 30 years ago, when we used to stay near the *baoli* on Ferozeshah Road. Now, there are a few feet of dirty water at the bottom. The well, however, is full of water though the level is low, around 10 metres below ground level. The water is stagnant and quite undrinkable but the fact that it has water shows that the groundwater levels are high in this part of Delhi despite the fact that most houses, apartments and offices have their own borewells.

"It used to be full of water till the third floor," says Anil. "The level has fallen since the Delhi Metro Railway Corporation began work here. They pumped out a lot of water and the water levels fell to this."

Agrasen's Baoli is one of many that dotted Delhi once. Most have decayed or have been filled up and converted into residential areas. Each *sarai*, or resting places for travelers, and many of the city's urbanized villages grew from *sarais*, had its own source of water that could have been either a *baoli* or a well. These *sarais* dot all the approach roads to the walled city of Shahjahanabad. There are remains of *baoli*s in Palam and Vasant Vihar in south west Delhi and a corner of Shahjahanabad. The rest, as they say, are history.

"Delhi had an estimated 794 water bodies, manmade and natural," says V K Jain, founding chairman of the NGO Tapas that he runs out of his farm-house in Mehrauli. He has surveyed the city and found these things all over the city, with a somewhat high concentration in the south. Jain has filed a petition in the High Court of Delhi to improve the quantity and quality of water in Delhi. Taking an average of two per village – one for human beings and another for animals – he has arrived as this figure. His figure, though does not take wells into account – it was too tedious to identify and count the exact number of wells that once were the sole source of drinking water in the city.

"Just 13 are manmade out of these. The rest are natural water bodies, usually depressions that have filled up with water. Many of them are not being used any more because the Delhi Jal Board promises water to everybody through tubewells," says Jain. "My contention is that they have to be preserved to augment water supply through tubewells. I have estimated that if they are all protected and restored, they can contribute to 15 percent of Delhi's water requirements."

Till the Mughals came and shifted the action to the banks of the Yamuna, Delhiites had to depend on water conservation and harvesting to meet their needs. The work of the Tomars, Chauhans and the Sultanate rulers is ample evidence of their expertise in using the rocky terrain to advantage.

Shahjahan made the Red Fort and the walled city, Shahjahanabad. This remained the capital till the British declared that Calcutta was the capital after the 1857 war of Independence. That short interlude ended in 1911 when the British shifted their capital back to Delhi, a little north of Shahjahanabad in Civil Lines.

Shahjahan was a builder par excellence. He planned for the water needs of his new city, the army and his palace. He made a system of canals and *dighis* – a small square or circular reservoir with steps to enter to divert water from the Yamuna. His engineer Ali Mardan Khan not only did this but also linked this canal with what has now become the Najafgarh drain that rises in the Sirmaur hills in Haryana, south-west of Delhi. The new canal was named after him. It charged the *dighis* and wells on its way into town.

People were not allowed bathe of wash clothes inside *dighis*, but could draw water. Most houses had their own wells or *dighis* for water. If the canal ran dry they fell back on wells. Water carriers, called *kahars* or *mashkis*, supplied water to households in hogsheads. They were either employed full-time, if the household was large enough, or visited houses with leather bags of water drawn from common wells. Some of the major wells were Indara Kuan near Jubilee cinema, Pahar-wala-kuan near Gali-Pahar-Wali, and Chah Rahat near Chhipiwara (the source of water for the Jama Masjid). According to the site, Rainwaterharvesting.org, in 1843, Shahjahanabad had 607 wells, of which 52 provided sweet water. Today 80 per cent of the wells are closed because the water is contaminated by the sewer system. This is the Jal Board's water cycle.

The Red Fort's intricate channel system is one continuous stream that goes from building to building. That and the river combined to make the place habitable. Given the abundance of water, it is unlikely that the Mughals had much need to set up elaborate water conservation and harvesting structures in Delhi, like their predecessors had done. Elsewhere in India, especially in the Deccan, they made some of the most elaborate rainwater harvesting systems. The Mughals built water systems for recreation.

Chandni Chowk, the Mughal's shopping arcade opposite Red Fort, is a contrast to the tranquility inside the fort. It's still one of Delhi's main shopping areas, some 350 years after it was built. The crowds, congested shops and tortuous streets crammed with shops make it hard to believe that this was once a fashionable promenade, designed by Shahjahan's daughter Jahanara. It got its name from a pond in front of the Fatehpuri mosque at the far end that used to shimmer in the moonlight.

Water ran short in Chandni Chowk a few years after it was completed, because it became such a prominent trading centre in north India. Shahjahan asked Ali Mardan for a solution and he renovated an old canal to supply water to the complex, and renamed it Faiz Nahar. It ran the length of Chandni Chowk and probably ended in the pond in front of the mosque. The British revived it in 1820 after the decline of the Mughal Empire, but it was finally buried in 1910. Now the main road of Chandni Chowk runs over the canal. It is said that when it was well kept, the canal could supply water to all of Shahjahanabad; when it fell into disuse, it bred disease and malaria.

Shahjahanabad was one of the Mughal's many contributions to Delhi; the other was the innumerable *sarais* that grew into villages and now, into shopping areas. *Sarais* were places for caravans to rest – Delhi dominated the east-west trade route. They offered shelter for the night, food and water. *Sarais* were set up by Muslims, *ashrams* by Hindus. *Sarais* were named after the person who set it up, usually an officer of the court or an entrepreneur.

O. P. Jain, convenor of the Delhi Chapter for INTACH, says, "The *ashrams* were completely free to stay and provided no amenities; you used what you brought. But *sarais* charged for extras such as bedding. They were run more like motels and named after the person who started them. So there is Yusuf Sarai, Ber Sarai, Neb Sarai and Katwaria Sarai – their namesakes long lost to history."

Each *sarai* had its own water source, either a *baoli* or a well. Nearly all have disappeared. There is one inside Lado Sarai, near Mehrauli, that is supposed to be the centre of this stopover. It's under a badh tree, duly covered with an octagonal concrete roof and all but eaten up by multi-storeyed buildings. The well has water and is covered with a heavy grill to keep humans and cows out. It's not been used for years, the locals assure me. All the roads in Lado Sarai seem to radiate from this well that shows it was the centre of life in the village in the not-too-distant past.

After Independence, Delhi grew at a phenomenal rate fueled initially by the influx of refugees from Pakistan and later, by India's economic prosperity. It's the only big town in north India and it took a little Punjabi enterprise to transform it into an economic powerhouse. From just 350,000 people before 1947, the National Capital Territory of Delhi has 15 million now. If you add the suburbs of Ghaziabad, NOIDA, Faridabad and Gurgaon, that's another 5 million people, making this the biggest urban sprawl in India. It takes three hours by road to drive from one end of this thing to another on a good day.

To understand where this is going, take a look at Delhi's geography. Delhi has three regions – the Yamuna flood plain, the Ridge and the Gangetic plains. The land slopes from west to east and from south to north. Delhi's highest point about 300 metres above sea level is near its southern border on the ridge, but the average altitude of the Aravallis is about 200 metres. The Yamuna has dykes about 4 kilometres apart, on both sides to control floods. The river cuts the city into two bits, one third to the east and two-thirds to the west. A lot of the ponds and lakes in east Delhi are depressions that used to accumulate flood water from the river but now are totally cut off from that source; the ponds are now garbage dumps and the only water in them comes from domestic and industry effluents.

The Najafgarh drain rises from west, flows north for a distance and then meanders north-east till it joins the river, just north of the Inter-State Bus Terminal. It was a major drain carrying water from the Najafgarh Lake to the river, and replenishing water sources in west Delhi. The British and later, the Indian town planners, found in it a convenient outlet for a burgeoning city's municipal and industrial waste. The result is that till the Najafgarh drain hits the Yamuna, the river is halfway clean. After their confluence, the river becomes one of the world's most polluted stretches of water.

The Yamuna Action Plan, or YAP, lives up to its acronym of being more hot air than action. The decades-long programme to reduce pollution by first reducing the number of drains pouring into the river, and then putting up effluent treatment plants to treat water from the Najafgarh and other drains before they it enter the river have come to naught because the authorities are simply not serious. Also, it's a milch cow with over Rs. 1,000 million having spent on it since 1993.

An immediate fallout of abandoning the *jheels, kunds, baoli*s and other traditional sources of water supply has been that Delhi, sprawling over 1,483 square kilometres, has little water to call its own. Groundwater is seriously overdrawn; the city draws twice as much as is available through natural recharge from rain and the river. It depends on dams in the Himalayas and the goodwill of riparian states for its water. The day Haryana and Uttar Pradesh decide they need more water, Delhi has a shortage. Supply has become completely inelastic, but the demand continues to grow – the urban sprawl is the second-fastest growing region in India.

The modern city of Delhi, founded by the British, was provided a water supply and sewage disposal system. The water intake for all the water treatment plants was upstream of the place where the Najafgarh drain runs into the Yamuna in north Delhi. After this point, the Yamuna becomes a highly polluted channel of stinking black water. The only water treatment plant in south Delhi at Okhla had to be closed down because pollution levels were too high for it to treat; South Delhi has been water-deprived since then. The trunk mains carrying water from north to south are old and pass through slums and illegal colonies where people tap into them. This wastes water and deprives the areas at the tail end of their supply system of water – the government acknowledges that 44 percent of water is lost in transit. Thus, Vasant Kunj in the south and Dwarka in the South West are perpetually short of water.

Delhi now needs over 5,000 million litres of water a day (MLD) but all its water treatment plants, including the new showpiece called Sonia Vihar, produce just 4,000 MLD; the rest comes from private tube wells. In other words, 70 percent comes from surface water and the rest from underground. Delhi is simultaneously home to the most under- and most over-supplied parts of India. The Cantonment area gets over 500 litres per capita per day (LPCD) of water but large parts of rural Delhi get just 1/18 of that. The norm is 225 LPCD but by this definition, just the New Delhi Municipal Corporation, Karol Bagh and Cantonment areas get enough water; the rest make do with less.

Delhi's traditional solution has been to dig for water, but even this isn't working in most places. O P Jain remembers that in New Delhi, the walls of houses would get wet because water from underground would seep up through the foundations. Groundwater was available just a few feet below the surface. That doesn't happen anymore. The Central Ground Water Board reckons that Delhi's water table was fallen by a foot a year, or by 8 metres in 20 years. If that does not sound like much, consider this: it is the height of a four-storeyed block of flats. And that is just an average figure.

The situation in some parts like Mehrauli in south Delhi is worse than average because it's the farmhouse belt. These are farmhouses in name. From Jasola in south east Delhi across to Najafgarh in the south west, a distance of 20 kilometres in a swathe about 2 kilometres wide, are the sprawling mansions of the city's super-rich. These have huge lawns and swimming pools; they are the city's largest water suckers. Not surprising that Mehrauli where most of these are concentrated, and Najafgarh, are the two blocks where the water table has plummeted the fastest. These are also hilly areas, so water was hard to find in the first place. It is also the region where life in Delhi could be said to have begun with the Tomar Rajputs 1300 years ago.

Being the national capital has its advantages. For Delhi, the government has spent Rs. 7,000 million to build the Tehri dam so that it gets 560 MLD of water and 1,000 MW of power. It already depends on high dams in the Himalayas for its water. Another three – the Renuka, Kishau and Lakhwar dams – will be built to provide another 4,000 MLD of water to the city. Now, if only others were as lucky.

Delhi's dependence on high dams in the Himalayas is disastrous for everybody concerned. The Himalayas are ecologically fragile and all the dams built so far have been faulty. Higher-than-calculated siltation rates have reduced their lives by 30-40 percent. Millions of people have been displaced and never compensated adequately for the loss of their lands or resettled properly. The Tehri dam alone has displaced 100,000 and drowned the historical town of Tehri, after which it is, ironically, named. But people living close to the dam get neither power nor water from the dam. They still have to make do with whatever scanty springs they had, or wait for the promised tankers from the dam to come. Dams like Tehri worsen an already inequitable water situation. They will lead to conflicts in the near future between all the states that have to share this diminishing resource.

Unfortunately, in Delhi there is little sense of responsibility about using water. Sonia Vihar commenced supply in August 2006 and dry Vasant Kunj heaved a sigh of relief. Water supply doubled from an hour a day. Nearly everybody in this affluent colony of around 20,000 houses has selfishly installed pumps on the main water lines to fill their own tanks, and beggar their neighbours. Now, tanks overflow while people refuse to spend the Rs. 100 needed to fix a ball cock that would save water. There is little recognition of the fact that thousands of millions of rupees have been spent, and hundreds of thousands have sacrificed their lands and way of life, so that these few could get some water. The story is the same across south Delhi that has benefited most from the new water treatment plant. Perhaps the government was right to attempt privatization because then, these same people would have had to pay higher rates for the water they so blithely waste.

As Delhi doesn't have much by way of water resources, rainwater harvesting is a viable alternative. The city gets about 610 MM of rain a year. A RWH system on a roof with an area of 100 square metres can yield 36,000 litres in a year. That's enough water for one person for 4 months, going by the government's water supply standards. If you reduce the water used for flushing toilets, watering plants and washing the house, this can be stretched to six months. Most DDA flats and private houses have that sort of roof area. Multiply it by millions of houses across the city and the quantity of harvested rainwater goes up substantially. However, as the managing director of DLF, a large private property development company, says, "Rainwater harvesting will not work in Delhi." With an attitude like that, it's no surprise that this has not caught on in Delhi save in a few pockets.

Delhi's continued splurge – people hosing down cars, owning private swimming pools, watering expansive lawns and wasting water in hundreds of other ways – is set to get worse. Malls and hotels are coming up across the city and these will strain an overstretched system further. Both are notorious for being intensive consumers of water and power. In fact, in water-scare Vasant Kunj, three large malls are to come up by 2008. On the other hand, area for water harvesting and conservation continues to diminish.

A combination of factors can ameliorate Delhi's disastrous water record. Rainwater harvesting, recycling waste water and a sensible use of this scarce resource can contain its continuously increasing demands. For any of this to happen, education has to begin at home. The government has tried to encourage RWH but it's not worked. Residents Welfare Associations in some parts of the city have used rainwater and recycled waste water for watering lawns. Best-case scenarios show that, taken together, these three simple steps can save a third of water needed by the city; that's more than the current shortage.

If Delhi's historical rulers took special care of the water supply, its current ones are marching in the opposite direction. Delhi wasn't dependent on the goodwill of four states for its water – it managed quite well, thank you. But when politicians, land developers and land sharks, the plethora of (un)civic agencies and plain citizens decide that their individual needs come first, things deteriorate fast.

Delhi has completely abandoned its rich and varied past of managing its water resources sensibly. Its citizens abuse water and waste much more than I have seen anywhere else in India. I have seen tanks overflowing in

Vasant Kunj, supposedly a dry area, while a few kilometers away in Dwarka, people still queue up for water. I have seen thousands of litres of water let out of full overhead tanks to flush them. I have seen leaking water mains turn streets into swamps in the height of summer. I have seen restaurant owners in Delhi convert ponds into parking lots and get away by bribing a judge of the high court. I have seen water flooding enormous lawns while poor people ferry the same liquid past these lawns to drink.

Perhaps this is due to the fact that it's a city of migrants who feel little empathy for it. Perhaps it's the city's commercial bent of mind, that sacrifices everything to Mammon. Maybe Delhiites just don't care because they know that at the end of the day, water will come from some distant land. They forget that this water comes at the expense of someone else, who one day will come knocking on their door for a job, and justice. And the former head of Delhi Jal Board, charged with delivering water to the city, had instead been charged with taking a bribe of $75,000 in kind for awarding Kaveri Infrastructure Limited a contract for renovating the water mains at an exorbitant amount of Rs. 36 million. A few enlightened resident welfare associations have taken matters into their hands and built rainwater harvesting systems – more such initiatives may yet save the city from a completely dry future.

4 TAMIL NADU: OF ERIS AND OORANIS

From a jet, I might be forgiven for thinking I am flying over a giant fish. At 11,000 metres, the basin of the Vaigai river in south Tamil Nadu looks like it's got scales on both sides. Giant blue scales. The scales are uniformly crescent-shaped, made against the slope of the land from west to east. On the ground, the story is very different.

The scales become water tanks, or *eris*. Each is semi-circular that approximates a crescent shaped. Earthen walls sometime lined with stones make up two-thirds of the sides of an *eris*; one-third is open, facing the slope from where rainwater flows in to fill it. The overflow of one *eri* fills the next and the next one's overflow fills the next – these series of *eris* called system *eris* is what I see as scales from a few miles up.

Eris as much part of southern Tamil Nadu's landscape as masala dosa and idlis. They have been around for a tad longer. *Eri* construction is recorded as early as the 3rd century BC but most that are still around are probably a few centuries old. The average age would be 700 years, though inscriptions near the walls of some make them older, going back to the Pallava dynasty that ruled this part of the country between the 9th and 13th centuries.

Eris were the mainstay of rural Tamil Nadu. They provided drinking water and irrigated crops – they were the centre of village life. Most *eris* were built by the rulers, either the king of the local chieftain, and looked after by the villagers. Some were built by the villagers themselves. They evolved a sophisticated system of sharing water that depended on the crops, amount of rainfall, height of the *eris* walls and area to be irrigated. This micro-level planning was possible because the village was administrative unit and everyone in the village was involved in the process.

My train, the Nellai Express, pulls into Madurai, the industrial and political capital of south Tamil Nadu, on schedule at 9 PM. The hotel is a stone's throw from the station, the pretentiously-named Madurai Residency. Situated in a small alley off one of the many radial roads that lead to the town's Meenakshi temple, Madurai Residency has a commanding view of the station. It also overlooks the main bus stand of the city; these two assets ensure that my room gets its share of city noisy 24X7. The view from the rooftop restaurant compensates for this though – at night, I get a spectacular owl's eye view of the city and the Meenakshi temple. It's all less impressive in the day, somehow.

Madurai has a temple in every street with garishly-painted spire adorned with religious figures – garudas, apsaras and gods selected from the Hindu pantheon – and monsters. The town is dominated by the 12 gopurams (towers) of the Meenakshi temple. Once, they were the only thing on the skyline; sadly, that's not true anymore with hotels like mine springing up a few hundred metres away.

The western gate is a 15 minute walk from the hotel through narrow streets with shops cheek by jowl selling everything on earth, and even things for the afterlife. There are as many beggars as there are sellers; both do brisk business from pilgrims on their way to experience god. At the western gate, a rapacious shoe keeper demands that I put my shoes in his, and only his, care. Irritated, I leave them next to the gate and walk, thinking that they are too old to be stolen.

The Meenakshi temple is dedicated to Shiva. Its complex sprawls over 6 hectares and has a massive central temple complex, a pond and innumerable smaller shrines. There is a wide walkway inside between the main outer wall and the inner temple walls. Each gopuram is richly carved with an assortment of celestial beings and the lesser gods. These are painted in all colours of the rainbow. Standing under one and looking up, I get the impression of staring at myriad painted pebbles with the occasional hand or head poking out against a blue sky. Pigeons abound and seem to nest in every crevice in the gopurams, decorating the heavenly bodies with their shit. Nobody minds – not the priests, the temple keepers, the pilgrims, the pigeons nor the statues. I fancy they have a nightly discussion after closing hours on the futility of keeping the birds away. The stucco figures have to be redecorated and consecrated every 12 years, which is why the paint doesn't look as old as the temple.

Entry to the temple is free. Under the massive gopuram is a relatively modest wooden gate of indeterminate age. The temple's website says it was originally built by Kulasekara Pandya, but it owes its current grandeur to the Nayaks who ruled the city between the 16th and 18th centuries. The complex is rectangular and entry is from four gopurams – north, south, east and west. The south gopuram is the tallest, at 530 metres; the others are around 500 metres high.

I walk around to the north side. Inside the north gopuram is a small shrine with a Nandi bull next to it. It's built around a kadamba tree under which Indira is said to have worshipped a shivling. The said shivling is under the tree, a rectangular wall surrounds it. On either side is two metal railings – worshippers have tied many little yellow cots to these. They reflect the desire for a son. An endless stream of people flows clockwise around the shrine, genuflects and repents at one end and goes about its business.

Further east is the hall of a thousand pillars. It's actually 985 pillars, each carved. The hall houses the museum with its impressive array of statues, pillars, paintings and carvings that reflect a millennia of history. Unfortunately, the lighting in the museum leaves one lot to be desired – it's too poor to photograph in and flash photography isn't allowed. Nor am I allowed to use a tripod. It's hard enough to see the rare sculptures; taking pictures is doubly hard. The only saving grace is the reasonable entry fee.

The east side also has a hall, the Meenakshi Nayaka Mandapa, where there are shops selling odds and ends for people visiting the temple – flowers, incense sticks, candles, lamps and cloth. There is a brass lamp holder that holds 1008 lamps which is lit on festivals. I imagine it's a sight to see, but at the moment only a few are burning. High up on the pillars, near the roof, a series of sculptures depict Meenakshi's life as the queen of Madurai and Shiva's miracles.

The story goes that a king of Madurai, Malayadwaja Pandya, who was childless, did a series of sacrifices (yagnas). Finally, his efforts were rewarded – a 3-year old girl emerged from the flames and the king adopted her. But she had three breasts. The divinity who gave the girl assured the king that the third appendage would disappear when she met her consort. Meenakshi, as she was called, grew to be a brave and beautiful princess. She met Shiva on the Kailash battlefield and the third breast disappeared because she was an incarnation of Parvati, Shiva's wife. They both settled in the temple as Meenakshi and Sundareshwar.

An elephant – it's alive but looks like another sculpture – greets me at the temple's entrance, to the east. I enter another hall, this one with 110 carved pillars. I walk around this and exit to the south. There is a small corridor that leads me to the temple tank, surrounded by a pillared walkway. The temple trust's office is to the right as I exit.

I perambulate the pond, called the golden lotus pond. It is said that Indira entered the tank and filled it with golden lotuses. Its steps are full of people, tired from walking around the temple, soaking in the evening atmosphere. There is a golden pillar in the centre and a large golden lotus to one side. A water treatment plant completes the equipment in the pond. As with all temple tanks in Tamil Nadu, this one too is fed by an underground stream. How that gets to the tank, in the temple, in the middle of the city is beyond me. Even the temple watchman, who catches me taking pictures and whisks me off to pay for using the camera at the trust office, is clueless.

"It is the work of god. This IS a temple, you know," he says.

The relationship between religion and water is clearest in the temples of Tamil Nadu. Each one has at least one large tank where devotees bathe before and after prayer. Bathe is a misnomer – in a public place, they rinse their feet and hands and wash their face as a substitute for a bath. The water in the Meenakshi temple is filthy – too many bathers and too little flow of fresh water.

In times past, the Tamil Sangam, the ancient academy of Tamil poets, used to congregate around this tank. Legend has it that the Sangam dates from when the gods roamed the earth. The tank was the testing ground for new poets. A new work of poetry was thrown into the tank. If it sank, it was worthless. If it floated, it was worthy of their consideration. Poetry was given divine sanction.

The story about Madurai is also linked to water. When Meenakshi and Sundareshwar got married, he arrived without any pomp and show, with just a dwarf called Gundodhara in tow. Meenakshi complained that they had put up a splendid show and retinue, while Sundareshwar had only brought along a gnome. Sundareshwar suggested his gnome was a match for the queen's retinue. He should be fed, Sundareshwar said.

Gundodhara ate everything the town had to offer and drank all its water. He cried for more but there wasn't anything to be found. Shiva called Mother Annapurneshwari to satisfy Gundodhara's hunger and Ganga, his thirst. Sundareshwar told the dwarf to place his hands on the ground and directed the Ganga to flow to that spot (Ganga had descended from heaven to earth on the tresses of Shiva). That river became the Vaigai River that rises in the Western Ghats and flows east through Madurai to the Bay of Bengal.

The road from Madurai to Ramnathpuram is allegedly a national highway number 49. It's an apology of a highway, with just a single carriageway that permits us to overtake if there isn't any on-coming traffic. We head south-south-west out of Madurai to see the fabled centuries-old *eris* and the water keepers of Tamil Nadu, the neerkattis. We are on the way to Mudukulattur where Dhan Foundation has a field office, about 100 kilometres away.

There is an abundance of tanks in Tamil Nadu, quite evident the moment we get out of Madurai. They are easy to spot and soon, I am an expert *eri*-spotter.

A. Gurunathan of the Dhan Foundation, a large non-profit organization based in Madurai, reels off impressive figures. "There are 150,000 tanks, ponds and dugouts in peninsular India used for irrigation, drinking water and animals, respectively. This excludes the temple tanks.

"Tamil Nadu has 39,000 tanks, Karnataka 30,000 and Andhra Pradesh,

75,000. The tanks provide water for irrigation and drinking, and recharge the ground water, that people extract to drink through wells and hand pumps."

Looking out of the Sumo's windows, it's easy to believe him. The crescent-shaped structures rise out of the ground outside nearly every village. Some are clearly in use as they are clean and their embankments clear of weeds and undergrowth. Others are overgrown with weeds as the villagers have probably found another source of water – they have fallen on bad times. The command area of an *eri* is called an ayacut and farmers who cultivate the area, ayacutdars. The *eri*'s embankments are called kanmoy.

The villages themselves are neat. Thatched houses made of either bricks of wood line streets, usually at right angles to the highway. Speed breakers before and after, and sometimes in the middle of, the villages ensure that nobody charges through, endangering humans and animals. The area is green with trees, though I am there at a time when there is no farming so farmlands are a desolate brown. We drive through many kilometres of acacia forests.

J Elamurugu is a team leader with Dhan Foundation in Madurai. He is also my guide on the journey to the *eris*. He says, "The forests are grown on wasteland and village commons. Farmers sell the wood to a wood-based power plant. They are assured of a regular income without having to work."

We reach Mudukulattur and the driver pulls into an impossibly narrow gate. Years of practice or sheer luck see the fat Sumo through and we disembark. The office is on the first floor. There is a large communal hall, a kitchen and toilet area and the actual office room with desks, chairs and steel cupboards. The walls are bright blue, and the lower half is painted a dark green with enamel paint. Elamurugu has called a well-known neerkatti, Ganesan, to speak with me. He is from Madeyini, a small village close by.

Neerkattis are the water keepers of the *eris*. Each *eri* has at least one to maintain it and distribute water. Neerkattis have been around as long as the *eris*. Their tradition is handed down from father to son – once a neerkatti, always a neerkatti. It's an obligation on the neerkatti's family to manage the *eri*'s water for the village. A neerkatti's decisions are never questioned, even by the upper castes, even though most come from the lower castes. Most are descended from the servants of the erstwhile *zamindars*. Neerkattis are pivotal to the success, or failure, of an *eri* in a village.

"Why is caste such a determinant?" I ask Elamurugu.

"If a neerkatti is from an upper caste, his decisions on water can create problems. Upper castes are also the land owners so a neerkatti from them will appear biased. Having a low caste person as a neerkatti gets around this problem because this caste has never owned any land. Their decision on water is taken as final and unbiased by everybody," he says.

"So traditionally they are all from the lower castes?"

"Usually from the lowest, the shudra caste. Some are even scheduled castes," he says.

It's strange that the most downtrodden should be chosen to control the most critical resource in villages, water. And everybody in the village should abide by his decision. There is no hard and fast rule that says only these people can become neerkattis; anybody from any caste can. Elamurugu's analysis makes sense but the neerkatti's word as gospel truth does not. However, that's a tradition and I let it pass. A neerkatti worth his water knows that effective tank management is key to social harmony.

Neerkattis know their village topography inside out. They know all the slopes and drains that the rainwater flows through. They know the distance from the eri to the fields and the amount of water needed to irrigate each field. They know which sluice to open in order to reach the furthest field. Years of experience has taught them the order in which to water the fields. They can suggest which crops to grow based on the amount of water. Some legendary ones even predict the amount of rainfall in a particular year even though weather prediction is an uncertain craft.

There are as many ways to appoint neerkattis as there are *eris*. Some have been hereditary. Others are selected by the village committee. Still others are appointed by the government. The common thread is their command over water – its sources, requirements and distribution – in their *eri*.

Neerkattis have a mile-long job list, even though their work is concentrated around the monsoons and the associated kharif crop season. In villages, with agriculture as the mainstay, water is the most critical input and the man controlling it, of prime importance.

"I have been born and brought up in Madeyini Patti," says Ganesan. "I know every inch of the land, every farmer and what he grows."

Madeyini Patti is a small village in the Madurai district. It's a few kilometres from where we sit in Dhan Foundation's office in Mudukulattur. The village runs along the *eri*, a long meandering crescent shaped structure with a very solid bund along its sides. The bund has many old tamarind trees and is remarkably clean. A group of women lounge under one, catching up on the gossip in the afternoon. The village stretches off to one side. The main access is the road along the *eri*'s bund and the village lanes lead off at right angles. It's a small village and beyond the houses are the fields, dusty and ploughed, waiting for the rains.

In season, Ganesan has no time to talk to itinerant writers but its late May and just before the rains start; Ganesan is free. He is a wizened white haired man of around 65 who's spent his years tramping around his village fields, ensuring they are watered, guarding them when needed and collecting his 'pay'. Ganesan does not own any land so in the lean season, he works as casual labourer on construction sites, a huge comedown for a man who is so plugged into the local water scene.

Elamurugu says, with a degree of pride, "He can predict the rains also."

Neerkattis maintain the *eris* in their charge. This involves mending the dykes (bunds) and checking and replacing the sluices. If the concrete base of the sluice is damaged, it needs to be fixed. Most importantly, maintenance involves clearing vegetation from the *eri* bed and deepening the *eri* so it can hold more water. As water in the *eri* dries, its bed is used for cultivation – farmers leave the stalks behind and these need to be cleared. Even when the *eris* are not cultivated, weeds and acacia grow fast and need to be cleared lest they take over completely. Then, rainwater flowing into the *eri* carries a heavy silt load that fills up the pond and needs to be excavated every so often. However, this has to be done so that the *eri*'s holding capacity isn't more than what the dykes will bear – greed and be the undoing of the entire village if the bunds break.

In addition to the *eris*, Ganesan has to clear the water channels that feed the tank. These often flow through the village and people dump garbage into them during the dry months. Ganesan has to clean all this out so the water from the rains that reaches the *eris* is clean and the *eri* doesn't get polluted with garbage. He also has to make sure that human and animal shit along the channels is cleared. In short, he has to tour the village and make sure that it is clean so the water entering the *eri* is also clean. Ganesan sometimes hires labourers to help with this if his family isn't available. He pays Rs. 80 for half day's work and Rs. 100 for a full day's work to each labourer.

"It is in my interest to involve my family," he says. "Otherwise, it affects my income."

He has a small family. One son works in a hotel and the other studies. Both chip in when needed, but their help is sporadic. Ganesan is quite sure he is the last of the neerkattis from his family. The village will have to appoint another when he dies. His forefathers were appointed neerkattis by the person who built the tank.

"Some 600 years ago, the tank was built probably at the behest of the local ruler. He appointed my ancestor as the neerkatti. It has been in the family since then," he says. From the original neerkatti, a clan of 20 families has descended. Each family gets to be neerkatti by turn, once a year. That means Ganesan's family gets its chance once every 20 years.

"Not quite. It's more frequent than that because others give up their right. Some work in government jobs and aren't interested in being neerkattis anymore. So I get my turn more frequently," says Ganesan. In lean years, he becomes a casual labourer. Sometimes, another neerkatti family hires him and gives him a share of their income. When his turn comes, he returns the favour.

On the output side, the first thing he checks is the sluices. These comprise a large conical stone that fits snuggly inside a concrete hole that is the water outlet. A rope attached to the top of stone lets Ganesan pull it up and open the sluice. It's a simple mechanism but prone to breakage because when he closes it, the stone usually cracks the concrete. The higher the stone is pulled, the more water the sluice lets out. He fixes the stone in place by pushing sticks between it and the hole. Ganesan also needs to clean the holes through which water flows out into the fields. If a sluice needs repair, it can cost up to Rs. 2,000. Dhan pays Rs. 500 and the village association pays the rest.

His *eri* has two sluices, one above the other. When the *eri* is full, he opens the upper sluice to water fields that are at the tail-end of the command area of the *eri*. Then fields nearer the *eri* get water. The lower sluice is opened only when the water falls below the level of the upper one. Then only fields near the *eri* can be watered by that time – the more distant ones have got enough water for the entire crop. The soil in this part of the country is black cotton soil which is very clayey and non-porous – crops don't need much watering to grow. This characteristic of the soil also makes *eris* successful here as water seeps very slowly into the ground.

Ganesan decides on his own whether to water fields tail to head or head to tail. Sometimes, farmers ask him to water their fields in a particular order and Ganesan has to factor in these requests. Ganesan has figured out how much time it takes to water each field in the *eri*'s command area. There is a complex system of channels that lead from the sluices to the fields. Ganesan 'opens' a 'gate' in a channel by the simple expedient of breaking the channel's mud wall and letting water into a field. When it has been watered enough, he closes the 'gate' by putting a few stones and mud and reconstructing the wall. Then he repeats this for the next field. Simple, but effective.

"How do you know when a field has enough water?" I ask.

He shows me his hand, a very wrinkled one with deeply etched lines. The veins stand out like small hill ranges on the back. These hands have watered countless crops for many decades.

"If the water is more than one hand deep, the field has been watered enough," he says. Water regulation is needed only after paddy has been transplanted.

"Does that apply for all crops?"

"No, it's for paddy. The other crops don't get much water and they don't need much water," he says.

Farmers grow mainly paddy in the first crop. If the rains have been good and there is water left, they plant gram and ragi (a coarse millet) as a second crop, neither of which needs a lot of irrigation. Paddy takes a lot of water and the water distribution expertise of neerkattis is tuned to the needs of this particular crop.

Ganesan does not get any money for his work. He can hire people to help with cleaning the water channels, but he has to pay them – the village will not. Ganesan gets paid in kind, as have countless generations of neerkattis before him. He gets 7 KG of paddy for every 60 cents of sown paddy. An acre has 100 cents. He also gets 4 KG from each farmer for operating the sluice gates. He also gets paid from the second crop, whenever there is one, but this payment is not fixed; farmers are free to pay him what they want. Ganesan earns a little extra by watching over the fields.

This rate was fixed much before Ganesan became a neerkatti and was accepted as a fair price for his labour. Madeyini's farmers pay him 10 bags of paddy every year, totaling 700 KG. He can do what he wants with the paddy – sell or eat it. That is a little less than what he should get as they farm a total of 60 acres of paddy. However, not all fields are sown with paddy every year. It sounds like a lot till I realize he had to feed and clothe his family from this; then it's not a lot. Then, if he hires labourers to help with the channel and eri cleaning, he has to pay them himself. Ganesan barely makes enough to get by between the paddy, his casual labour and his wife's work weeding fields. She makes just Rs. 30 a day for working in the hot sun. But he would not be anything but a neerkatti.

"I'm paid only if the crop if good. If it's bad, and the farmers have no surplus, they don't pay me. Then, I have to find work as a construction labourer to make ends meet." He says. "Sometimes, farmers don't pay even if the crop is good. When that happens, I don't water their fields the next season. I cannot fight with them," says Ganesan.

The *eri*'s walls are made of mud with a stone covering in places where it has to face the direct flow of water. This makes the walls porous. When the *eri* is full, water seeps through into the adjoining fields. But this isn't cause for concern for either the farmers or Ganesan. They know it keeps the fields moist and helps with crop growth; it also reduces the actual irrigation required. The water is deep and Ganesan has to swim to raise or lower the sluices because there are no steps down to the gates, nor a place to stand.

Each *eri* has its own little shrine. Some are regular temples with a small garish tower that seem like wannabe Meenakshi temples. Others are little triangular constructions under a large tree, preferably peepul or a banyan tree, with a small platform in front. The idea wasn't so much to pray as to purify the water and keep people from shitting or pissing in the eri's catchment.

Elamurugu says, "In some places, the irrigation department has cemented the *eri*'s walls to strengthen them and increase water storage. This has not gone down well with the villagers because water seepage stopped. Their fields have gone dry and need more irrigation. The department also constructed cement channels from the eri's sluices to the fields. Even this wasn't welcomed because it makes watering fields more difficult."

Ganesan says, "Earthen channels are easy to use because I just need to break a portion of the wall and then fill it up with stone and mud later. A concrete channel is hard to break and block again."

Ganesan won the Best Neerkatti Award, handed to him by then President of India, K R Narayanan. He wears his fame nonchalantly.

Concrete channels do serve their purpose – they ensure that fields at the tail end of the system get water. This increases equity and where it has proved beneficial, villagers have welcomed it. In most cases, though, they have not been happy with concrete channels.

Neerkattis are not always appointed in the same way nor is their functioning always autonomous. In Madeyini, it is hereditary and Ganesan knows what to do. In Aiyankoila village of Madurai district, the farmers tell the neerkatti how they want their fields irrigated. Periyarswamy the neerkatti is responsible for three *eris* though typically, it is one neerkatti per *eri*. The village has three hamlets and each one has its own *eri*. Once he has been told the pattern, he irrigates fields according to his own assessment of water needs.

"I've been a neerkatti for 40 years," he says. "My family has been neerkattis for many generations. We are responsible for irrigating the entire ayacut of the three *eris*."

His job is similar to Ganesan's – he closes the sluices before the rains and cleans the *eris* and the channels. Here, though, the farmers share the cost of cleaning, unlike in Madeyini. Periyarswamy oversees the work but does not pay from his pocket. Unlike Ganesan, Periyarswamy convenes village meetings – he is something of a village secretary. He guards the ayacut and keeps cattle off the fields. When he needs additional manpower, he hires his sons but never gets non-family to help. In Aiyankoila, neerkattis do not work by rotation as Periyarswamy's is the only family in the village in this line of work.

Sometimes, Periyarswamy has to settle disputes over sharing of water because the feeder channels for the three *eris* are common. Ayacutdars of one want theirs filled before the next one; the neerkatti's word is taken as final in these disputes. The ayacuts for the three *eris* are different – there is no overlap.

"There was a dispute a few years ago between different groups of ayacutdars. One group diverted the feeder channel to their tank. I brought the two groups together and we worked out a compromise," says Periyarswamy.

Periyarswamy earns considerably more than Ganesan. The pattern is the same as Ganesan's but the cultivated area is more, at 40 hectares. He makes 1,500 KG of paddy in a good year.

We drive along a long, narrow winding road in Madurai district. On one side runs the Sowdarpatti tank, an enormous expanse of grass and stone. On the other side is a series of villages. An impressive banyan tree dominates a turn in the road – the builders decided to go around it rather than cut it down. The wall that the road runs over is made of stone, two sides are bounded by hills and the third is where the water enters from. There is a small puddle in the middle of the tank – the rest is dry. It's an impressive tank that must be several centuries old. The outlet at the far end has a series of four sluices. The tank is very much in use; it's not been cleaned yet to store water but will soon be.

Sowdarpatti is a village named after the tank. We stop on the road under the tree. Elamurugu and I walk down a lane to find Dorai Pandi, the head of the village TFA. His house is unpretentious; a single storeyed building made of bricks, plastered with adobe and covered with corrugated iron sheets. The sheets come way down so I have to bend double to get into his verandah, where there is some more head room. The main door is painted a bright blue that contrasts with the white of the wall. The door's locked but a young man appears under the roof sheet at that moment.

"Where is Pandi?" asks Elamurugu.

"He has gone to the town. He'll be back in a little while," says the youth.

We decide to wait under the banyan tree as its hot in the verandah. The youth is packed off to get Pandi from the town. He pedals off. I look around – there are a few outhouses that accommodate labourers. Dorai's fields stretch beyond them for a great distance. His house is somewhat removed from the village as is sometimes the case with village headmen or *zamindars*. The village is typical, with fairly clean swept streets and houses made of stone, adobe and thatch. Its late morning and most people are in the fields, preparing to sow. The odd dog or child are the only occupants of the village.

"He will take at least an hour. Should we wait?" asks Elamurugu.

I wiggle my head, in the south Indian equivalent of a nod. We get into the Sumo and drive to the banyan tree.

The youth returns before the appointed time is up with Dorai in tow. Dorai is clad in typical fashion, white shirt with a white lungi.

Elamurugu introduces me. Dorai is obviously a man of some importance in these parts. We sit on the tank's wall to chat. Dorai says the tank irrigates six villages. That's easy to believe given its size; when it's full of water after a good monsoon, it looks like a lake. The neerkatti tradition here is different, in keeping with the needs of water.

"So you must have more than one neerkatti to manage so much water," I ask.

Pandi wiggles his head. "Four families are selected out of 20 neerkatti families by a draw of lots every year. Each family gets its turn once every five years. We need so many to control the water from the tank. Each neerkatti controls one of the sluices. The heads of the other villages have a meeting here every year to chart out the neerkattis' duties."

Sowdarpatti, a Brahman-dominated village, is also headed by a Brahman family. This family has been responsible for perpetuating the neerkatti tradition. The neerkattis for the tank have always been from Sowdarpatti village and not from any of the other five that it irrigates. The 20 families live in hamlets scattered through the village. They are all scheduled castes, in keeping with the general neerkatti pattern, and have been neerkattis for centuries.

This happy picture gives way to one of utter desolation a few kilometres on. We drive off the road and bounce along a dirt track through picturesque countryside – ancient granite rocks perched atop red rock mounds, with gnarled tree trunks making a living on their burning sides; elephant grass growing on the margins of small ponds; a little stream dancing through large rounded pebbles. We emerge on a small plain bounded at the far end by a low ridge. To the left is a smallish tank with grass reaching to its edges. This is the Chinna Veer Sudmanai tank. Cattle graze and buffaloes wallow in the pond. I walk to the ridge.

It's the check-dam that created the Peri Veer Sudamani tank, near a village of the same name. The Peri tank (larger of the two) is of great antiquity – two carved stone pillars stand a little distance from the check-dam that is actually a pile of rocks that has become a little ridge over the centuries. The granite pillars have inscriptions on them.

Elamurugu says, "These tell of the builder and lay down rules for the use of water. The tank's builder had made rules that villagers needed to follow when using water and maintaining the tank. There were punishments for violating them. There were rules for appointing neerkattis as well. I don't know what the inscriptions say exactly, but that is their meaning."

The pillars were connected to the check-dam once, as I can see from the slabs of rock lying at the bottom of the tank. There are other carved stones scattered on the bed of the *eri* so there was probably a building in times past. The bed of the tank is red rock, sloping upwards to a row of low hills on the far side. To the right, the edge of the tank merges into a little forest that separates it from the village named after the tank. The tank must hold water for several months and water an enormous area. A group of village girls frolics in the water some distance away, quite unabashed by the men working the rock quarries some distance away.

The Peri tank is used by humans for washing and bathing. Elamurugu tells me there is a well on the far side from where villagers draw drinking water. The Chinna tank, that gets the overflow from the Peri tank, is used by animals for bathing and drinking. It's easy to see why – animals would find it hard to scramble up the steep slope of the check-dam. From this one, water is released into the fields beyond.

It's a pretty picture and all would be perfect. But for the rock quarries on the hills across the tank. Hammers falling on anvils and rods sing out a rhythm that would do a jazz drummer proud. Here, though, they are sounding the death knell of the two tanks. In a few years the hills that are the tanks' catchment area will have disappeared under the greed of the miners and the government's stupidity in granting mining concessions. In just a few years, the miners have substantially whittled down the hills. The legacy of centuries is being hammered away at the Sudamani village. The villagers are part of this plunder, having abandoned farming – and use of the tanks – for short term gains from the mining. After these hills are mined into the ground, there will be others, then more.

In many places, *eris* are linked through channels that follow the contours of the land. The overflow from one fills the next, then the next and so on. These are typically called system tanks or cascades. It's another show ingenuity in tapping rainwater and not letting much escape – an *eri*'s capacity is limited but by building a set of them along a natural drain, people have managed to maximize the impact and multiply the quantity of water that can be stored.

Saviourpatnam, a Christian village around 20 kilometres south of Ramanathapuram, has an *eri* and two *ooranis*. *Ooranis* are smaller than *eris*, usually rectangular in shape about 30 metres by 20 metres. They are fenced with barbed wire and gated to keep animals out. Most that I see have been recently built and have steep mud walls on three sides. *Ooranis* are built on the surface of the land, not excavated, by raising walls. The walls are 2-3 metres high. The fourth one, nearest the gate, slopes gently to the water or a well at the edge. People collect water from here. The International Water Management Institute in Sri Lanka has listed *ooranis* as one of six most innovative water management practices globally.

Ooranis are exclusively used to store drinking water for humans. Unlike *eris*, that have feeder channels to collected rainwater from a large catchment area, ooranis have high walls and no channels. They only collect rainwater that falls directly into them. As they are on the surface, there is no chance of water from outside seeping through the walls to contaminate what is within. The fences ensure that no animals get into pollute the water. Animals and human shit cannot be washed into the *ooranis* either. The water is reasonably free of bacteria and people drink freely from a well-kept *oorani*.

The clayey soil of the region ensures that the water does not seep into the ground in a hurry. Villagers determine their drinking water needs and the size of *oorani* needed to meet them. Sometimes, a village can have more than one. Elamurugu says this ensures water security; I suspect caste equations in the village necessitate construction of more than one *oorani*.

The clayey soil is a blessing and a curse. It keeps the water on the surface, where people can use it. It also makes the water extremely turbid. I draw a bottle of water from the *oorani*. It's got so much suspended clay that

I cannot see through the bottle. A woman draws water from a well to one side of the *oorani*. I peer into the well – the water is as murky as that in the *oorani*. The *oorani* is fairly new, a couple of years old. The fence wire still has a shine and is good repair right around. A gap in the fence suffices as a gate; villagers take it upon them to keep animals out. We have parked next to the *oorani*. Across an open patch of land is the village church, an old tumble-down structure. Next to the *oorani* is a large spreading tree, the Therran.

Elamurugu says, "The well doesn't filter the water much, only a little. It is easier to draw from the well so we built a concrete slab on which people can stand and draw water rather than walking into the *oorani* to draw water. It keeps the water cleaner." In some places, Dhan has made a slow sand filter through which water flows; this is a bio-sand filter that removes both turbidity and bacteria. Water collects in a trough outside the *oorani* from where people take it.

"How does anybody drink this? They will get all sorts of diseases." I say.

A group of men has gathered in the few minutes we have been there. Most have only multi-coloured lungis (sarongs). One has a white lungi and white shirt. A couple are in trousers. One of them is Xavier, an oldish man of some authority in the village, who gives me a toothless grin. He rattles something in Tamil to a man, who returns a while later with a mud pot and a few dried seeds. They are blackish-brown, hard and oblong, about 1 CM on the longer side. Xavier soaks one seed in the water for a minute and then rubs it against the pot's side for another. He pours in the water and swirls it around; then he sets the pot on the ground.

"Wait 10 minutes," he says in good English. I am taken aback. He used to be in the army but left after five years to farm. The seeds are from the Therran tree.

Nothing seems to happen immediately. In a couple of minutes, the water looks like spoilt milk, albeit slightly yellow. The coagulant in the seeds is working in real time. The flecks of coagulating mud get bigger and bigger, and then the process slow down. They settle at the bottom. The water is still somewhat murky when we set the pot down and walk off.

There are two such ways to coagulate floating impurities in water and the people of this region know about both. One involves local trees and is extremely simple – wet the seeds, rub them on the inside of the pot a little, pour in the water, wait a few minutes and decant the reasonably clear liquid into another container.

That spreading tree is the Therran, one of the family of Loganiaceae of plants. The tree is native to the Coromandel coast. Botanically, it is called Strychnus potatorum – homeopaths may find that familiar. Other varieties of Strychnus trees also produce the deadly poison curare that was used to coat tips of arrows and spears to kill an enemy. Strychnus produces alkaloids that are extremely poisonous but are also used as a medicine. According to the Eclectic Materia Medica, in small doses they form a bitter general tonic. In larger doses, they act stimulate and tone the body. In regular doses, they increase reflex action, enlarge lung capacity and raise the pulse rate. In higher doses, they can kill. When he wet the seed and rubbed it, Xavier released the alkaloid that helped the mud floating in the water to coagulate. This principle of using proteins for coagulation has been well-researched and there are at least 10 known plant sources of coagulants.

Another popular one is the seeds of Moringa oliefera, locally known as the drumstick tree. It produces long, thin and ridged vegetables that are used primarily in sambar (lentils cooked with vegetables) in Tamil Nadu. The fleshy insides are a tasty treat. The locals also cook its leaves as vegetables.

These are cheaper than the chemical-based way that uses chemicals such as alum for commercial water treatment. The seed process produces no toxic sludge. Sludge from Moringa-treated water is only 20-30 percent of what is produced from alum-treated water.

I walk around Saviourpatnam. The village does not have a tarred road – a dirt track is the main road of the village. On either side, single storeyed houses open onto the road that ends at the square between the church and the *oorani*. Beyond are the fields and an *eri*. Most people in Saviourpatnam are farmers, growing the typical single crop of paddy and the occasional crop of gram or coarse millets. I would not call them poor, though by urban standards they would be. Nearly everybody is well clothed and fed. The houses are made of bricks and thatched with straw. The village is clean even though the road is muddy in patches. Saviourpatnam grows enough to provide for itself and has a healthy surplus.

"In a good year, each family grows enough to last for two years. So if there is no rain the next year, we can all manage easily," says Xavier. He takes me to his house, a rambling single-storeyed structure with a large courtyard in front. The courtyard is swept clean and has been recently plastered with a mixture of cow dung and mud. I take off my shoes at the entrance and walk across to his house. We sit on cane chairs in the shade of his verandah.

He points to a room behind us. It's full of sacks of rice – his bank. There is enough for his family of three for the rest of the year to eat and buy other stuff with. It's farming time from the onset of monsoons till winter, then harvest time and getting the paddy to the market. The early part of the year is the slow time, full of festivals and leisure, unless they have water for a second crop. It's also a time of uncertainty – will the rains be good, what will summer be like, will we have enough water to tide over the hot season. At this time of year, people migrate to towns and cities for work or rear goats and poultry to earn a little extra.

"Last year, we decided to build another *oorani* because this one isn't large enough," he says. "We have raised our own money and are building it on our initiative. We have not taken anything from the government or Dhan."

Tractors and bullock carts ply up and down from the *oorani*'s site, bringing in mud to build the walls. The rains are only a few days away so work has to be completed soon.

"We will be ready in two days," says Xavier.

I look at the frenetic activity and believe it is possible. We return to the mud pot under the Therran tree. I peer in, expecting to see murky water, and almost drop the pot in surprise.

The water has completely cleared up, and at the bottom of the pot are a few blobs of congealed mud, looking like mud-coloured yoghurt. I put my hand in and shake them – they float up momentarily and settle down again. I pour the water into the plastic bottle that has a little bit of *oorani* water still in it. The turbid water swirls up into the clear liquid but the mud quickly coagulates and settles at the bottom. The water is faintly yellow but tastes nearly as good as the bottled water I have along with me from Madurai. The coagulated mud is left behind in the pot – Xavier throws it away.

The process depends on people using the right sort of pot. You cannot use the seeds on water stored in plastic pots or metal pots. The coagulation does not work in either case. It only works if water is stored in earthen pots.

Elamurugu explains. "We make the paste by rubbing the seeds on the side of the pot. Only earthen pots are rough enough to let us make a paste. Plastic and metal pots are not. In addition, the commonly used metal is copper. The chemical in the seed would react with that to form a compound that tastes bad."

I see little evidence of earthen pots. The woman who was drawing water a short while ago from the well at the *oorani* was filling a yellow plastic pot. Most others carry multi-coloured plastic pots, with the occasional metal providing relief. There are no earthen pots. The reason is simple – plastic is lighter and cheaper and they don't break as easily as mud pots.

In the event that people are switching to plastic pots – I saw this in all villages in the region – it is necessary to find other ways to clean *oorani* water. Dhan Foundation has adapted a Canadian sand filter. This contraption has a small container on top, the filter in between and a container at the bottom with a tap. The entire thing is fitted in a cement cylinder. You pour the murky water into the container on top and collect filtered water at the bottom. They are fairly cheap to make and each household is supposed to get one under a programme of the Foundation.

"Why not adapt the Therran seed paste instead?" I ask Elamurugu.

He shrugs. "It's hard enough to get people to contribute to the upkeep of *ooranis* and *eris*. They want time-saving devices and feel that collecting, drying and then using the seeds makes no sense. Then, you need to get the proportions right – a little bit of Therran seed paste for a whole pot, no more, else you can fall sick."

That despite of the fact that Therran seeds have been used in alternative medicine for millennia and are free. The Canadian filters won't be.

Nearby, in the Pusari village, the *oorani* used to hold enough water for the entire village for just seven months. Villagers went thirsty for the rest of the time. They asked the government for a desalinization plant that was set up and it worked for a while – the groundwater is saline here because of the ingress of seawater. When that broke down, they had nowhere to go because in the years that the desalinization plant worked, they let the *oorani* and the *eris* go to seed.

What happened next is typical of the tank revival movement that has quietly crept across large parts of Tamil Nadu.

Dhan Foundation promoted a Tank Farmers' Association (TFA). This includes people from all families of the village, regardless of caste. The TFA decided to revive the *oorani* and *eri*. The total cost was Rs. 105,000 including labour and material. Dhan gave the TFA Rs. 75,000; the villagers contributed their share in kind as labour or by sending their tractors for earthmoving work. Each family contributed between Rs. 80 and Rs. 140 a day. In five days, the *eri* and *oorani* had been restored.

Dhan Foundation works on the principal that a third of the total cost has to come from the village; they chip in with the rest. Villagers can contribute in kind or cash. If they contribute in labour, it's called shramdaan. This 25:75 ratio applies to all tank rehabilitation work in the region. Restoring a tank costs just a fifth of what making a new one does. It is faster and more practical than constructing a new tank. Restoration also makes sense because most villages don't have the land for new tanks.

"It gives the people a stake in the work so they maintain it when we leave. It breaks the cycle of dependency on an external agency. It also changes their mindset that 'the government will provide'. The government has not provided and people have started realizing that their contributions have revived their water structures," says Gurunathan.

Dhan Foundation raises some of the money from the District Rural Development Agency or other government sources. These wings have money for minor irrigation schemes that the *eris* fall under. Dhan has catalysed these funds and mobilized the villagers – its acted as a catalyst.

Gurunathan says, "We have tried to revive the traditional social structures that existed before the arrival of the British. For this we have promoted Water User's Associations (WUAs) that map onto the village assemblies as they have representatives from every household in the village. This is the first step towards reviving traditional water management systems. It can take us up to six months to mobilize people and set up a

WUA."

That is after Dhan has worked in the region since 1994 to set up self-help groups (SHGs) that lend small amounts to individuals for starting businesses. In many places, these SHGs have been instrumental in setting up WUA or TFA in the same village. Once a TFA is set up, it can open a bank account to get funds for restoring *eris* or *ooranis*, depending on the village's need. SHGs keep the TFAs alive during the dry season by meeting every month; the idea is to keep the organization going even when there isn't a need otherwise it will fall apart. These TFAs are still nascent and villagers have not fully caught onto their utility.

The TFA determines what is needed in the village – revival or construction of *eris* or *ooranis*. Dhan helps it make a project proposal that is given to the DRDA. DRDA appoints a project manager who forms an implementation committee. The money from DRDA comes in installments into the TFA's bank account. The final installment is released after the DRDA does a final assessment; sometimes this amount is less than what is actually needed for the project. In such cases, Dhan makes good the difference. The project lifecycle is usually 18 months.

Issues vary from village to village. In Kothaluthu village, upper caste farmers had encroached on the feeder channel for the *eri*. Others in the village had tried to move them since 1972 and succeeded five years later when the district collector intervened. The supply channel was cleared and the *eri* rehabilitated after that.

In Silamali, a man called Kurinchiyappa Gouder made the *eri* on 20 acres of wetland six centuries ago. It had been neglected for years in recent times. In 1997, Dhan formed a TFA, to revive the *eri*. It had 60 ayacutdars. They spent Rs. 120,000 to rehabilitate the tank; their own contribution was Rs. 24,000 and the rest came from the DRDA. The eri now irrigated 25 acres. I am surprised the people here remember Gouder as the man with a vision who built the tank. In most villages, all I get is a shrug when I ask who built their tank.

Rehabilitation work has helped soothe caste conflict in some cases, as in Manavaikudi village that is part of the Vallakulam cascade. It is dominated by the Servai caste, two groups of which fought over land for a temple. The scheduled castes of the village support one against the other. In the process, it was impossible to set up a WUA. It was critical to rehabilitate the village's *eris* as it was part of the cascade and affected the cascade as a whole. Dhan, neighbouring villages and the district administration jointly got the villagers to settle their differences and get on with forming the WUA. The process took two years but now all is quiet and people have enough water to farm rather than squabble.

Kadambankularm village, in the same area, has an *eri* that was renovated in 1997 with an ayacut of 60 acres. After renovation, the ayacutdars found they had more water and expanded the area under paddy. The *eri* is large enough to grow fish, that gives the TFA more income. Farmers now grow rice for their own use and chili and cotton as cash crops. The eri was built by the local *zamindar* about 200 years ago. The *zamindar* ensured its maintenance with labour from the villagers.

In all these villages, a pattern emerges for Water Users Associations. WUAs work best if the population is about 200 families. Smaller villages don't have the critical mass needed to raise funds for *eri* maintenance but nonetheless have vibrant WUAs. They squeeze their requirements into what their WUA can afford to do. However, the system seems to break down in villages that have larger populations. If the number of households is much above 200, WUAs appear to be ineffective. This is perhaps because in larger villages, there is a higher percentage of people who do not farm – they are traders, craftspeople, or work in jobs. Their links to the land are tenuous and need for water is less than farmers. They do need drinking water but see investments of time or money in *eris* and *ooranis* as unnecessary; they would rather get their water by tanker than put aside time or money to build something that will provide for them for free. The task of forming WUAs in larger villages has been harder for Dhan. However, the average village size seems to be 200 households and the model has worked well.

I recall this as a problem elsewhere in India. In Rajasthan's Alwar district too, where Tarun Bharat Sangh has worked to form village associations to build *bunds* and restore *johads*, the model has worked in small to medium sized villages. Large villages have not banded together as well to work for the restoration of water management structures.

The well-bring of the village's water resources and the neerkatti depends on how vibrant the WUA or TFA are. The better the Associations, the better the village's tanks. If agriculture does well, so does the neerkatti. Conversely, if the Association and neerkatti are good, agriculture does well. In other words, if the modern Association has been mapped successfully onto the village association of yesteryear, things look up for the village.

The associations have well-demarcated roles. TFAs enroll farmers who own land in the ayacut, plan and implement development work such as rehabilitating tanks and build wells, undertake fish rearing and tree plantation or brick making to raise money that will pay for eri restoration and build up a corpus of funds to pay for tank maintenance.

To reinforce its work at the village level – reconstituting WUAs and TFAs, Dhan has banded groups of TFA together into Tank Cascade Associations (TCAs). Cascades are a series of interconnected tanks – the success of restoring one depends on the others and there are frequent problems of water sharing between villages. Cascade associations are a way to resolve these disputes. They also clean and repair feeder channels, mobilize funds across villages to improve tank irrigation systems and provide better services on agriculture and water management.

Another step up is setting up Tank Farmers Federations (TFFs) as apex organizations. These are groupings of TFAs at the district level. For example, the Madurai federation has 100,000 members from 198 villages. The federations mobilize funds from the DRDA and other sources, organize training programmes for their constituents and monitor the operation and maintenance of tanks systems. These federations are registered under the Societies Act, giving them a legal status.

The movement to rehabilitate *eris* is two-pronged, therefore. On the one hand, it involves restoring physical assets.

Gurunathan says, "These can divided into three activities – acquisition of water, system restoration and improvements in water use efficiency."

The first includes removing encroachers, cleaning and desilting feeder channels and clearing vegetation from the tank's bed. The second includes rebuilding tank *bunds* and strengthening them to withstand heavy rains or floods; repairing water regulation machinery such as sluices and surplus weirs to reduce water loss; involving the landless under wage employment and; planting and preserving fodder, fuel and other plants. The third activity involves replacing damaged or missing shutters in sluices and restructuring the water distribution channels to improve the efficiency of the water distribution system.

On the other, it involves rebuilding village-level social structures such as village associations that, in centuries past, were the mainstay of rural organization. They ran the village, made rules and maintained the *eris* and ooranis. Under this system, the village was considered an administrative unit and paid taxes as a whole, collected on behalf of the ruler by the village headman.

The British undid this system with the simplicity of genius that only rulers intent on maximizing gains can display. They levied tax on individual farmers rather than the village. In a single stroke, they drove wedges into the village republic to prise this socio-economic unit apart. One of the fallouts was that they appropriated control of water resources and made water a commodity, to be paid for. This implied that farmers who had maintained their own water structures no longer had a stake in doing so; they also had to pay to use the water. Gradually, the traditions that bound village communities to their water resources withered away.

The network of *eris* and *ooranis* in Tamil Nadu, and elsewhere in India, is so intricate that no centralized system can effectively look after it. It survived only because villages looked after their own systems because they saw value in it and water a common good. By making water a government service, the British, and later the Indian, governments alienated local communities. On the other hand, they did not allocate enough money to pay for the upkeep of this network. Villages could manage with extremely small investments comprising chiefly of labour. The government had to contract everything, including labour – this pushed up its cost of maintenance. As with all government systems, corruption ensured that most of money never reached the *eri*. Centralised management of water resources still remains the cause of India's water crisis.

Over the past 200 years the network slowly decayed till the early 1990s when organizations such as the Dhan Foundation decided to reverse the rot. During the first phase from 1992 – 95, the Foundation rehabilitated a few tanks to increase their storage capacity and improve the reliability of water supply. This gave it the experience and the confidence to launch a second phase from 1996-99. During this, the Foundation executed 500 development works including tank restoration, digging wells and providing drinking water. They covered nearly 56,000 farmers.

The ancestors of the people of Madurai and Ramnathpuram certainly had the right idea when they started digging *eris* and *ooranis*. Rainfall is erratic and agriculture here is completely dependent on this making it a game of Russian roulette. *Eris* and *ooranis* evened out the rough spots by making water available for most of the year. This helped farmers tide over drought years and avoid famine as they could grow enough in a season of good rainfall to last them a couple of years.

Eri builders studied the contours of the land before picking a spot to make an *eri*. The size of the *eri*, the height of its *bunds*, the ayacut and command area were an integrated package, each designed to maximize the irrigated area while minimizing the submergence area. None of the tanks were made with sophisticated measuring or construction equipment, which makes them all the more remarkable. They were so successful that *eris* once irrigated a third of all land in the state.

The ray of hope for *eris* and *ooranis* comes from the government's inability to provide water. Rainfall has become more erratic in recent years. It has finally dawned on the local people that they have to revert to the wisdom of ages to make ends meet if they want to live in the land of their ancestors. Else, they have little option but to find greener pastures in the slums of Madurai, Chennai and other cities. The movement started by the Dhan Foundation has gathered speed – it is spreading across the state and to other parts of Peninsular India, bringing with it renewed hope for *eris* and *ooranis*.

5 CHAMBAL: WATERING DOWN DACOITS

Brij Mohan Gujjar and I squat in the shade of a stunted desi babul (native thorny tree), dodging three-inch long thorns. It's a hot afternoon in Karauli ki Dang a little north of the Chambal River. The tree provides a minimal amount of shade. In the heat and dust, Brij Mohan tells his tale.

"I am a reformed dacoit. In the eight years that I practiced dacoity, I murdered, kidnapped and extorted from people in the Chambal ravines.

"I became a dacoit with my brother to avenge our father's murder. When I was seven, and brother Bhagwan Singh was 11, people who we considered our neighbours and friends came and killed him. They said, 'Sign your land over to us' but my father refused and they killed him."

The setting sun turns a darker shade of orange, dyeing the red earth underfoot nearly crimson. The muddy green checked headgear that Brij Mohan has on, to help balance heavy loads, becomes brownish in the orange light. His white cotton vest, also muddy from the day's work in the field, and checked cotton lungi, acquire the lowering sun's hue. His eyes seem to glow redder and the black moustache bristles. He has a white stubble beard, black moustache and hair. The moustache is impressive – it arches away from his face like the horns of a wildebeest. He follows my gaze.

"Yes, I had a big moustache. It was bigger than this and straight. What else was there to do as a dacoit save twirl my moustache. The size was in keeping with my status in the gang. All dacoits have moustaches. It helps pass the time – twirling is a threatening gesture and makes us feel we have dressed for the day. The twirling also kept the moustache in shape without the need for any wax or oil. A dacoit was always known by the moustache he kept. If he wasn't worth his whiskers, his sardar would have him chop them. But now, in civilian life, I have reduced this to less menacing proportions."

Brij Mohan's was a land-owning family from the village of Rajpur in the Sawai Madhopur district of southern Rajasthan. Sawai Madhopur is better known for the Ranthambhore wildlife sanctuary than its dacoits but these 'tigers' are more a fact of life for the locals than their striped counterparts. The Gurjars were traditionally herdsmen of the region and migrated from place to place in search of greener pastures for their cattle. They made money selling milk and tending the cattle of others. Over the centuries, their lives became more settled and they acquired land and became agrarian. Land led to disputes, like the one which killed his father.

"My brother and I became dacoits 12 years after my father was killed. We were small then. We had to learn to use the gun and become strong men before we could endure the hardships of being a dacoit."

Hardships? After a life of twirling moustaches? No horse-mounted cavalry charges for the Chambal's dacoits. It was a hard life of tramping miles on foot through sandy ravines to extract money or execute a contract killing. Unlike the dacoits of Hindi films, where they gallop in and out of villages and take what they want at will, the real life of a dacoit is hard.

"The money was good, which compensated for the hardship. I used to make up to a 100,000 a month at times. But I never saved a penny."

Ill-gotten gains benefit no-one.

"We avenged my father's death and fled into the ravines. We joined a gang of men led by Jagdish. For eight years, I led a life on the run.

"One day, we had camped near a stream in a heavily wooded area. We were bathing. Suddenly a scout shouted 'police' and then we were attacked. We had to pick up whatever we could and run. The gunfight lasted the entire morning but made our getaway."

Brij Mohan smiles at the memory. His paan-stained teeth also seem to glow orange in the light of the setting sun. Is it cold, or is it just me, I wonder. The summer evening isn't cold by any yardstick, but with the sun down, its noticeably cooler. The Dangs aren't what you would call typical dacoit country. There is little forest cover despite deep ravines so men would find it hard to hide during the day when they could be observed from a height. Across the Chambal River, though, it's a different story. The Madhya Pradesh portion of the ravines is more forested.

"We would cross the Chambal in rubber tubes after an operation. If we had done the operation in Madhya Pradesh, we would cross into Rajasthan till heat was off. On the other hand, if the hit was in Rajasthan, we would go across to Madhya Pradesh. We preferred MP because the forests are denser there and policing lax.

"I did not murder anybody except my father's killers. The rest of the time, I spent in extortion, dacoity and kidnapping. The mine owners of Dholpur, known for red sandstone, were out primary targets. We also picked up the relatively rich farmers in the region and small businessmen.

But other gang members did kill people for money."

The gang varied in size from 10 to 15 men for the eight years Brij Mohan was part of it. When Jagdish died in a police encounter, a man called Pritam Singh took over. He surrendered to the police and Maharaj Singh became the sardar, or leader. Brij Mohan decided he had had enough of a life on the run during Maharaj Singh's tenure.

Brij Mohan takes me and my two companions down a path. We reach a row of trees and path abruptly dips and descends steeply to the valley floor. It's a narrow path, passage made more difficult by the sand and loose rocks on the way. I pick my way down carefully, weighed down as I am by camera equipment, so as not to land on my backside.

Across the valley is a 10 metre high mud wall.

It spans a *nallah,* a drain, some 25 metres across with a sandy bottom. Scrub trees on both sides break the sandy monotony. The sides of the ravine have more trees than usual, anchoring the sand and stabilizing the slopes. The mud wall is actually a check dam to stop rainwater from running off into the rivers, deepening the ravines in the process. It is part of a system of check-dams that Brij Mohan has worked to erect across some ravines near his Rajpur village. A group of men and women transfer stones to each other to build a low stone wall on one side of the wall. The side that will eventually face the onslaught of water has a stone face.

"This is what I do now," says Brij Mohan. "Conserving water."

"I left the gang and surrendered to the police. There was an amnesty scheme under which I served a couple of years in jail. The police dropped charges against me in exchange for my surrender."

Brij Mohan joined the ranks of hundreds of surrendered dacoits.

"I thought, 'I have achieved my goal as a dacoit to avenge my father's death. Why fall to a police bullet when I can return to my former life'. I approached the station house officer of the local police station in Rajasthan and gave myself up."

This reason for joining a giroh, or dacoit gang, has made it easier for those working for the surrender of dacoits to get them to return to a normal life. It is honour or revenge that drives the men and women of the region into the ravines. In an interview to The Tribune, Dr. S. N. Subba Rao, founder of the National Youth project of India, says, "Once I had figured out that it is not money or the lack of it that made a person take to weapons but revenge for an injustice done, I knew what had to be done to convince them to come back to the mainstream. For example, there was this 16-year-old boy, Khunta, one of the youngest of the lot. He told me that ever since he was five, his mother had ingrained into him that he had to avenge his father's death. The day when he was strong energy to hold a gun, he shot the man dead and joined a giroh. But we were able to bring him back."

Dr. Rao has been the man behind the surrender of nearly 670 dacoits between 1960 and 1976. He recalls, "It was a historical moment when in 1972, 189 dacoits surrendered before Jayaprakash Narayan at Mahatma Gandhi Seva Ashram, Chambal, which I had established with the help of some volunteers in 1970. I worked with the help of Tehsildar Singh, Man Singh's son."

But water seemed to have softened Brij Mohan's heart. He is now a family man, with around 20 bighas of land behind his house and another 30 or so downstream of the checkdam. His checkdam. About four bighas make an acre; bighas are an Indian measure of land and vary from one place to another.

There are other check-dams upstream of this one, but Brij Mohan took the lead to get this one constructed.

"Most of the farmland owned by Rajpur's villagers is downstream of this checkdam. We have always had a water problem – too much during the monsoons and too little at other times. The checkdam will even out the availability of water and let us grow more than one crop," he says.

He has seen how this works elsewhere. The water table is low so tubewells don't work well. Handpumps in his village dry up every summer. So the idea is to catch rainwater before it runs off into the rivers and make it stand – standing water percolates to the water table. Therefore, the checkdam.

The villagers toiling at the site look up at him. Brij Mohan pulls on an olive shirt with epaulettes – totally undecorated as if to mark the uneventful life he led in the ravines. Were he to change from the coloured lungi to a pathani pajama of the same colour, he would look like he had just walked in from the hunt. The man has presence. At 5 feet 10 inches and 80 kilos, head topped with black hair streaked with a little white, he looks much younger than his 40 years. His arms are hairy and powerful; I can well imagine them gripping and using the crude double barrel guns that some of the dacoits still prefer. Most, he assures me, use advanced weapons including AK 47s, though some have the older shotguns and rifles. He personally preferred rifles because they were easier to handle.

The man is easily the leader of the group of around 20 working on the checkdam. He sits on his haunches and directs the others, occasionally lending a hand to lift a heavy stone to a labourer's head. Stones fly and the wall rises slowly. The wall forms the downstream face of the checkdam. When full, it will hold water for several months.

Brij Mohan says, "I motivated the villagers to build this dam. Our farmlands are downstream of this. We have some wells to irrigate the fields but they run dry soon after the rains. The soil is sandy and does not hold rainwater. When this is complete, our wells will have water longer so we can grow a proper crop, maybe even two. We will also have more water to drink. Already, the checkdam upstream of this one has brought up water tables in the region. It's good to be a labourer again."

It's a help to the women folk as well. They had to walk six or seven kilometres for water; the older checkdam has reduced that to 3 kilometres and this one will reduce it to less than one.

"Giving water is the highest form of service," he philosophizes.

I ask, "So what made you, a man who spilt blood, into a man who saved water?"

This story begins in a village some distance away, Rawatpura, from where his wife comes. After he got out of jail, Brij Mohan married and became a farming man. The family has a fair bit of land and he did well growing rice, wheat, mustard, millets and gram. He bought himself a tractor that was used for carting construction material, when not ploughing fields. Brij Mohan made ends more than meet.

An organization was helping people at Rawatpura reclaim ravines by soil and water conservation. They needed equipment and labourers, both rare in a region where there is little activity other than subsistence farming. The only other activity in the Dangs is sandstone mining.

"I offered my tractor and labourers to the organization for their work at a daily rate of Rs. 750 plus diesel," he says, solemnly. "That was three years ago. It was the start of a long involvement with water. I used to be an angry man then. My eyes used to be red and my moustache, hennaed and long. I looked every bit the dacoit that I wasn't. It was a reminder to everybody about what I had been."

My guide in the Dangs, Karan Singh, nudges me at this point. He has been a mute listener, nodding in agreement with all Brij Mohan has said.

"Actually, he demanded that we use his tractor. He said, 'If you need men and equipment, you have to take them from me and nobody else'. So we agreed even though his rate was higher than the Rs. 500 that others were willing to provide tractors for. But we wanted the cooperation of the entire village and saw this man could ensure it."

This, during a lull in the story when Brij Mohan is called away by the construction workers for a bit of advice. Wheels within wheels.

He returns to his story. "They were making a tank for the village to collect rainwater so that instead of running off into rivers, the water could be used for irrigation. It was also the revival of an old system that we had here for irrigation that had fallen into disuse as men migrated to towns for work. I thought this was something good that I should try and do in my village."

Brij Mohan spoke with this village Panchayat and persuaded them to construct the older checkdam in 2003. It has worked wonders for water in the area. The region is noticeably greener than other parts of the Dangs. In the ravine, trees are taller and there is some grass – better for the Gurjars' cattle. Now, they have a second checkdam to store more water for crops. This one, though, will work indirectly – the stored water will recharge the wells in the fields that will be used for irrigation and drinking water.

Tanks here are called *talais*. Those in fields are called *khet talais*. A majority of tanks are made in fields or common lands. Nearly all are used for irrigation, drinking water and watering animals. Wild animals also quench their thirst at these oases. The land is dry but stunted trees indicate that water is available a few feet down. This is what handpumps exploit in the region. But we shall return to *talais* later.

We turn for Brij Mohan's village. I walk along the bottom of the checkdam while he, Karan and Sunil Sharma, my companions, walk along the top. Flanking Brij Mohan, the threesome could well have emerged from the ravines that very minute. He makes an imposing figure, in contrast with the relatively shriveled physiques of my two companions. Against the setting sun, it's a great photo-op. We scramble up the bank and the inevitable happens – I slip and slide backwards on my butt. The camera is safe thankfully inside two bags but not my dignity. Brij Mohan helps me up. We walk through thorny brush and my trousers gather many spiny seeds from the plants. The three-inch thorns threaten to shred my arms but, following these three, they easily find a way around the bushes. The soft sand of the ravines gives way to broken rock underfoot – red and flaky. It's sandstone.

We cross a road. The jeep we had driven three days and 250 kilometres to locate our elusive reformed bandit has had a puncture – from a three-inch thorn. Its comical almost – a vehicle designed for life in the rough immobilized by a small piece of wood that looks daunting to me, but to it? Who knows how many tyre punctures these have caused. The driver was sure careful about not driving over branches with these projections but on tracks it was usually impossible to be 100 percent certain. The driver has fixed the puncture and is waiting on the road, not taking chances. We tell him to switch off and follow; the village is a five minute walk on the opposite side of the road. He gratefully complies – the last three days have been hard on everybody.

In the village, it's evident that Brij Mohan is a man of respect, notwithstanding his shady past. Dacoits are also called baghees in the Chambal region, meaning rebel. It's symbolic of their rebellion against something – society, the government. They are looked upon more kindly by their fellow villagers than the law, understandably. People know behind every dacoit is a sound reason. The most famous of them all, Man Singh, became a bandit after he and his family killed a bunch of Brahmins in his family. It was the climax of a family feud. He ruled the ravines for 20 years before he was killed. In his time, legend had it that Man Singh was invincible. He ran a parallel administration, settling disputes among villagers and earning the title of Raja. At Independence in 1947, a general amnesty was announced and Man Singh returned to his village. Blood lust made him kill afresh and he died in an encounter with the army and police. His lieutenant Roop Narain Sharma, aka Roopa, ran his empire after Man Singh's death. Roopa ran a larger and more ruthless operation till the law put a bullet in him in 1959.

In more recent times, the infamous Phoolan Devi turned *baghee* after she was gang-raped by the Thakurs of her faraway Behmai village. She was from the lowly Mallah caste and this atrocity was the latest in a line of centuries of abuse. Phoolan avenged herself and ran a ruthlessly efficient gang of bandits till she surrendered in the early 1980s.

This tradition of avenging an insult or righting a wrong has earned dacoits respect. Even reformed ones are well-respected and their arbitration skills called upon regularly in villages.

Sitting in his house, Brij Mohan offers us sickly sweet tea in tiny cups, almost too small to hold. It's a departure from the usual tea drinking procedures that takes place out of glasses. But guests need special treatment, so the microscopic cups. He has two sons and two daughters – no regrets about the girls here.

"My eldest son is with my sister in Niwera, studying in high school. I hope they never have to go through what I did," says Brij Mohan.

***

The Dangs, essentially highlands north of the Chambal river, extend over seven tehsils in the districts of Sawai Madhopur, Dausa and Karauli in Rajasthan. The Ranthambhore plateau, between 300 metres and 600 metres in height, is deeply eroded in places. A lack of forest cover in most of the region has left it open to erosion by water during the monsoons and strong summer winds. The soil is red, originating from the red sandstone that lies beneath. Most of the highlands have no roads – there are dirt tracks that connect villages. These are ideal for cross-country racing and little else. The main transport in villages is camel cart – seldom does a jeep or any other mode of powered transport reach the interiors. There isn't any electricity or telephone. In the Dangs, I was well and truly cut off from the outside world. Not that I minded being in the place that time forgot.

But not the people.

They cling to life. They rear cattle and goat on the precarious greenery of the highlands. They eke a single crop from the soil during the rains, if the rain gods are kind – if they aren't, they migrate in search of work to nearby towns or villages. Their villages have houses made of piles of stone, bound together with a mixture of cow dung and mud, like it used to be in rural India several decades ago. Their villages are clean and there is little of the overflowing drains that I saw in many other parts of the country. The men of the Dangs work as hard as the women, again a pleasant change from other parts of India where women slog while men play cards. Of course, social segregation of the two exists. Remote villages have schools, albeit two room structures, where teachers actually come to teach and students attend classes. Seldom do teachers bunk – the place sets great store by education and both girls and boys attend at least primary school. The people ask nothing of the government, and get nothing.

The region gets around 800 MM of rain between June and September, enough to support human and animal life. However, the ravines ensure that most of this runs off into rivers and very little stays behind to sustain life.

The Chambal River is Yamuna's main tributary, rising in Madhya Pradesh at Bar Nagar. It flows north till Kota in Rajasthan, where it turns north-east. For a distance it forms the border between Rajasthan and Madhya Pradesh. This is also where the ravines are. Before joining the Yamuna, it turns south-east in Uttar Pradesh and flows through more ravines. The river's basin covers 31,000 sq. kilometres in the three states. Centuries of erosion have created an incredible maze of mud cliffs – the ravines of Chambal. Some are several hundred feet deep – you cannot see the bottom from the top. This extensive, interlinked system shelters countless species of birds and animals. The rivers have several varieties of fish and reptiles. The ravine part of the Chambal river basin is roughly rectangular in shape, around 300 kilometres long by 100 kilometres wide. This huge area has thorny, dry deciduous vegetation. It is a peculiar situation of adversity in the midst of plenty though urban or western yardsticks of poverty do not apply here.

In 1979, a 400 kilometre stretch of the river Chambal and an approximately 2 km wide swathe of the river ravines on either side, an area of 635 sq. km, was designated the National Chambal Sanctuary (NCS). The NCS, an IUCN Category IV (Managed Nature Reserve) lying in the Indus-Ganges Monsoon Forest belt, begins downstream of the Kota barrage in Rajasthan. The sanctuary's lower limit is after Pachnanda near Bhareh in Uttar Pradesh where the river flows into the Yamuna. The entire river basin is a haven for flora and fauna. Apart from the Gangetic dolphin, the other inhabitants of the sanctuary include magar, ghariyal, chinkara, sambar, nilgai, wolf and wild bear.

There is a legend that says the Chambal originated from the blood of cows that an Aryan king sacrificed, seeking supremacy. Unnerved by this ambitious king, the Brahmins cursed him and the bloodied river. That's probably why you will not find a single temple town along the Chambal.

Whatever the legend, the river remains clean enough to bathe in and drink straight from, even half-way down its course to the Yamuna. In the height of summer, it carries up to 10 times the quantity of water that its principal does, restoring to the Yamuna the respectability of a river after Delhi and Haryana have done their utmost to reduce it to a drain.

My staging point for the Great Daku Hunt is a small village on the north-west fringe of Karauli Ki Dang, Rewali. It's a seven-hour drive from Delhi, or you can take a train to Dausa and bus or jeep from there. The best way to get there is to drive up to Jaipur and take the highway to Agra. Dausa is 57 kilometres from Jaipur. I turn off the highway here, cross the tracks and drive through the dusty town. Its claim to fame is that it's the constituency of one of the Congress Party's 'promising' young Members of Parliament, Sachin Pilot. Then it's another 40 kilometres on a fairly good road, lined with enormous mango trees to Lalsot. Traffic is light though the occasional jugad – a vehicle made by marrying the motor of a diesel water pump to a tractor trailer – hogs the road, forcing me to move over. At an under-construction temple on this road, I turn left onto a narrow but well-paved village road. Fields that are beginning to sprout, interspersed with brown ploughed ones, line the road. Some 10 kilometres down this village road, dodging jeeps and jugads out to drive me into the fields, low hills rise on either side, some four or five kilometres distant. They increase in height and when I reach Lalsot, they seem to fill the sky on three sides; I am in a valley of sorts with hills on three sides. The only open side is from where I have come. A veritable cul-de-sac and a great place for a kingdom. It's lush and green, the trees are tall and varied. Tube-wells and handpumps point to an abundance of groundwater. The hills on either side keep the valley well-supplied. There is power and while the mobile does not work in Lalsot, there is an abundance of public phone booths. However, the lushness hides a grim reality – the water table has fallen from 10 metres to to 40 metres over the past 10 years because of the tubewells; people have deepened wells and put tubewells into them as well. Handpumps are for drinking; tubewells for irrigation, bathing and washing. Nobody uses wells anymore – its cumbersome. Most houses are made of stone or brick. Nearly all the villages have cemented roads, built over the past couple of years under the Prime Minister's Village Road Project. There aren't any villages with dirty drains flowing all over the place – they have cracked the elementary problem of waste water disposal.

I reach in the afternoon in early May; it's been a hot drive and the coolness of the building is welcome. My destination in the village is a school. Its head teacher gives me a glass of cool water, slightly metallic to taste. Then, a surprise.

"Will you have a cold drink?" he asks.

I know what campaigners for community ownership over water resources feel about aerated drinks. But it's tempting to be naughty. I nod and a little later we have cold drinks in our hands. The empties are promptly returned.

I wait for my trip planner, Chaman Singh, who heads a project in the region to restore water resources, and my two companions Karan Singh from Amavra and Sunil Sharma from Nai Basti. Karan is a thin dark man of around 35; Sunil is older by a decade and well built, with light eyes. They both know the Dangs like the back of their hands, having worked in villages there for around five years.

The hills to the west of the school form what is called the Kochar Ki Dang. They are a part of the Lalsot hills. The Karauli Ki Dang are further south and part of the Ranthambhore plateau.

Karan and Sunil arrive a little later and after a round of introductions, they call Chaman to find out when he will come. He will be late, he says. So Karan suggests we visit Godh village where a local Baba lives, in a little roadside Hanuman temple. It's a 20 minute drive from Lalsot, nothing compared to the 300 kilometres one I've done earlier that day. I had ham sandwiches from home for lunch, so am not hungry.

Karan says, "The Baba is a character. If you have come all this way and have time on your hands, let's go and see him. He is well known in these parts now."

So we reach the Baba's nondescript temple. It's a small, two-room construction with Hanuman's statue in one and his abode in the other. A well stands to one side and a cement platform in front, separating the temple from the road. There is a young man sitting on the wall of the well. The baba is inside with Hanuman. We wait while he finishes his prayers and emerges.

He's wrapped in dirty rags – everything about him is disheveled. From his black flowing hair, through his black beard, to his once-white kurta pajama and his bare feet. He is the archetypal baba of a thousand pictures. His eyes shine through the mess of hair on his face – they are piercing and shrewd. They contrast with his general, spaced-out behaviour.

Karan, always the talkative one, begins, "This man has come from Delhi to see you baba. Tell us your story."

Godh Baba gives me the once-over. The young man brings out a filthy rug from the baba's quarters and spreads it on the cement platform. He pulls a little water from the well and pours it into a steel lota, which he passes around. Then there is a round of beedis, local smokes of tobacco wrapped in leaf.

Godh Baba says, "In the winter of 2003, I got a call from Hanuman. He said, 'Come with me' in a dream. When I got up in the morning, I found myself in a temple some distance from my village. I started walking towards this temple – my family tried stopping me but Hanuman gave me strength to overpower them all. I lost my mind here, resisting Hanuman's call. He spoke to me daily. He kept me going. Eventually I gave in. Seeing me at this temple, that was broken then, people started coming for help. They came to find out about their stolen property, sort out health problems and find solace in life. When a person asks me a problem, I feel Hanuman speaking in my head and giving me the answer."

Karan interjects at this point. "Tell us the camel story."

Baba says, "A man who'd lost his camel came to me to help find it. I told him the animal was tied on top of a particular building in a village. He located it and with the help of the police, got his animal back."

Sunil breaks his silence at this point. "The baba became famous after this."

As if from nowhere, a gust of wind blows sand over us. After a short lull, it gets windy and we are soon in the middle of a dust storm. We move into the Baba's dwelling. Lightening flashes on the Hanuman idol next door and through a stone lattice window, I see the orange monkey god light up with every flash. We sit for a little while longer and then take our leave. I place a tenner in front of the Hanuman idol.

It's dark, dusty and drizzly as we drive back. The road has disappeared under a thick cloud of dust and the headlights barely pierce the gloom. A couple of times I come close to driving into the fields around a sharp turn in the road. Sunil, sitting next to me, cautions me in time so we stay on the road. By the time we reach the school, the storm has blown itself out. Chaman Singh has arrived.

"Nityaji, how nice to see you. No problem getting here I hope?"

"Not at all. Your directions were very precise."

Chaman is distracted the next moment. "Bring tea, boy." Then to me, "What will you eat?"

"Whatever. I am not particular."

He tells the boy to get vegetables from the market and then we sit together on a charpoy to plan my travel over the next three days. He knows I want to meet reformed dacoits who have started working for soil and water conservation in their villages in the Dangs. I also want to see what traditional water harvesting and storage structures exist in this part of the country. That part is a very pleasant surprise.

I eat a simple but incredibly tasty dinner, the first of many, of daal, vegetables, roti and a powder made of ground red chilli, garlic and salt. There is desi ghee (clarified butter) on the chapattis too. Then we lock up the downstairs and take mattresses and thick quilts up to the roof for a night under the stars. The sky is ink black and I can see the heavens clearly – a contrast to Delhi where light pollution blanks out all but the brightest stars. It is, well, heavenly. The hills are dark forms in the night and the fields behind the school, devoid of crops, glow in the starlight. There is no moon to spoil the view. We go to sleep. Around 2 AM, a storm brews and we have to run downstairs – I have the privilege of a room to myself.

The Lalsot hills are some 700 metres high, too daunting to climb. There are villages up there, Sunil assures me.

"There are *talaabs* on top of the hills that were made centuries ago.

They are used by villagers who take their herds up for grazing. Gurjars are primarily herdsmen so they spend several weeks in the forests with their herds and use the water from these *talais*," he says.

The hill *talaabs* are the first line of rainwater catchment. There are small check-dams on the *nallahs* that flow down from the hills that serve the same purpose – checking the flow of water to give it time to percolate into the ground. Then there are *khet talais* on flat ground that traps the remaining rainwater near fields and villages. These are sort of end-users of water and directly benefit the fields they are built in. The hill and *nallah talais* have indirect benefits. I can make out where there is a *talai* by the vegetation; it's much greener around a *talaabs* or a *talai*.

We leave for the Dangs at 6 AM. The jeep comes at the crack of dawn, an hour earlier. It's a Mahindra Commander, just the vehicle for the cross-country ride we will face over the next three days. We load up and are off to Sapotra, the village from where we enter the Dangs in our quest for the reformed dacoits. Karan tells me how he began his career here.

"I had worked with Tarun Bharat Sangh in Alwar for a few years. I wanted to do something for my own area so returned here in the mid-1990s. I had heard of a village in the Dangs where water was a problem – they had a *talai* that had broken. I offered to help them rebuild it. Most villages have *talais* but they have not bothered to look after them.

"The villagers told me to supply them cement and artisans and they would contribute labour. I did so and got the *talai* repaired. While the work was on, a dacoit kidnapped some of the artisans and demanded a ransom. I met the man in his lair and told him he had committed a grave sin by kidnapping artisans who were working for the good of the local villagers. The man wanted my watch but I told him if he set right his wrong, he would get many watches. The man gave in eventually and release my artisans but didn't reform himself. He was killed in an encounter with the police."

That was Karan's first brush with dacoits, one of many. He has been responsible for turning reformed baghees water conservation. He is an unlikely campaigner, wiry and self-deprecating.

We reach Kachaheda village, 25 kilometres from Lalsot. It's small, with 20 Gurjar families. The village claims to be 600 years old and was once was part of the Jaipur kingdom. The houses are scattered any old how. Dusty fields surround the village. We take the only road through it – its concrete, built under the PM's scheme barely a year before. The village's claim to fame is the secondary school that gets students from many villages nearby. One side of the road has the school's compound, stretching from end of the village to the other. The other side has houses and lanes leading into a maze of buildings. The road ends in a steep drop, barely negotiable by the jeep.

Just outside the Kachaheda are a series of *talais*. They are ground-level ponds, surrounded by 2-3 metre high mud walls and open on the side that faces uphill. The land is nearly flat so it's hard to see what's uphill and what's downhill but Sunil tells me the villagers have it figured out by watching the flow of rainwater. The crescent-shaped *talais* stop water outside the village and hold it for several months. This prevents flooding inside the village and recharges their wells, provides water their animals and irrigates their fields. The main *talai* is on common ground, is about a hectare in area and used to water animals, not for irrigation.

Gokhalendar Gujjar, a tall man with an impressively white turban, greets me at the *talai*. He is the physical training instructor in the local secondary school. The village has mostly stone or brick houses – I see a few towards the periphery that are thatched, probably belonging to poorer people from lower castes. The Gurjars are all fairly well-off.

"The groundwater here is brackish. We have to depend only on rainwater for irrigation and for drinking. The *talais* have helped reduce the brackishness in the village wells so we can drink that water for part of the year now," he says.

Gokhalendar has about 50 bighas of land, with two *khet talais*. One wasn't enough to irrigate all his fields so he made another. Now, he says, he gets two crops a year where earlier he got only one. Some of the *talais* go back several hundred years. Where the land is hilly, there are *talais* in the hills – called *talaabs* here – that trap rainwater in the heights and help to recharge wells in villages in the plains below. There exists an old and intricate system of *talaabs* and *talais* in the villages around Kochar ki Dang. Nearly all the fields have *talais*, built by the farmers with local labour. The mud extracted from the *talai* goes into building the walls and the field. Every year, the *talai* is excavated and the mud from its bed makes good manure.

He says, "Next year, I am going to grow fish to make more money."

It seems innovative uses of water harvesting, an age-old tradition here, is catching on. The spread is slow but seeing is believing – as more farmers use *khet talais* to water their fields, others are following suit. Hopefully, the water table and brackishness in the groundwater will disappear one day in the not-too-distant future.

We drive south from Kachaheda village towards Thali village. This is at a major crossroads – one road goes to Ranthambhore, another to Gangapur. I am about to meet my first reformed gangster – Jagdish Prasad Gujjar or Niwera village. He looks like an extremely unlikely dacoit – there is no moustache, he is neatly shaved and his hair is cut short. He's literate, having passed the 10th class. He looks around 35. The man is slightly built, dark and dressed in a shirt and trousers that have accompanied him through several fields. He carries a red cloth shoulder bag. At first, when Karan greets him by the roadside, I think it's another of his many friends – Karan seems to know every other man in the place – but then he gives me a wry smile and jerks his head towards Jagdish.

"This is the man you want to meet."

"A reformed dacoit?" I ask Karan, sotto voce. Karan has told me never to use the D-word loudly or ask dacoits questions about their past directly. The rule apparently doesn't apply to Jagdish, though. I am told I can talk openly with him. We enter a thatched tea shop by the roadside and side on red sandstone benches – everything in the region seems to be made of red sandstone.

Jagdish's underworld career began as a go-between for dacoits and mine owners in Dholpur. He used to negotiate with the miners on behalf of the dacoits. They influenced him to join them with tales of the good life – an income of Rs. 50,000 a month, little work and complete authority. Jagdish spent a fairly short, but intense, time as a bandit, more so than Brij Mohan. The former was in the business for just two years but 'accomplished' much more.

"I joined the Bane Singh group six years ago. I killed people for money, kidnapped and extorted from the same mine owners with whom I had negotiated deals earlier. If a person didn't pay, he was shot. Many times, I did the shooting.

"Two years after I joined them, I went on a mission to a village called Ratnapura where an NGO called Tarun Bharat Sangh ran a school called Tarunshala. I entered the school to rob. There, I saw a book on 'Water on the Mountain' that changed my life. Instead of robbing, I decided to quit. I went and surrendered at the Karanpur thana to Ramnath, the thanedar."

Jagdish spent two years in jail. During this time, the police resolved the cases against him, dropping most of the charges. When he came out of jail, he met Karan Singh soon after and joined the NGO.

"I think it's better to earn Rs. 10,000 honestly than Rs. 100,000 dishonestly. All my gang members have surrendered. I found it hard after coming out jail to get accepted back into society. I also thought of surrendering because sooner or later, I would have stopped a bullet. Why die unnecessarily?"

In this, Jagdish differs from Brij Mohan. The latter had little problems being accepted back while Jagdish did. But the chance to win respect came soon. One day, a marriage party came to his village. Four people from the group fell into a well. Jagdish jumped into rescue them as the others just looked on.

"That won me much-needed respect. Since then, I have built several water harvesting structures in many villages of this area. This so much better than being a dacoit," says the slightly-built former bandit. I try to picture him in black, with a red tilak (vermilion mark) on his forehead, bandoliers across each shoulder and shotgun in hand, striding the ravines. Somehow, I cannot conjure up the image as we sit in the thatched shade of the tea shop, sipping sickly sweet tea out of tiny cups. The cold drinks stalls across the road look infinitely more inviting and I am dying for a smoke. Leaving Jagdish with Sunil and Karan, I quickly buy myself a cigarette. The others light beedis. We bond over smoke. Jagdish doesn't normally smoke or drink tea, saying these are reminders of his past that he'd rather forget. But with the conversation concentrated on his past, he gives in and has a half-cup of tea and shares a beedi with Karan Singh.

"You must see my work," he says. "It's just a short distance from here."

Then rising, he excuses himself. "I have to go to Gangapur." And turning to Karan, he asks, "Are you going that way?"

Karan says we are going to Sapotra that is further south. Jagdish and I shake hands and he slings his cloth bag over his shoulder.

"When you come next, stay at my village," he says, signaling a bus to stop. Then he's gone.

The roads are fine and we make Sapotra by lunch-time. Sapotra is the end of the road – after this, we go off-track into the Dangs. There won't be any more roads for the next two days. Sapotra is a small town where farmers get their vehicles fixed; it also has many ghanis, or mustard presses. Opposite the dhaba where we eat, there is a ghani – the reek from the freshly extracted mustard oil wafts into the dhaba. Sunil goes off to meet a local contact.

Sapotra is dusty town, and qualified as an urban centre because it has a municipality. I see evidence of this entity when a tractor loaded with garbage pulls up near the jeep, that's parked next to a large pond, and upends the trailer so the rubbish pours into the pond. Karan Singh shakes his head.

"That is how they manage their water resources. We tried working with the municipality here but you can see the results."

The pond has water and pipelines lead from it to a water treatment plant that supplies the town. Garbage in, garbage out, I think to myself. One day they will get sewage to drink.

Sunil's man has disappeared into the Panchayat office. It's getting late – we have a long drive to a village where we'll spend the night. We give the man a few minutes and are about to leave when he emerges, looking hassled. He's a short man in his mid-fifties in a white kurta-pajama and Gandhi cap. I marvel at his clothes' whiteness in the dusty landscape – must have a ready supply of clothes to remain so white. He looks cool – both mentally and physically.

Netaji, also known as Dhojia Semriwale, has had a long association with both sides of the law. Like Jagdish, he was a go-between for people on both sides of the law. Unlike Jagdish, he didn't get tempted by the dark side despite a 15-year long association. Karan offers him a lift as we are headed into Karauli Ki Dang towards Kalyanpura, village in the Sapotra tehsil, where Netaji wants to go. The man is a little wary of our offer, specially with a Delhiite in the vehicle. Karan assures him I am not a government official and Netaji's secrets are safe with us.

Netaji is extremely voluble thereafter, his enthusiasm tempered only by the dense clouds of dust that seem to swirl around as much inside the jeep as outside. We have Sapotra and, it seems, civilization behind. There is not road, just a camel track with dust so deep and fine that only a jeep-sort of vehicle can pass. There are a few scrub trees and plenty of thorny bushes but no shade. The afternoon is hot and even though I want to roll the window down, the dust puts paid to any such notion.

"But Netaji," says Karan Singh. "You have been a clever man. Making everybody believe that you have left your former racket."

Netaji replies, "I have. It's not a question of making people believe something. It's true. I decided rackets are best left alone. I've earned enough."

Karan says, "Netaji, it's rumoured you made a killing on a deal. The mine owner gave you a fat ransom but the dacoit who demanded was killed by the police in the meantime. Where have you hidden the booty?"

Netaji squirms. "No ransom was paid. The miner learnt of the killing and refused to pay."

"How could he? Come on, we won't tell anybody."

The driver chips in. "It's just us Netaji. We are all employed and not interested in these matters."

Netaji sticks to his story. "Do you think such booty would have gone unnoticed? Somebody would have come to claim it."

Sunil chimes in, "Oh Netaji. You are an old player. You would know how to hide it in a safe place and help yourself to it once in a while."

"Besides," he adds with a wink at me. "You are always well turned out and never seem to work."

"You guys are just pulling my leg," says Netaji. "I stopped being a go-between many years ago. This ransom thing happened much later."

"Yes, but your name came up as the intermediary, the dalal," says Karan, using the derogatory term for go-between to provoke Netaji.

The old man isn't moved. The conversation revolves around the ransom and what became of it. We reach a sort of crossroads, rather cross tracks. Netaji wants to get off here and Karan obliges. I have listened silently to the conversation, letting Karan extract information while filing it away. I felt butting in would make Netaji shut up. It has been informative.

"He is still in on it but won't admit to us," says Karan. "We have a goody goody image among the villages here so people don't like talking about extortions and kidnappings with us."

I ask, "But you are sure Netaji is still on the take?"

"Quite," he replies.

I shut my mouth – its full of dust. The others follow suit and Sunil wraps a cloth – his gamchha – around his face. He stares out of the window. We have left the extremely dusty trail but it's still dusty. And hot. The rocks over which we are driving have splintered in the heat of the day and cold of the night. Its over 40°C in the day and around 10 at night. There is no road, only a faintly recognizable trail that wends left and right, leading us about eastwards across the Dangs. Progress is slow because the driver has to dodge vicious thorns and large rocks that dot the track. It's a camel track. What a wonderful place for a car rally, I think to myself. Miles of back-breaking trail with no break, no traffic and no facilities. It would test the mettle of the best of drivers and vehicles. I have to complement the Mahindras for making a contraption that, while extremely crude and uncomfortable, covers the trail with ease – that's the important thing. The trail would test the best of 4X4 vehicles and drivers. A Raid De Chambal. I glance at the jeep's instruments, expecting to see the temperature gauge in the red but its pleasantly in the blue. Everything is fine, it seems. The trail becomes a rocky gully as it descends from one level to another – the beginnings of a ravine. In the rains, this would become a raging torrent, carrying water from the higher level to the lower and in the process, carving out a deeper niche. The gully is full of loose rock and is quite deep in one place. The driver skillfully maneuvers two tyres of the jeep along one side of the cut and the other two on the other side. Then, with all of us holding our breath, he drives over the cut in the first gear. There is a collective sigh when we're past the deep cut.

Its cooler in the lower part of the trail. The trees are taller and vegetation is denser. The trail starts to descend to what seems to be a plain. The vegetation gets denser and suddenly, we are out of the thickets and into a field. It's unploughed. In a corner is a *khet talai*. Bouncing over the field, we see more and then the first cottage of Rawatpura village. The cottage is a mud and thatch affair, surrounded by a four-foot high fence of thorny bushes. One side has a wooden gate – two posts with a rectangular piece of wood lashed to one of them. A woman sees the jeep and goes inside the hut. We bounce on and more houses appear.

There is no power in Rawatpura, no phones and no running water. Rawatpura could well be the place time forgot, but not quite. There is a single tractor in this village of around 500 people. There isn't any approach road, just the trail through the fields that ends in an open space at one end of the village. A long low house made of stones and topped with large slabs of red sandstone (again) runs along the left of the clearing that ends in a compound with buffaloes in it. To the right are the backs of other houses. One double-storeyed structure has a small balcony sticking out the rear – a woman leans out on hearing the jeep. A buffalo gallops away from us into the clearing.

People appear – from the long low house, the lanes in the village. The village elder is Ramlal Gujjar, a farmer who owns around 45 bighas of land. He is quite old, possibly 60. His white kurta and dhoti tell of long use – both have turned off-white. We sit outside the house, under an awning, and the others of the village gather round. Karan and Sunil engage them in conversation about crops, weather and *talais*. I wander off into the village.

Save for one house that's double storeyed, all the others are single, and low. The double-storeyed one is much older, possibly a couple of centuries old, and belongs to the local *zamindar*. It's an impressive structure made of stones and mortar with a large sloping courtyard and lattice-work windows on the first floor. The ground floor has a row of four rooms set back from the verandah. The others houses are made from roughly hewn blocks of stone held together with a mixture of clay and cow dung. The insides are plastered with the same stuff as it the floor. The roofs are made of sloping slabs of red sandstone that are supported in the middle by a central beam, running the length of the room. The roofs also serve as storage areas for food and to dry seasonal vegetables.

Nearly all the woman have a *ghunghat* on their heads, partly covering their faces; the *ghunghats* are thin enough to see through but too thick to let their faces be seen. The men almost uniformly wear short white kurtas and dhotis. They are mustachioed and grizzly – the daily shave just isn't something they do in these parts. All the houses have courtyards where the animals stay, with a raised portion in one corner to wash dishes. They all have verandahs that serve as a lounging area and kitchen – all have blackened walls and roofs and at least one chulha, or fireplace. Most households keep their store of firewood in the front courtyard.

A baby lies in a cot, hanging from the ceiling of one courtyard. Flies buzz around him as he sleeps and the mother lurks protectively in the background as I satisfy my photographic urge. Below him, a bitch suckles her pups. The village is slowly winding down for the night, the only discordant note being our arrival before dinner time. I return to the jeep and see quite a crowd sitting under the awning.

Ramlal orders a hookah and his wife, also of indeterminate age, delivers a freshly stoked one. He draws first and then passes the pipe around. Karan has already done introductions.

I ask him, "What do people do here? How has farming been the past year?"

Ramlal lets the smoke trail from his nose. Contemplating the middle distance, he says, "Nearly everybody farms in this village. Everybody has land. Usually chana and wheat. Sometimes we grow vegetables and daal. The rains were good last year so we managed a good crop. If there are no rains, the young men and women migrate in search of wage labour. The old stay here – who will employ me."

By everybody has land, Ramlal means the Gujjars, Rawatpur's dominant caste, has land. The others don't count even as persons.

"What have you done for conserving water?"

"With their help, we have built several *talais* in the fields. These have helped us to grow more. Since 2000, we have doubled our crop output," says Ramlal. The village is reasonably well-off by their standards as my stroll shows – there aren't any jhuggies made of mud and straw or jute bags sewn together.

"Any trouble with dacoits?" I ask him.

All the men shake their heads, some more vigorously than others. It's suspicious, and Ramlal's denial is almost too quick and rehearsed. "Not here. They operate far away from here."

We leave Ramlal to his hookah and head for Nainiyaki, where we will stay the night. The sun is a red ball hovering above the horizon when we arrive. It's an hour's drive from Rawatpura over more punishing tracks. Karan knows his way around the wilderness – he sees tracks where there are none, only hard rock.

Nainiyaki has the only primary school in the entire place, a two-room affair atop a small mound. It has a rooftop water harvesting system that channels rainwater into a concrete underground tank. A handpump helps people get water out – its dry now because all the water has been used up. The handpump was put in to help school children get water without the risk of hauling a bucket out of a well.

I ask Karan, "Do you think the teacher comes to this place. It's so far from anywhere."

He nods. We walk from the school to the edge of the settlement. The village is set against highlands on a stretch of flat land – behind it, low hills rise, covered with scrub vegetation. Before it, there is an unbroken expanse of red rock that slopes down to the village's fields. The jeep follows us and the driver's told to park inside, where it cannot be seen from outside the village. Nainiyaki consists of two rows of low, single-storeyed houses stretching some 1 kilometre with a road in the middle. It has around 1,000. A few trees on either side give shade during the long hot summer. The street is made of red sandstone slabs placed unevenly together – I have to watch my step. At one end of the street, from where enter, an upended camel cart keeps watch. Then come the camels – all the village camels are parked at the entrance to the village. Crossing these sullen-looking creatures cautiously, I reach a sort of enclosure as the end of the village where the reception committee is waiting.

Karan takes me into a thatched hut, a sort of tea shop. A large group of men, women and children has gathered there to see us and perchance to talk. No dacoits here, warns Karan, so don't say the D word. There aren't any men with handlebar moustaches, I notice.

In the centre of the hut is the inevitable hookah. I sit on a charpoy and the others arrange themselves in various corners of the hut, accompanied by noise coughing and throat clearing. Karan begins.

"He is from Delhi and writing a book on water. He wants to know what you have to conserve water here. Now you tell him your story."

A man in his sixties with shrewd eyes, stubbly hair and beard with a large dent on his forehead, opens the batting. He is Shishpal Gujjar – you guessed it, this is also a Gujjar village – the headman. The others arraigned around him are his brothers, nephews and their children. A handsome well-built dark man of around 35 with an athlete's build enters and squats opposite me; the others make space for him. He is Shishpal's son. In different circumstances, Shishpal junior could be in the movies, I reflect. His hair and moustache are jet black and well-trimmed unlike those of most others in the hut. Tea arrives and the hookah pipe does its rounds before Shishpal speaks.

"We have been conserving water here for generations. You will see very old *talais* in the highlands above the village built by *zamindars* and rajas many years ago. They are all crescent shaped, the open side facing uphill, to catch and store rainwater. They have a small gate at the bottom through which we can let water out into our fields. These *talais* help us recharge groundwater and give water to wild animals. Then, we have *khet talais* to store water for irrigation and for animals to drink. Together, they form a system where very little water is wasted. This has been around for generations," he says.

"What can you grow with this water. Agriculture must be good here?" I ask Mr. Handsome.

Shishpal answers, "Chana, mustard, daal, wheat, jowar and bajra mostly. If the rains are good we grow vegetables and rice."

Shishpal junior add his bit. "When the rains are good, the place is full of life. We have enough to sell and can live well. If the rains are bad, we migrate in search of work. Most of us go to the sandstone mines near Dholpur."

I've seen there are no roads in the place. "How do you get around here. There are no roads?"

"We use camel carts. It is extremely tough. More than 10 women from out village have died in childbirth because we could not get them to Sapotra in time," says Shishpal. The others nod. Accessibility is a major issue here. Even by jeep it's a good five hours to Sapotra; by camel cart it takes two days over extremely rough terrain. It would tax a healthy person, and I can only imagine what it would do a woman in labour.

Their farms are about a 1 kilometres from the village where it's less rocky. The only source of drinking water is a handpump a five minute walk from the village sunk in the red rock face; there are none inside the village. Actually, there are two but one always remains out of order. For 1,000 people, it's a shameful ratio – and the government claims that nearly all villages have drinking water. Sink a handpump and forget about it; good for officials figures, bad for the people. The officials take weeks to respond to complaints of breakdowns so having two isn't a bad idea. It's closer than the stream they used earlier, that is 4 kilometres from the village through forests. The handpump yields a bucket of water, after which the next person has to wait 10 minutes for it to recharge to extract the next bucket. I banish the thought of bathing. People use the handpump strictly for drinking; bathing and washing is done at the nearest *talai*.

Night falls and the verandahs in all the huts glow with cooking fires. That's the only source of illumination. The stars are the other source. Once my eyes get used to the darkness, I stumble less. I walk the length of the village road. Low walls of the courtyards line the road. All the courtyards open towards the road with the backs of the houses forming the boundary for the village. At the far end, the road peters out into nothingness and I turn back – I have gathered a silent crowd of children and dogs. I walk back through the street lined with flickering verandahs. In places where the houses are lower than the road, I can see over their roofs into the wilderness beyond. There is no space between the houses to exit the village – the only exits are at either end.

A man hails me from his house to have a glass of milk. I shudder but accept. It's fresh and warm from the buffalo and smells of the animal. There is sugar mixed in it – a luxury for them as they have to buy sugar from the nearest market that is also a half-day walk distant.

The women guards their water containers as they would their children. Most are earthen pots; the slightly better-off have steel of brass pots. The village is bone dry, that also accounts for its cleanliness and the lack of drains flowing down the street.

Dinner is in Shishpal's verandah. The three of us sit on the floor, flanked by other men of the village. It's a feast in our honour, lit by the hearth fire. His wife piles extra wood on the fire so we can see what we're eating. A firelight dinner in this place is an exotic idea, even to me. The food's tasty – daal, potato curry and chapattis. Then there are the inevitable chillies and onions. Water is poured straight down the throat, presumably to save the water used in washing glasses. I estimate the per capita use of water at 20 litres a day – 3 to drink, and the rest of bathe and wash clothes. Extremely economical, for the people are washed and their clothes are clean. Everybody eats well and to the noise of loud belches, we get up. I'm not ashamed, for once, to belch loudly. There is another round of conversation about local projects after which the charpoys are dragged into the clearing for the night.

There is a thick cotton mattress below and a heavy cotton quilt on top. The night is warm to start with but get progressively colder. I lie awake listening to the drone of talk and watching the stars move across the heavens. Slowly, I drift off.

It must be 3 AM and I wake up, totally disoriented. The stars are still where they should be. But there is a steady scrunch-scrunch sound, followed by a pause and a scraping sound from behind my head. I twist around but cannot see anything in the pitch darkness. The scrunching invades my dreams and I spend the rest of the night in semi-sleep. Day break solves the mystery – it's a buffalo that's spent the night chewing the cud a few feet away. Fanciful images of a carnivore feeding on a carcass evaporate.

"Let's go to the jungle," says Sunil.

"What for," I ask in alarm. Maybe he feels this is a good place to get rid of me.

He laughs. "To get fresh."

In other words, to shit, brush and wash. After the crap, I wash with mud at the handpump and we walk back. Even though they don't use toothbrushes and toothpaste, they have remarkably healthy teeth, attributable to constant twig chewing. Not an advert that Colgate would want, though. Twigs are free and need less water; you can chew while working the fields. The village is bustling, if you can call it that, when we return. A woman churns milk to extract cream and ghee using a wooden rod twice her height with paddles at one end sunk in a mud pot of milk. Her body sways to the rhythm of the churning – left and right, left and right. Near her, a boy of six or seven sucks milk from a buffalo's udder. The men have already left for the fields and the women will follow later with their morning meal. We have tea and leave, thanking Shishpal for his generosity.

Nainiyaki is indeed a place where time has stood still. Its people live without anything that can be called modern, save for a lone radio, as they have for centuries. No motorized transport, power or phones. The school is the village's sole claim to fame. It's as if the mists of time parted to let me in for a night and have closed behind me to hide Nainiyaki.

A large *talai*, bigger than anything I've seen so far, opens up to my right. We have driven up a small hill where there is a government rest house about 2 hours from Nainiyaki. The *talai* is behind the hill. It's got plenty of water, unlike the smaller ones I've seen so far. A woman stands on the far shore, drying her done in the wind – it flutters red and long behind her. Her hair flows from her head and merges with the odhni, a thin cloth worn around the upper body and head. This is one built under a drought relief project of the government. Uphill from this is a small hill *talai* with a gate at the bottom. The gate is a large stone block set in the ground with a hole in the middle. Into this hole, a cylindrical stone is lowered to stop water, or raised to let it flow. Simple locally made device. Even this *talai* has a little water at the deep end.

***

The ancient king Mayur Dhwaj ruled in these parts. His palace is half way up the Kochar ki Dang plateau. The story goes as follows. His queen was a woman of great beauty, but arrogant. She refused a long line of suitors till her father, fed up with her excuses, ordered her to marry the first creature they saw the next morning outside the palace. This was a peacock.

After the wedding, the peacock flew up the hills and its bride followed, till it alighted on a *badh* tree where it nested. A storm came up that night and the peacock died in the storm. When Yamraj, the god of death, came for the peacock's soul, the wife refused to let him so. Yamraj eventually gave in and returned the peacock to life. The peacock turned into a man – Mayur Dhwaj, a king who had been bewitched and turned into a bird.

This king was a great devotee of Lord Shiva, indeed he considered himself to be greatest on earth. The king and his wife had one son, who was dearer to them than life itself. Shiva decided to test his majesty's faith and appeared outside the palace gates, riding his tiger, in the guise of a sadhu. The king, being a pious man, invited the sadhu for a meal.

"I'll eat only when my tiger's been fed," said the sadhu. "And he eats only human flesh."

So the king offered various people for sacrifice but the sadhu turned them down. The sacrifice, he said, had to be of somebody dear to the king and the king had to perform the sacrifice himself. The king got the hint. He called his son and said, 'Sit on this rock'.

Then he and his wife got a saw and cut the boy into pieces, had him cooked and fed to the tiger. The tiger was satisfied and Shiva the sadhu sat down to eat. The king and his wife joined him but the sadhu wouldn't start his meal. He told the king to call his boy. The king lost his temper, thinking the sadhu was making fun of him. But at the sadhu's insistence, he called, and the boy came running to eat.

The sadhu assumed Shiva's form. "I am convinced you are my greatest devotee. You sacrificed your only son to please me."

Karan points at a large rock lying in front of the palace. "That's where the sacrifice took place." Who knows.

As I enter the palace, two peacocks walk past an archway in the distance. By the time I reach the arch, they have disappeared. I see them through a window later, sitting on a wall outside a temple far below. Eerie. Maybe Mayur Dhwaj's spirit still lives in these birds.

Below the palace lies a large village, once Mayur Dhwaj's capital. Now it's known for its Hanuman temple. Next to the shrine is a tank which, according to legend, never goes dry. Its filthy now, from overuse. The entire village bathes in the tank, rather than taking water out and bathing outside it. Its murky water looks most uninviting.

Outside this, in the middle of nowhere, is a *baoli*, or step well. I drive off the village road, into a gully that seems to lead right into the hillside. At one point, Karan tells me to climb the side of the gully and the car barely manages the climb. We stop under an ancient peepul tree. A goatherd is pulling water from the *baoli*. We remove the thorns from the entrance to the well and walk to the bottom, dodging roots and massive cobwebs. The water is just below stair level, too risky to bend down and touch.

The well's fed by underground springs from the Kochar ki Dang. Karan assures me the water is drinkable. The goatherd proves it by pouring some down his throat. We return to the surface.

Karan asks the goatherd for water. He drinks and tells me to follow. It's the most refreshing drink of water I've ever had. It's cool and slightly sweet, thanks to the lime mortar used to build the *baoli*. One of the ironies of life — here, forgotten by all but the occasional goatherd, is this *baoli* that still provides clear, drinking water in the middle of a dusty, hot plain.

Truly, something that Indians made before the concept of India, or Bharat, or country arrived on the scene.

***

Chand ki Baoli is a spectacular step well, its age variously dated at 1200 to 1500 years. It's in a village called Abhaneri, corrupted from Abha Nagri, or town of light. It was probably built by the Pratihara kings who ruled here in the 9th and 10th centuries, AD. Another line of thinking attributes the founding of the village to Raja Bhoja, a Gurjar ruler, in the 9th century.

Chand ki Baoli is at least 30 metres deep, with a maze of steps leading down to a greenish puddle of water at the very bottom. I drive off the Jaipur-Agra highway and head over bumpy roads to Abhaneri. Outside the village is the step well. The concrete wall hides the spectacle within.

At the entrance, the chowkidar, or watchman, has spread his charpoy in the shade of a shelter, built for people who would come to the step well. He and his lackeys follow me into the complex. A few steps to the left and I turn into the step well complex itself. Its aptly named because there are thousands of steps made of stone blocks placed on top of the other. They form an interlocking pattern on the far side; getting down is easy but getting back up is tough. Each step is about 45 centimetres high and narrow so it's certainly not for the faint-hearted.

One side of the complex is given to a complex of rooms where, the chowkidar informs me, the ladies of the royal house would come to bathe. There are platforms are various levels that allowed them access to the water in privacy. The rooms are richly carved with figures of gods, flowers and animals. The whole place is made of granite, held together with mortar in places and blind faith in others. There are five levels of rooms, each with its own set of carvings. The top levels have very basic carvings. The lowest level has richly carved pillars and walls. The outside walls of the room complex have stone carvings of various gods and goddesses. Obviously, the royalty preferred the lower levels. The place is cool in the mid-May sun.

The rooms mostly smell of bat-shit and their cries echo in the halls. Thankfully its daylight and I don't run the risk of being dive bombed by vampires.

The step blocks hang together by force of gravity. The precision of the craftsmen in building the step well is quite amazing. Each step is the same size. Each terrace of stone blocks is fitted exactly the same distance further out so the structure narrows to a small rectangle of water at the bottom, from its square mouth that is some 80 metres to a side. The stones look new – I cannot believe they have weathered sun, wind and rain for more than a millennia.

The step well has a stone bottom, which means there are no springs feeding it. It only stores the rainwater that runs into the compound and into its depths. The chowkidar, who's been there for 30 years, confidently tells me the well has never been without water.

"The true beauty, sir," he says, "Is to be enjoyed on a full-moon night. the moon lights up the well and the steps glow."

I marvel at the feat of engineering, so vast in its scale and so detailed in its execution. It's hung together for 1200 years at least. Chand ki Baoli was one of many such built back then. In modern terms, it would be a small water harvesting structure, but the skill and foresight of its builders sets it above even the largest of India's dams. Besides, nobody was displaced when Chand ki Baoli was built and people are free to use its water. All they need is a bucket and a rope.

6 SHILLONG: BETELNUTS AND BAMBOOS

Lan Pohtam is the unlikely looking owner of 20 hectares of farmland in the Amlynpiang village, near the Bangladesh border. It's in the Wār Khasi hills of Meghalaya, overlooking Bangladesh, in the middle of dense moist deciduous forests, that he cultivates arecanut, oranges, bay leaf, broomstick bamboo, and other fruit. Wearing a vest that barely hangs together over shorts in the same state, the 55-year old farmer deftly assembles what I've traveled some 2,500 kilometres to see – the *shyngiar*.

Shyngiar is Khasi for their traditional drip irrigation system, fashioned from bamboo. It's an age old way to build a network of bamboo canals that ferry water from a hill stream to the roots of individual plants in a plantation. Bamboo grows abundantly in the Wār Khasi hills, as indeed in large parts of north-east India. It's used in everything – pickles, as a vegetable, for building houses, a weapon of war, and irrigation. The last is the most fascinating use of this extremely versatile grass.

Shyngiar is well-suited to the hills and their method of cultivating plantations. The Khasis, that are the dominant tribe in Meghalaya (the other two are the Jaintias and the Garos), follow the pattern of shifting cultivation. They clear a part of the forest of large trees and undergrowth and plant plantation crops. These yield for between five and 10 years after which they are left to die and the plantation shifts to the next plot. The land is hilly and even though they chop the large trees, there is a lot of forest still left behind. The streams to irrigate the plantations are usually a few kilometers away. They have to get water to their crops using bamboo channels because the land is hilly and rocky – digging canals is harder than making the *Shyngiar*.

Lan's patch earns him about Rs. 200,000 a year, plenty to get by for the entire year. It takes him about half an hour to set up a *Shyngiar* for demonstration, that irrigates two arecanut trees. But even that tiny sample – it covers an area of 10 square metres – is enough for me to appreciate the

78

intricacy of the system that extends over 20,000 square metres, of undulating plantations and forests. It is so precise that water fed in at one end produces a steady trickle at the individual plant.

The raw material is completely free. Lan cuts bamboo growing in the forests of varying thickness and uses these to make the *Shyngiar*. It's like the human arm. The system has three or four stages, from the shoulder to the fingers. After cutting the bamboo, Lan uses a local axe called a dao to slice it in half to make a channel. Sometimes, he only cuts a slit in side of the bamboo without halving it. He uses another type of dao with a curved head to remove the internodes save the ones at the two ends of the bamboo. Lan makes a set of bamboo channels of different thickness with the internodes removed. Some have small slits on one side and the bamboo runs whole for a few centimeters before it is slit in half. Lan thus painstakingly fashions the raw material for his *shyngiar*.

The thickest piece of bamboo is placed into the source of water, either a stream in the nearby hill or, as it the case now, the supply tank of the irrigation department. For Lan and a few other farmers, the irrigation department has laid pipes from the Amlynpiang stream over the hill to their farms. Lan does not have to labour to build a long bamboo channel to get water from that stream to his farm anymore, a distance of around a kilometre. He sources water from the irrigation department's tank next to his farm.

The bamboo used to make the main channel is as thick my arm at the shoulder and is stuck into one of the many holes on the side of the tank, held in place by a 'washer' of plastic bags. It is sliced open along the top, but not cut in half, to maximize the quantity of water it can carry. This runs for a few metres into the plantation from the irrigation tank and connects with other thick bamboos that form the main irrigation channel. The primary and other channels are supported by pieces of wood, to which they are tied with thin strips of bamboo.

Along the length of the primary channel, pieces of bamboo as thick my forearm, each cut at an internode, are placed on top at right angles and tied in place with bamboo strips. These are secondary channels and they have small rectangular slits in their sides where they cross the primary channel. One end is closed by an internode; the other is slit in half and the internodes removed. A narrower piece of bamboo, as thick as my wrist, sits in the primary channel and lifts the flowing water from it into the slit of the bamboos of the secondary channel. Some of the water flows into the secondary channel through this lift mechanism – the rest goes onto the next secondary channel. Water flows from the lower to the upper channel under its own momentum.

The secondary channel slopes steeply towards the plants. At intervals, tertiary channels tap water from them at right angles and irrigate individual trees in the plantation. Here again, the bamboo used to make the tertiary channels are tied above the secondary channels. They also have small slits on their side. Even thinner pieces of bamboo placed in the secondary channels lift water from these into the slits on the tertiary channel bamboo pieces. These are also cut in half and go from the secondary channel to the roots of the trees. The tertiary channel bamboos are about as thick as my thumb.

The bamboo pieces used to make all the channels are lashed together with extremely thin strips of bamboo. When these strips dry, they harden into place and make for a fairly permanent bond. The channels are supported by an equally intricate network of branches stuck in the ground.

When complete, the *Shyngiar* forms a tracery of bamboo across the plantations. They are so well constructed that very little water is wasted. The internodes at the ends of the bamboo pipes ensure that all the water is channeled to the plants rather than flowing out of the end of the pipe.

To begin irrigating one part of the plantation, Lan connects the network to the mains by shifting the bamboo that taps the source to that network's source. The network is designed to irrigate two hectares at a time.

He says, "It takes a couple of hours to irrigate all the trees in a particular area. Then I shift the water to another part of the plantation by simply removing the little piece of bamboo that lifts water from the primary channel to the secondary channel. I usually irrigate the whole plantation in two days. In the dry season, I spend nights on the plantation."

He sleeps on a low bamboo platform. Lucky for him there are not large predators around. His dao is a constant companion, stuck in the waist band of his shorts even when we are around. It's a menacing, two-foot long implement and in the right hands, can lop of a human head. Daos are multi-purpose – in the Kamakshi temple in Guwahati, priests use the same thing to slice off the heads of goats and buffaloes that are sacrificed to Kāli. Lan manages alone even though he has his family around to help. Khasis are matrilineal, and the women work at home while the men labour in fields or elsewhere.

June Lyngdoh, my guide on this outing, is from the Jowai irrigation department. She says, "It takes him about a month to build a system that will irrigate 10 hectares if he works alone. He hires people when it's time to build the *shyngiar* to speed up construction."

"You mean he has to build it again and again?" I ask.

She puts the question to Lan, who says, "The system lasts only for a season. The bamboo rots in that time and has to be replaced. We replace the entire system rather than parts of it because it is easier."

That is a lot of labour for a few months' irrigation. The upside is that the raw material is free and there are no running costs – fuel or power. The downside, in addition to the labour needed, is the need to cut bamboo. In this area alone, June says, there are 800 hectares of plantations. There is little agriculture save for plantations here – the locals buy all the food they need from Bangladesh that is a 20 kilometres away at the border town of Dawki.

This scale of plantation uses up a lot of bamboo just for irrigation every year. Last year's *shyngiar* lies scattered all over Lan's plantation. He uses bits of old bamboo to support the new *shyngiar* but the rest just rots away. In the warmth and humidity, it quickly returns to the soil.

Lan has not been trained as an *shyngiar* engineer – there is no such thing. All the plantation owners in the Wār hills of Meghalaya – Khasi, Jaintia and Garo – where bamboo irrigation systems exist, build the systems themselves or with the help of skilled local labour. Its construction is literally by rule of thumb. The ratio of the thickness of the primary channel to the tertiary one determines the quantity of water that will reach the trees. It's a fine balance that comes with years of watching and experience, something no degree can provide.

"How did you learn to make the *shyngiar*?" I ask him, through June.

Lan grins, showing gumless teeth. They have long fallen to the incessant use of lime, betelnut and betel leaves. "I watched my father and uncles and learnt over many years. If you stay here long enough, you will also learn."

The bamboo system is used after the monsoons, when the dry season begins. It is assembled in October and is in place by November. The plantation owners use it till April or May, or till the first showers start. Then they dismantle it because it rains here for a good five months. Excess water can kill off the plants more easily than under-watering can. For these five months, water gushes through bamboo channels from stream to the plantations in the Wār hills of Meghalaya.

June takes me across the road. "Let's see where the water comes from."

The forest across the road is very grim and foreboding. It was tropical rainforest a few years ago, with tall and dense growth. Most of the old growth trees have been cut and sold but the undergrowth is very dense. I see many of the trees coming back, but it will take a few decades of a total ban on logging to restore the forests to anything close to their former glory. The Khasis has bartered their future for a few bucks; rainfall has dropped and the climate has grown considerably warmer. Their system of shifting cultivation hasn't helped matters either. They admit to water shortages after clearing a patch of forest near the crown of a hill but continue to do it. There is a ban on logging following an order from the Supreme Court some years ago, but people cut trees on the sly.

The sun disappears – its evening – as soon as I step into the forest to see the headworks of the irrigation department. The dense forest closes around me as I desperately climb the slippery slope behind my guide. She is fleet footed; I have a twisted ankle. I cannot see the ground because it's hidden under shrubbery so have to assume that by following him, I am treading on solid ground; many times, I am wrong. Sweating, heaving, ducking, pulling and pushing myself along, I clamber up the slope. The path thankfully levels off around 50 metres up and then climbs gradually into even denser forest. She's warned me of leeches but I am more worried about getting there and back.

We descend as steeply as we climbed – more treacherous because it's along the water course. The stones hidden in the undergrowth have slippery moss on them and I slip many times. I can hear the stream and smell the water but cannot see it even though my ears tell me it's a few feet ahead. Abruptly, I come upon it. The irrigation department's pipe runs along the stream like a python. This bit of 'civilisation' is out of place in the forest. The pipe ends in a small check dam, about a metre high, that ensures there is enough of a head of water to keep the pipe supplied.

I catch my breath balancing on rocks in the stream. They are red and peculiarly pockmarked, as it the earth caught small pox in some bygone era. The stream is quite dark and the forest is settling for the night. Birds call and beetles creak. The stream roars down the hill to join another river and flow into Bangladesh.

The forest abounds in an amazing variety of trees and plants. I seldom see two of the same species close together. I am no botanist but can tell the species apart from their leaves and bark. It's hard to compare this plethora of plant species with the red pine monoculture that Khasis practice in the higher slopes of the Khasi hills. But, they have extracted all the valuable timber from this forest, leaving behind saplings and secondary growth.

The National Highway 44 connects Shillong to Guwahati on one side and Silchar on the other. Jowai is about 50 kilometres from Shillong on this tenuous artery. It's the main trucking route for coal mined in the Jaintia hills destined for Guwahati or Bangladesh. It's the only for people to get from one part of the state to the other. At night, returning to Shillong, it's totally blocked by truckers parked on both sides of the road. They have retired for the night to amuse themselves drinking and whoring. Late travelers have to contend with traffic jams that can last half the night.

The highway and many of the smaller roads that connect villages around Jowai are in fairly good shape – the state government ensures this. But the bridges are World War 2 vintage and in extremely poor shape. They are made of steel girders overlaid with thick planks of wood. Trucks weighing up to 30 tonnes carrying coal to Bangladesh use these and the bridges give up the ghost with regularity. I get stuck getting out of Jowai to see the *shyngiar* in the War hills because a bridge at Myntdu has collapsed. This is also a national highway, leading to Dawki on the Bangladesh border. Even though June says it will be fixed in a few hours, it takes a few days to repair. The diversion takes us through pretty pine forests and rolling countryside, the sort you see in British postcards, tiny villages and farmland.

The idyll lasts till we regain the main road. At Amlarem, where the Wār Jaintia hills start on the route from Jowai to Dawki, we drive past an endless line of trucks – I count 332 – waiting with loads of coal to enter Bangladesh. They enter the border town of Dawki 100 at a time, cross and unload and return. The first part of the drive is through fairly steep mountains that descend to a plateau. The mountains have rudiments of forests left but the plateaus are completed bald. The hills from the plateaus to the Bangladesh border are called the Wār hills – Khasi, Jaintia or Gao, and have new growth and few stretches of forest.

At one point, I see a quarry sculpture. The land owner, digging for limestone, has left a portion of the hill standing, with a network of interconnected caverns that remind me of a cathedral. Its stands on the junction of the two roads, a sentinel to the forests that cling on.

The *shyngiar* is caught up with the cultivation of arecanuts in Meghalaya. Arecanuts plantations are the main source of livelihood here, says Biswarup Chowdhury, manager of the State Bank of India's branch at Pomshutia village in another part of the Wār Khasi hills. He is an old, plump balding man who has spent the better part of his life in areas as remote as this. We are about 60 kilometres south of Shillong on another route to Bangladesh, that also leads to Dawki. The road is good and traffic light and I cross maybe 20 vehicles, mostly taxis conveying Bangladeshi tourists to India. These are the legal visitors, not the hordes of illegal immigrants leaving their benighted country to work as labourers in India. There are very few trucks conveying low grade coal to Bangladesh from the East Khasi hills. Public transport comprises Maruti taxis, Tata Sumos, jeeps and the occasional mini-bus.

"About 40 percent of people here work in the arecanut industry," Biswarup says. "Another 30 percent is involved in the coal industry. The other sources of employment are limestone mining and stone quarrying."

I am sitting in Raja Khongshit's house in Pomshutia, a hill village of about 300 households. I cannot see most of the households because they are scattered up and down the hills, hidden in dense undergrowth and plantations. Raja is the local strongman, owner of the largest everything, house and plantation. He is building a petrol pump a kilometer uphill and plans to have a resort next door to it as well.

"Here?" I ask. "Who will stop here?"

"The Bangladeshis will. There is no place to stop on this route between Dawki and Shillong," says Raja. The petrol pump he is building sprawls over an acre of his land. The resort is up a small hill, above the pump. He stands sweating on his land, listening to the radio playing music from Bangladesh. The government of India has obviously not covered this part of the country, lacking a strategy to reach India's border areas. He is wearing a vest a couple of sizes too big and trousers. Raja is a man with a belly, and grimaces when he smiles. His eyes disappear into this face when he laughs, which is just once during our meeting. He is also suspicious of strangers.

"Who are you?" he asks. My driver Sharma who has brought me here, introduced us. But Raja does not buy the story and wants to see some evidence. I produce an old identity card from a newspaper I used to work in two decades ago. It satisfies him and he drops his dour demeanour and becomes almost amiable.

Raja owns 50 hectares of land but wants to earn more than plantations can provide. Therefore, he is diversifying, like any good businessman. Having the State Bank of India as a tenant helps to get loans.

Biswarup says, "The arecanut plantation industry has been recognized as a cottage industry. It is eligible for loans."

Areca nuts are orange nuts, like small coconuts the size of a small chicken egg that grow on the betel palm. They are harvested by September or October and spend the next six months underwater, 'being processed'. They are dunked in enormous bamboo baskets, about 6 metres tall and five across, that are stood in streams or tanks of water. Neither Raja nor Biswarup tells me what happens to the areca nuts during their submersion but I presume their alkaloids are drawn out. Areca nuts contain two alkaloids, arecaine and arecoline, that stimulate, intoxicate and suppress hunger in much the same way that nicotine does. Areca nut cultivation here is fast becoming uneconomical though. Market prices have halved while cultivations costs have gone up. A kāni of nuts (400 nuts) used to sell for Rs. 300 in 2004; now it's Rs. 140. The larger measure is lynti, that is 16 kāni. The large bamboo baskets hold 20 lynti. The nuts come out smelling of smoked natural rubber. Women grade them by hand and then they are sent off to the nearest market.

The nut cultivators do not own the processing centres. They pay the processing centre Rs. 1000 per season per basket for 20 lynti of nuts. It's cheaper than buying their own baskets, each of which costs Rs. 500 and lasts just a couple of seasons. Even Raja does not have his own baskets – he used the processing centre outside Pomshutia.

You cannot eat an arecanut straight off the tree. It makes your head spin," says Sharma. "Submersion takes some of the sting out of the nut but in its processed form it is still very potent."

only smiles his eye-hiding smile when I ask him if he has got a loan; that says it all. But his eyes don't smile – they regard from behind uplifted cheeks.

is the traditional form of welcome in all households here. The Khasis eat pān that is a bit of betelnut along with betel leaf and a bit of lime. There are no other add-ons as elsewhere in the country. It is also something that poor people can afford to give visitors, in addition to water. Nearly all the betel nut and betel leaf grown in the Wār hills is consumed locally, even though both are of high quality and would probably command good prices in other markets.

A local legend has it that there were once two very close friends, one from a rich family and the other from a poor one. The poor family used to visit the rich one regularly and get the royal treatment. One day, the rich family's man and woman came to the poor household. The poor family had nothing to offer them. Ashamed, the man killed himself; his wife saw what he had done and followed him and finally, the daughter of the house joined them in the afterlife. The man was reincarnate as the betelnut, the wife as the leaf and the daughter as the lime. Therefore, paan is served to guests even by the poorest family. More likely, the poor eat it when they cannot afford food and the legend has been spun to give chewing paan respectability.

"Gastro-intestinal diseases including cancer are much more common here than elsewhere," says Dr. Edmund Khongthaw, the doctor in charge of the large primary health centre at Pongtung, a village about 10 kilometres from Pomshutia, between Shillong and Dawki. He loves the hills and asked to be posted back here, unusual for a doctor in India. He's been treating patients for years, and nobody takes his advice to cut out paan seriously. Its tradition, you see.

"There is no traffic between Jowai and Shillong. We will get home soon," I tell Sharma, the taxi driver.

He doesn't reply. A little further, we hit the first of the trucks and are soon in the middle of a midnight jam. It takes four hours to clear.

***

I take a bus from Guwahati to Shillong. The person who arranged it, a constable with the Central Reserve Policy Force, has chosen the lousiest, slowest bus that takes four hours to cover the 100 kilometres. The drive through the busy NH 44 takes me through extremely dusty and polluted parts of Assam's state capital. Once out of this, it is a pretty sight even though the road is narrow. Bamboo is the construction material of choice here though the hills don't have much of it left. They don't have much of anything left, though they are greener in Assam than in Meghalaya.

The 100 kilometre drive from Guwahati to Shillong contrasts with what I see in the Khasi hills. The hills are mostly forested and there is an abundance of bamboo. There is so much bamboo that nearly all the buildings use bamboo screens for walls and bamboo thatch for roofs. They are strong screens and look like they could withstand a fair amount of battering. The houses have frames made of some hardwood into which these screens are fixed and roofs mounted. The structures are simple, yet elegant. Nearly all the houses are built on stilts – the smaller ones have wooden or bamboo stilts and the larger ones have concrete pillars.

Most of the houses along this part of the highway are made of bamboo – bamboo walls, bamboo roof and they even have a bamboo floor. No, it's not number 64. some are on foundations of stilts, others on packed earth. Bamboo pervades all aspects of life for the Assamese but the people in Meghalaya now regard it with disdain – it's for poorer folk.

Nearer Shillong, the terrain is hillier and terraced farms more in evidence than in Assam. They are pretty, with vegetables growing on the terraces. Potatoes, cauliflowers, cabbages, tomatoes, peas, brinjal, ladyfinger, spinach and chilies – all are grown locally and promptly sent out of the state from these market gardens. The locals do not get to eat what they grow as they fetch a better price in the markets of Calcutta. They get their food from Assam. The potatoes are so good, and available for such a short season, that they command a high price outside. It makes economic sense to send the vegetables out. Potato fields have raised rectangular patches. In the valleys, narrow canals carry water from the nearest spring or tubewell to the fields. On the hillsides, fields are irrigated only by canal and very carefully, because some of them tend to be quite steep. But the agrarian dominance is misleading.

Most land in Meghalaya is privately owned by the resident tribes – a Khasi can own as much land he or his forefathers could grab – has resulted in a very peculiar situation. This has been interpreted as having the license to do what they want with it. Farming and pine plantations are just two of the activities that people do with their lands. Many have set up stone quarries, other mine coal or limestone from their land. The state government turns the other way and levies a nominal royalty on what they extract. Most of the income goes into pockets of the quarry owners and some to line government officials' pockets so they look the other way. Agriculture is not the main employer here – quarrying is. At Rs. 100 for a six-hour working day, a local labourer does not have it too bad. Bangladeshis, though, get paid a fraction of this and make up the bulk of quarry and mine labour.

The other problem with the lack of accountability is that people have clear-felled the forests, that once were of a dense sub-tropical variety, and planted pine trees. Fast growing, they are more valued for fire wood and house building than the indigenous species of oak and other trees. The Khasis love pine – they are the dominant tree species in these parts.

This is more in evidence as I near Shillong. To my horror, native moist deciduous forests give way to pine, and quarries. It's a different image of the north-east from what I have read in books. The undulating hills are largely bare save for patches of these plantations. Quarries cut an unsightly white swathe in the remaining greenery. It's a steep climb into Shillong and things improve somewhat once on the outskirts of town. Large parts of the town are under the army cantonment, that retains some magnificent old trees, mostly pine unfortunately, but also oak and other native species. The pine grows fast and is used for construction now that all the old hardwood trees have been logged.

My hotel, the Tripura Palace, is part of the palace of the Tripura maharaja. He lives in the front part of the sprawling complex on a hill, surrounded by a beautiful garden and some 25 dogs. The hotel is to the rear of his highness's residence in what was the guesthouse. It's got few rooms but all are very well appointed. Next door is the Birla residence, also swathed in foliage and mist. His highness is extremely fond of black – all his cars are black and have black-tinted glasses. At night, the house is dark save for a light in a couple of windows.

The taxi from the bus stand to the hotel takes me up a steep drive and pulls into the hotel's small parking lot. My room is on the lower level but nice and large. It's wood-paneled and has a tiled floor that must be cold in winters. It's pleasant enough in summer though I need a heater when it threatens to rain, as it does on two days.

You can walk through Shillong in about 45 minutes, though parts are not pedestrian-friendly at all. It's got all the problems of India's hill stations – overcrowding, narrow streets and traffic that is in a hurry to get somewhere. If you are planning to spend an evening out, forget it because the town hasn't grown out of the years of anti-tribal violence and everything shuts down by 8 PM.

It's a two-hour comfortable ride to Sohra, or Cherra, from Shillong along steep hills. The 56 kilometres that separates the two places is pretty badly denuded. My driver on this route, Suren Chamling, from Darjeeling, tells me that there were forests in these parts once. He has been a cabbie here for 15 years. He blames it on the land owners, who are free to do what they want with their land. For most of the journey, the hills are bare, covered with little but a thin layer of coarse grass. They have lost their ability to attract rain and store water. It's a matter of a few years before they lose their ability to sustain life. The land owners have preferred to make a quick buck by selling timber or firewood. There are a few trees left in scattered clumps on the hillside. Even bamboo, which once covered large parts of these slopes, is conspicuous by its absence. Their crowns are bare but most valleys still retain some foliage. Bare-headed hills have heart-attacks and kill not themselves but the people who live on and around them.

A little before Cherrapunji, on a plateau between the highlands the Wār hills, I chance upon a fishing tank, again privately owned. It's rectangular, the side facing uphill open to let water in, lined with stone blocks and concrete. The perennial springs ensure that it never runs dry even in the short summer that bridges winter and the monsoons. It's not very big, with the longer side around 15 metres long and the other one, around 10 metres. At the deeper side, a cut in the wall whose height can be regulated lets water overflow into the fields below. These structures are local fisheries and while the water may also be used for irrigation, human consumption is ruled out. Fish is an important part of local diet and these tanks are their main source where there are no rivers. I see itinerant anglers with thin bamboo fishing rods waiting patiently at these tanks for the fish to bite. The tanks exist in either isolation, or in cascades where the water that overflows from one fills the next and so on.

"These tanks are one of the newer modes is sport fishing. Several people have made small ponds, between 800 and 1600 square metres in spread and 2-3 metres deep, lined with stones and usually with a board or slab of rock sticking out over the water, where people can fish for a fee. They stock these with fingerlings from the nearest government hatchery. Once these fingerlings grow, the pond owners charge Rs. 100 for a rod to let people fish. They make much more this way than catching and selling the fish on the market. It's an idea that is catching on really fast – water is abundant and if you have the land, why not turn it into a productive asset. A fish pond owner can made Rs. 50,000 in a season, and its tax-free agricultural income. He needs no permission or license," says Edmund.

Water isn't in short supply in the region. Even in Cherrapunji, that supposedly has a drought every summer before the deluge, there is enough water from streams flowing down from the hills above, to keep the town supplied. It's hard water, as is to be expected if the liquid has been stored and released in an area rich in limestone – but sweet. Washing and bathing are tough as soap forms a persistent slime that is hard to wash off. Limestone also purifies the water so whatever falls from the heavens gets cleansed, stored and released over a long period. Even in the height of summer, the streams do not run dry. Yet.

I am surprised there is enough water, given the ecological degradation that has taken place here. Virtually all private lands have been stripped of their trees. Forests existed here till a few decades ago but now, bald hills greet me. Cherrapunji lives on its reputation as the wettest place on earth, but that sobriquet has moved on. Rainfall has decreased, say locals. The few tourists who do visit to get a glimpse of the waterfalls around seldom stay the night. Perhaps that is why residents do not face a water shortage. The town begins and ends before I realize it. One road leads to the bazaar, a misnomer for a small collection of shops that sells clothes, vegetables and trinkets. The only place to eat is an unnamed restaurant that Suren knows, but I would miss as being another house.

The view from Cherrapunji towards Bangladesh is marred by a cement factory. Cherra Cements Limited is a government entity that feeds off the locally-available coal and limestone to manufacture cement for local use. It's so remote that transporting cement anywhere would be unprofitable, but then, the government has its own strange logic for siting industries. This one is clearly there for political reasons to employ Khasi youth. Its twin chimneys spout bilious clouds of white smoke that drift west over the Noh Kalikai falls.

The government has made an eco-park in Mawsmai Nongthymmai that purports to show how water is harvested, forests regrown and waterfalls generated. It sprawls over about 5 hectares of land a little outside Cherrapunji, overlooking the Bangladesh plains. The overall effect is exactly the opposite. A couple of streams flow into the eco-park; one is collected in a water trough from where it goes into making a water fall. The streams cascade into the forests that run from here to the border. However, the toilets for the eco-park empty into this trough; somebody with a lot of sense designed the park.

The Mawsmai cave, a few kilometres back towards Shillong on the highway, is awesome. It has 150 metres of stalagmites and stalactites, formed through millennia of hard water dripping from the ceiling. In most places, the stalagmites and stalactites yellow and deeply furrowed. At one point, they form a small arch, that looks like the head and trunk of an elephant. The cave narrows to a small passage at one point, and reaching it, I wonder if it makes sense to go on when the entry is so tantalizing close. I walk through an am richly rewarded. The passage opens into a marvelous cavern, a veritable cathedral of stalactites. There are a few stalagmites also, but they are restricted to the sides of the cavern. The cavern is lit by a halogen lamps that caste harsh shadows on these marvels of natural sculpture, while not giving enough light to take pictures.

Just inside the entrance to the right is a recess in the wall with what looks like a very black (what else) shivling. It's dark and wet, appropriately, and wholly unapproachable. The floor is full of large limestone rock, pitted from centuries of water dripping from the ceiling. In some places, the water has formed stalagmites while in others, it's made craters in the rock. The cave's ceiling drips water right through making it an incredibly cold and damp place. I pick my way over the slippery floor, balancing carefully on outcroppings to get from one cavern to the next. The stone on the floor has been polished and rounded by water flowing over millions of years. It looks soft and fluffy, what with the craters that dot it, till I put my foot on it – then it's hard rock. In between, there are many places where I have to go down all fours to get through. Getting up, I am careful not to bump into any sharp rock projections – the last thing I need in there is a bleeding head. When it rains, the caverns fill with water and become impassable. It takes a few hours for the water to drain away after that.

The absence of natural light makes it difficult to make out colours and the artificial lighting does not help matters. Yellows appear grey, whites appear yellow. And everything is gloomy in the light. Without the light, the caves would be closed to all but the most intrepid caver; ordinary people can walk and crawl through thanks to the lighting. I just wish somebody had used their creativity in lighting.

At the far end, cold, wet and muddy, I emerge into the welcome sunlight in the middle of – nowhere. There is no path, only forest. Then I hear the generator and walk towards its sound. The forest is dense, probably as it has always existed. It's also the reason there is a continuous drip of water inside the cavern.

The Siemlah sacred grove stands outside the eco-park. It covers 40 hectares and is an amazing collection of biodiversity, fenced and protected by the locals. Sacred groves have been protected by the local community for generations and represent the best collection of local biodiversity. They are a microcosm of the forests that existed once upon a time in the region. Sacred groves are the last repository of the rich biodiversity that once covered most of this place. They are important watersheds, places of religious importance and a source of medicinal plants and herbs. Local healers would be at a loss if sacred groves were to totally disappear.

I step into the sacred grove leaving my taxi driver staring behind me. If a spirit were to nab me, nobody on earth would be the wiser – my money is in the car, unknown to the driver. Almost immediately as I step inside the grove, an eerie feeling of being watched comes over me. The trees are tall and leafy, cutting out most of the sunlight on the ground. Rocks blackened by aeons of water flowing over them peep through the tree trunks and in places, resemble the faces of spirits that are supposed to live there.

"Don't be silly," I tell myself. "There is no restriction on entering a sacred grove, just on taking stuff out it. The spirits won't mind an itinerant visitor wandering about."

It's still and humid in the grove – the feeling of being watched follows me as I walk up the small hill and climb down the other side. There is a wealth of biodiversity here; these were the moist deciduous forests of the north-east before they were cleared for agriculture, plantations and mining. They remind me of similar vegetation on the other side of the country, in Goa. I breathe easy only when I emerge from the grove into the sunshine.

Cherrapunji was the wettest place on earth, testified the British over a century ago. A board still attests to this fact. Standing on a bluff next to the Noh Kalikai falls, with the plains of Bangladesh in the background, it proudly proclaims that I am at the wettest place on earth. A few feet beyond the board, a pipe runs down to a dilapidated hut – the few drops of water coming out of the pipe are gathered in an aluminum pan. Presently, these stop and the water stands in the pan, against the stark, barren plateau. There isn't a tree on the plateau.

The wettest place.

A woman sits in the hut with piles of firewood next to her, entertaining her grand-daughter. She calls to her like a goatherd calls goats – aa, aa. She's as oblivious to Cherrapunji's claim to fame as its fall from the pedestal.

Behind her hut is the source of the firewood – forests in the 200 metre-deep valley of the Noh Kalikai falls. A small stream runs down to Bangladesh from the falls. The falls themselves are breathtaking, plunging in a thin stream some 100 metres. It's not the rainy season yet so there isn't much water but even then, it makes for a spectacular cascade. A small green pool at the foot of the falls lies placidly in the sun, gathering the water and letting it flow onto the ocean through the next country. The river reaches the falls through a forested valley that stretches a few kilometers upstream. It is one of the few forested areas left in this part of Meghalaya. On the other side of the plateau, another few streams cascade down their valleys.

People grow vegetables – potatoes, cabbages, tomatoes, lettuce, spinach, gourds, chillies – and rice, a thick red variety of rice. There is some crop all the year round and the place is very affluent. I see no huts, only houses made of stone blocks and wood. People here have stopped using bamboo for construction. Bamboo is a poor man's building material, and these guys aren't poor by any stretch of imagination.

The Khasis channel water flowing from the upper reaches of the valley down one side of a field. Feeder channels running across the valley take this water to all parts of the field. The vegetable or paddy patches are built in terraces from the highest point that flat land is available right down to the road or the rocky bottom of the valley. Whatever water is left in the stream emerges at this point to scurry across the rocks and disappear into the foliage in the valley.

Farming is just one of the things this rich land yields.

"Meghalaya is the richest state in the northeast," says Suren. "It has minerals like iron ore, limestone, coal and extremely fertile soil."

The hills are pockmarked with limestone, rock and coal quarries of varying sizes. Both are still on a comparatively small scale in most places though some 20 kilometres from Shillong, I see that an entire mountainside has fallen to the quarrier's picks. No dynamiting here, because the quarries are right next to the highway. Instead, labourers drive iron rods into rock and pry large blocks loose. These are hammered into smaller bits and carted off in tractors or trucks. There are many stone crushers on this small stretch of 20 kilometers, doing brisk business enveloped in fine, deadly dust. The workers have no protective gear. They produce gravel that can be coarse, or as fine as sand.

"They take the material to the towns. The crushers produce gravel that is very good for building. The slightly brown gravel is Rs. 2000 for a jeepload. The white gravel is costlier, about Rs. 3500 for a jeepload. A truckload of rocks is about Rs. 15,000 to 20,000 and coal can be as much as

Rs. 50,000 for a 30 tonne load," says Suren, a treasure trove of facts on quarrying in the Shillong area.

Quarrying yields better returns in a shorter time than agriculture. A person with some 30 hectares would make Rs. 250,000 or so in a year from agriculture. If he digs it up to sell rock, he can make that amount in a few months if business is good. The argument locals give is that they need the material to build their houses. That's clearly not the case – the quantum of quarrying is way above what the thin population of the region could use. The stone is sold in nearby towns and the limestone to local cement factories. The coal is used locally. The Khasis use rock and wood to build their houses. I see little bamboo, so presumably this plant has fallen on hard days here. There is little use for it either.

The quarries stand in stark contrast with the surrounding greenery. There have been a few showers and early growth shrubs have turned the hills green, where they have been allowed to grow. The quarries are a glaring white against this, and the green of the vegetable farms. In most places, I see the entire gamut of economic activity – quarrying in the hills, vegetable farming in the flatlands and fishing in small tanks that dot the flatlands.

Many hills and valleys have the entire gamut of economic activity in rural Meghalaya. The same hillside will have a quarry higher up and vegetable patches in the lower reaches. A muddy stream provides water for the vegetables. Clumps of pine and a few other trees make up the rest of the scenery. The non-quarried parts of the hillside are clothed in coarse grass.

Water to drink comes out of community taps, set up the water department. These are supplied from a concrete tank common to the entire village. A spring, that could be a few kilometres away, is the ultimate source, from where a 10 centimetre-thick pipe conveys water to the tank. This pipe is embedded in the headworks – a fancy name for a small check dam about a metre high that stops the flow of water and gives a small head of water to keep the pipe filled. Then, inch thick pipes take the water to different taps in the village. Water supply is regulated because often, a single stream provides for many villages. The Khasis bathe and wash clothes in any of the hundreds of perennial streams in the hills.

However, not all water is safe to drink and there is a high incidence of gastro-intestinal infections – diarrhoea, cholera, dysentery – among the people. That's because they don't boil the water before drinking, even though they collect the water in aluminum vessels from the community tap. The assumption is that if it's out of a tap, it must be clean. The truth is that the water supply department does not treat the water in any way before supplying it to the public. The costs of this are debatable but minimal training on hygiene is not. The people should be told to boil water before drinking.

Once the sun is up, I see women and children washing and bathing with abandon in the streams, oblivious to the vehicles passing by full of interested onlookers. Of course, the women bathe with clothes on. The men finish their baths earlier and get to work. In this matrilineal society, the men get to do all the work that women traditionally do – chopping wood, cleaning, tending animals, and farming. Women restrict themselves to cooking, fetching drinking water and commerce.

In places, forest fires have wiped acres of forest clean. These brown swathes contrast with the surrounding greenery. En route Cherrapunji, there are many such swathes and they usually are surrounded by forests; it's the common argument trotted out by the forest department that locals start the fire to get fuelwood. There could be some substance in the charge as most forests are privately owned; these forests have very few trees left. Most of the surviving trees are on government-owned lands and one of the ways to get at them is to start a fire that kills them off.

The villages are small and scattered with maybe a few dozen households arranged in an untidy jumble, but land holdings are large. There are terraced fields in the valleys in which run streams. Despite deforestation, streams continue to flow through summer. The land around them is extremely fertile and terracing helps reduce soil erosion and water runoff. The terraces reach down to the stream in giant steps from the upper reaches of valleys. Above them, in some places, villagers have retained some tree cover.

Khasis traditionally used bamboo and wood for their houses. A traditional Khasi house is made of straw – straw walls and roof – on a wooden frame. They make a hut-shaped frame of wood, put in the frame for the roof and then tie the straw thatching to the frame. It's all locally available material, cheap and quick to assemble. An improvement on this is a house with a wooden frame and steel sheets as covering, instead of straw thatch. The steel lasts longer and is more water-proof. Further upscale, the foundation and walls are made of stone blocks and the rest of the house, from the windows up, is wooden; a frame to which wooden planks is nailed, with a roof of corrugated iron. Even better, the entire house is made of stone blocks and the roof of reinforced concrete cement. The construction reflects the wealth of the owners.

Regardless of what they are made of, all houses have a small verandah or covered sit out. The straw ones have a tiny place, big enough for one person to squat in. the size increases with the economic status of the owner. The larger houses have an open window behind which the women sit and stare at the world going by. All Khasi women above 40 seem to chew paan; their toothless mouths appear as red gashes in their otherwise fair, if weather-beaten, faces. They have amazingly pink cheeks and if not paan stained, their lips are defined by bright red lipstick. On the higher slopes, the villages cling to the hillsides. Most people in these villages make a living quarrying and selling timber; smalls bundles of firewood are the evidence. Farming isn't possible, the houses are smaller and the people are poorer.

In the valleys, houses are larger. Farming is the economic mainstay. Quarrying and selling timber are incidental sources of income. In some places, I see piles of coal by the roadside. This is mined locally and sold mostly for domestic use as it's of low quality.

The Khasis carry their belongings and babies in conical bamboo baskets, suspended on their backs with a cord that goes around their foreheads. They plod forward, hands folded in front. The traditional Khasi dress for women comprises of a maxi-like dress called dhara with a toga cloth called jainshien wrapped over it, toga-style. Women also wear shawls called tamoh. The men wear pants and shirts or straight pajamas and a short kurta and a variant of the Gandhi-cap. Everybody carries an umbrella – the weather is as unpredictable as the people.

Mornings are for field work, washing clothes and bathing as well as that bane of Indian womanhood – collecting water – where piped water isn't available. Outside large villages, there is no piped water and women have to trek to the nearest stream. The men mostly work the fields or graze livestock – cows, few goats and pigs. The women wash clothes and cook; a very traditional division of labour. In the villages I actually saw men working in contrast to other parts of India where the women do all the work and the men play cards. By the afternoon, the scene of action shifts to the quarries as nearly everybody here seems to own land that has been stripped of trees and now is good for digging. Both men and women dot the fields. The women are colorful, in their traditional red shawls, and stand out in the green of the fields. The men are dowdily dressed and were they to stand still, I would mistake them for rocks in the field.

Meghalaya is a Christian-dominated state and nearly all villages have a church of some sort, situated on a hillock. They are nearly identical – a small spire, hall large enough for the small parish, a little verandah outside the main entrance and a couple of steps up from the surrounding ground. The church bell isn't in the steeple but suspended from a concrete structure just inside the church compound. I don't see any house that could belong to the priest so presume that the priest stays in the village and not around the church.

Khasis do no work at all on Sundays. The fields are empty, the quarries silent and the traffic thin. We pass a dozen vehicles on the drive to Mawsyngram that was 56 kilometres. In contrast, the churches are packed with people in their Sunday best. The women are painted to their gills and well turned out; the men look better than their usual sloppy workaday clothes. It's easy to make out Christian burial sites on the bald hills – the top of a hill will have graves marked with crosses. These are in open spaces, away from any settlement. A lonely cement path leads to the fields of crosses.

The no-work attitude is so bad that the boys at a restaurant near a hot spring called Lowblie at the Jakrem village, about 64 kilometres from Shillong refuse to give us lunch even when offered Rs. 50 over the regular price.

To get to the springs I pay a fee of Rs. 10 and walk down a cemented pathway 250 metres long, that goes through a small forest. The springs are at the bottom of a hill with an interesting combination of large black rocks and pine forests. They ooze out from under some rocks and are immediately gathered in a small pool. From the pool, pipes lead the water to the bathing area. The local hill council, the administrative body of the Khasis, has made separate bathing areas for men and women and piped the water to these 'bathrooms'. The men have separate cubicles, the women a communal area. The water is fairly warm, hot enough to bathe in without needing dilution even in the height of summer. It's rich in sulphur and supposedly has medicinal properties. It tastes sweet and is faintly perfumed. The water flows into a stream a few below through channels that have a coating of a hard green substance, presumably caused by the minerals in the water – it looks like the sulphate of some metal. The rocky bed of the stream has deep pools and the water is clean.

J Nongseij, the Khasi man who maintains the sulphur spring complex, says, "The ideal thing to do is to have a hot water bath and then dip yourself in the cool stream water."

I take a rain cheque. But one of his tribesmen does precisely that after a vigorous bath in the hot water. Three naked Khasi children play in the spring water and disappear into the stream shortly thereafter.

The Khasi Hindus follow largely tribal burial customs. These are the 'original' Khasis, called Shen Khasis. Their distinguishing mark is a black chicken painted on a red flag. The Khasis traditional erect a menhir, or monolith in memory, of their dead, accompanied by a special prayer. It is said should the prayer go awry, the stone will fall and crush the erector; therefore, it is extremely important that the priest does a good job of the prayer to please the spirits and ensure his benefactor's longevity. These menhirs are long and flat granite stones, up to 6 metres long and rounded at the top, which are sunk into the ground. They stand any old how – vertically or tilted at a crazy angle. One, in Cherrapunji town, has a fluted round stone atop it. Most menhirs are old, but the custom persists. Sometimes, they erect a set of monoliths – four upright and one horizontal – like the fingers of my hand with the thumb folded in front, or just three or four vertical stones. It all depends on the occasion.

From Mawphlang to Jakrem, I see more smaller villages with houses of straw or wood covered with steel sheets. These belong to much poorer people and they are generally dingy. There are fewer houses made of stone, perhaps one of two in an entire village comprised of houses made of cheaper material. Even here, I see neither use of bamboo in house construction nor any clumps of the plant. In some places, a species of bamboo is used to fence plots. The wood for house-building is usually pine or other fast-growing variety.

I see myriad small streams oozing out of rock, collecting and getting bigger. Even though the hills are denuded, they still retain enough water to feed these streams. These streams are the substance of life here. Three-inch thick pipes run down hillsides, presumably tapping streams at source for villages and towns. These pipes empty into concrete tanks from where smaller pipes supply community taps. I see no pipes going into houses so the concept of individual piped water supply hasn't yet percolated here. Most taps provide water at a fairly good pressure in the mornings and evening; despite this, they have the inevitable line of pots stretching away from them. A few women tend to the line to make sure nobody jumps the queue; the rest show up when they estimate that their turn for filling has come. The chowkidari rotates, with a different person guarding the pot line every day.

Perhaps the most famous of the sacred groves in this part of Meghalaya is at Mawphlang, 25 kilometres from Shillong on a good but narrow road. Its centuries old and covers several hundred acres of rolling hills. There are no pine trees, these being a British introduction, but an amazing range of indigenous plants. These include aroids, ferns, pipers and orchids, all native to Meghalaya. Sadly, the grove contrasts with the balding hills and underlines in bold the degradation of the hills.

Mawphlang is also the place where a dam, built in the early 1990s, supplies water to Shillong. I do not have permission to see the dam; permission is needed in case I decide to just walk up to the dam and toss in poison to kill every person in town. But from behind the inspection bungalow, I get a bird's eye view of the river as it flows into the dam.

There are different types of protected forests here, preserved for different reasons. Edmund describes them. "The one at Pontung is on land owned by individuals. This type is called a Law Kyntang. People needing wood or land can be allotted resources from here. Sacred forests where locals believe a demi-god lives are called Law Lyngdoh. Some are under the care of the village headman, called Law Adong; these don't have any religious significance."

I drive atop the Khasi hills plateau. At Siatbakon village, where the Wār Khasi Hills begin, I see women sitting next to piles of stone and coal, waiting for customers, outside each rock quarry. Women squat next to piles of small rocks, breaking them into smaller pieces with hammers. A day's labour produces a 20 KG pile of rock that fetches around Rs. 50. Stone crushers produce smaller pieces and gravel and are usually operated during the day when there is electricity. These are made on order and shipped to the consignee immediately after the rock is crushed. The quarrying industry supports nearly 40 per cent of the population in these parts of the Khasi hills – quarry workers, crusher operators, labourers, truck drivers and loaders. Some of the quarries have been around for years and the denuded mountains, some of which have nearly disappeared under the crowbars of the quarry workers, bear testimony to this.

Elsewhere, it is king coal. Individuals dig black gold out of their patches and sell the stuff to Bangladesh. It is of inferior quality and not suitable for anything other than domestic use. The locals contemptuously say this coal is only good for Bangladesh, not for Guwahati.

A little further, there is abundant horticulture. In the valleys and even on hillsides, people grow a variety of vegetables. The countryside is picture-pretty. Rolling hills stretch into the distance, valleys tumble down to my feet with green potato plants or other vegetables sprouting. Clumps of bamboo or stands of pine dot the fields. Streams and brooks gurgle their way down the rocky hills and into the fields below. The population here is small and villages are correspondingly far apart and tiny, usually between 20 and 40 dwellings. The dwellings sprout any old how and are extremely varied. The rich have concrete and stone houses. The middling rich have stone and wood houses. The not so rich have thatch and wood houses. And the poor have houses made of thatch or bamboo. Most dwellings are far apart in the smaller villages, and clustered together in the larger ones.

Mawsyngram is a village 1000 metres above sea level near the Bangladesh border. It's a 25 kilometres drive from Weiloi, a crossroads where one road goes to the hot springs at Jakrem and the other to Mawphlang. The narrow road passes through spectacular mountains. Mawsingram has a spectacular limestone cave with one large and several smaller shivlings – stalagmites formed by millions of years of water dripping from the roof.

The cave is actually a massive overhang of rock that covers maybe 2000 square metres of a rock filled cavern. A long crack in the ceiling has let water drip over the aeons and this mineral-rich water has built up the shivling. The stalactite atop the shivling is nearly as long, but thinner. The tips of both are painted red. Behind the larger one are a series of smaller stalagmites, with corresponding stalactites; all the tips are red. Even here, far from maddening crowds of tourists, water and religion are mysterious and inextricably interlinked. The roof on the sides and back of the cavern have collapsed sometime in the past. From the back of the cavern comes the sound of rushing water. The man at the ticket counter – it's a two rupee ticket – says nobody has found the source of the sound. It must be an underground river. Did water, then, create god?

Mawsyngram is a small village of around 130 houses, dominated by two huge churches. It's unusual for such a small place to have such large churches. But it's the only village after Weiloi with a sizeable population; it's the local parish. From the village, I can see the plains of Bangladesh as it is at the end of the Khasi hills.

Nearby, a stream flowing down the hillside is channeled onto the road via a bamboo rod that has been sliced in half and the internodes removed. It flows in a steady stream of sweet water, tempting in the hot afternoon sun. Here, the locals have not yet rendered the hillsides bare so they are beautiful shades of green. However, I do not see any tree that would be over 15 years old; the larger ones are cut for furniture. Piles of firewood at every turn stacked neatly between vertical bamboo stakes tell me where the other species of wood have gone. The Khasis are burning both ends of their natural resources candle. Still, there are forests in this part.

The traditional system of channeling water from streams on the heights to fields in the valleys using a system of bamboos is slowly giving way to another one. The new order comprises the thick plastic pipes used to channel optic fibre or power cables. These are tougher than regular plastic pipes and flexible enough to run over rocky terrain from the source of the spring to the fields, supported over ditches with bamboo sticks. Once laid, they can last many years before they need replacement. They are easier to put in place – just unroll the pipes. Bamboo systems on the other hand have to be painstakingly constructed.

However, the plastic pipes do not achieve what the bamboo systems do – progressively reducing the quantum of water reaching the plant to a level where each plant gets just what it needs. These systems reduce waste and maximize the use of available water. Plastic pipe systems do not. It's a single pipe, ranging from one inch to three inches in diameter, that brings water from the source to the user. These modern replacements are beginning to snake up and down hills.

People like Lan aren't familiar with the plastic pipes. They are hard to cut and are seldom straight. They are heavier and tougher to work with than bamboo. They last longer but fashioning a *shyngiar* is out of the question. Plastic pipes will remain a means to transport water from the streams to the *shyngiar*, but the *shyngiar* will live on.

Meghalaya's immense water resources have to be nursed. Its natural resources need to be conserved. Locals have perfected the art of using what they have, with the *shyngiar* and terraced farming. They have a long, long way to go in learning how to conserve what they have. Trading the future for a richer tomorrow won't work, even though it may let the Khasis, Jaintias and Garos buy that fancy car or colour TV. Once gone, tropical rainforests never return and eventually, their streams will dry up. When that happens, an entire way of life will flow into the sea.

7 SHEKHAWATI: UNDERGROUND TANKS OF THE SETHS

Shekhawati in eastern Rajasthan has produced virtually every business family in India – steel baron Lakshmi Mittal, cement man Dalmia, cloth man Singhania, Poddars, Ruias, Khaitans. The list is long. Traditionally traders, each developed a town or a part of a town. Shekhawati occupied the old trade route between West Asia and the sub-continent of which water was a vital part. The seths of old built complexes with a tank of water, a temple and a well, many of which survive today in the desert as ghostly images of the past and conjure up images of caravans.

Forests once covered this place but have disappeared – there is no living memory of them. Now most of Shekhawati is desert, sandy or scrubby. People farm – growing dryland crops like bajra, gram, mustard, pulses or jowar – or live off animal husbandry. There is little industry despite having spawned the core of India's industry. It's a dry and inhospitable land, with the underground water having turned salty – so deep have tubewells gone. Where it's not salty, it's high in fluoride. In either case, its unfit for drinking by man or animal. The trees dotting the landscape are gnarled, of indeterminate age. They are prized possessions, feeding animals through the year and people when the rains fail. But they aren't treated as prize possessions and new trees are seldom to be seen.

Shekhawati's towns – Jhujhunu, Churu, Sikar and Chirawa, Ramnagar – are more famous for their painted world-famous havelis, or large houses, that now barely echo the grandeur of the past, than for water conservation. Yet, one wasn't possible without the other. The seths and the rulers took care to ensure a steady and adequate – if not abundant – supply of drinking water, and where possible, irrigation water, for the people. Shekhawati thrived as a trading area till the early 20th century. Then the seths moved away, to Bombay, Delhi, Calcutta and Madras to tap into rapidly expanding commerce and the opportunities it brought. They abandoned Shekhawati, their beautifully painted and carved havelis and the sandy towns to the locals, who continued to live as they had for eons, growing dryland crops of gram and millets and rearing camels and more recently, goats. The goats finished off what little greenery there was left; the forest department and locals completed the destruction by cutting and selling or burning trees. Shekhawati now is a backwater – a handful of seths have returned to give back to the place of their ancestors the gift of water.

****

It's a short overnight journey to Jhunjhunu in the heart of Shekhawati in eastern Rajasthan. The metre-gauge train starts from Delhi at 11 at night and gets there at 5 in the morning. Its second class air conditioned is as good as first class a/c in broad gauge trains with doors to lock passengers in. The first class a/c differs in that it has carpeting. It feels like a toy train, narrower and somewhat more derelict than its broader cousins.

At quarter to 11 the train silently slides onto the platform, much like the hulk of a ghost ship. It is dark, the windows are shuttered and the doors are locked. A few coolies and sundry touts hang onto the doors, struggling to push their hands through their window bars and open them so that they can grab seats to sell to passengers later. Most of the coaches have these leech-like appendages as they are second class ordinary. There is no first class, having being dumped by the Railways some decades ago as a vestige of the Raj. My second air-conditioned coach slides into view and I pick up my suitcase to follow it.

There is the usual rush to board the train, with men and women scurrying up and down the platform searching for their coaches and seats. Most simply want to board the train to get from Delhi to their destination as the train services the Rajasthan hinterland from where a lot of migrant labour comes to Delhi to work in the construction industry. These people dominate the passengers; they crowd out any reserved ticket holders with their bundles of food and clothes and their little bedding rolls. As soon as the train moves, they spread their bedding on the floors, regardless of where they are, and after a little jabbering, go to sleep.

I don't get much sleep even though I have set an alarm to wake me before getting to Jhunjhunu. The attendant comes however, a little while before we get to Jhunjhunu, on time at ten past five in the morning, to get me up.

Jhunjhunu's station isn't anything to write home about – a platform and a half with a narrow exit and entrance. Then a portico where you are supposed to be picked up or dropped off. Only, the crowd of people there makes it impossible to get a vehicle; instead, the jeeps and shared diesel three wheelers wait in a dusty courtyard beyond the portico, engines idling, for passengers to lumber up. They have fixed rates and given the size of the

100

town, these sound ridiculously low. I pay 5 rupees for a kilometre's ride to the pretentiously named Hotel Shekhawati Heritage.

My host in Jhunjhunu, Niranjan Singh who heads the Shekhawati Jal Biradari, had asked me my budget and when I said anything under Rs. 1,000, he chose this hotel. The others, he assured me later in the day, were more expensive. Shekhawati Heritage is an extremely basic hotel, more a lodge, at Rs. 600 a night, including taxes. The gate is locked and its dark inside at 5:30 AM. There is no bell to push so I find a stone and rap on the gate. Presently somebody hurries to open the gate and lights come on. I am ushered into the portals, down the drive, into a hallway and to my room at the end of the hall. It's a bare hall with another four doors, all leading to rooms.

I get a largish room with a TV and phone. There are shelves that are painted with stuff that comes off on whatever I place on them, so lining them with newspaper is a good idea. A curtain separates this well-appointed area from the rest of the room, serving the purpose of a cupboard door. It has seen cleaner days in the dim and distant past. The bathroom is large enough to shit and bathe in, but not two people together. There isn't any hot water, I gather quickly, from the presence of just a single tap in the bath area and the sink. Thankfully, there is water.

But the water is salty. It's not brackish, it's salty. Impossible to get a shave in that water as nothing will lather. Hard to bathe because the tiny soaps that the hotel has given run out before I can work up a decent scrub. Still, it will have to do what with my budget. The drinking water, which a tall, gaunt and haunted looking attendant brings in, isn't salty thankfully. It looks safe to drink but as I still have a bit of my bottled water left, I finish that off, ask for tea and proceed to get ready. Niranjan calls me at 7:30 to find out when we should meet. 9-ish I tell him and he rings off.

Its 9 and I am waiting outside the hotel in the bright hot sun. A jeep in reasonably fine fettle clatters up. There are two men inside, one of whom will be my guide for the day. Niranjan arrives around 10.

"Nitya bhai, sorry for being late. I got caught in a meeting. Can we spend half an hour fixing your programme for the next few days?"

"Yes, let's. And also who will be with me. Are you going to come along?" I ask, wondering what meeting he had at 8 in the morning. Niranjan a 50-ish man, tall and well built, with salt-and-pepper hair and large piercing eyes. He smiles a lot and speaks Hindi that even littérateurs would need a dictionary to translate. Niranjan is always in khadi kurta-pajama; they are his trademark. He owes his physique to his days in the army.

"I beg forgiveness for the first three days but on the last day I will come along with you. On all three days, you will see a mix of old and new water harvesting structures. Some of the old water structures are hundreds of years old. Most of the new ones have been with support from a seth. At

Chirawa, the Dalmias built a school many years ago, and they have recently installed a large rooftop rainwater harvesting system. Its remarkable."

And, turning to my guide, "Is that OK with you Parshuramji?"

Parshuram has a few clarifications on where we have to go. Then, "You had better get going, it's already quite hot," says Niranjan.

We get into the jeep, a Mahindra Commander. It's in reasonable shape and the driver has put clean white cotton seat covers. The jeep, Parshuram tells me, is the only vehicle that will comfortably go to the area we have to visit – a bunch of villages and the towns of Shekhawati. It's not the most comfortable vehicle to get around in, though, and in the heat of the desert day in May, it gets worse. However, the noise, heat and dust are just beginning.

Parshuram's advice is, "Take plenty of water". Right. But Niranjan is opposed to bottled water, as indeed are most people campaigning around the country for local community control over water resources. It's not too much of a dilemma for me – I'm carrying a flask that I fill with cold water. The others have a harder time refilling a bottle of Bisleri on the quiet. Anyway, water and other formalities over, we leave. A final word from Niranjan.

"Nityabhai, I will see you in the evening."

I nod, "I'll call you around 9 or so." And we are off.

We make a quick tour of Jhunjhunu itself, while getting out of town. It's quite unremarkable as towns go – dusty, wide open spaces and a small market place. Jhunjhunu has its share of havelis – the residences of the rich traders who have long since migrated to larger cities. Without exception, these rambling mansions are elaborately built, copies of palaces of kings, and richly painted. The paintings are usually gods and goddesses, hunting scenes and depictions of the Ramayan and Mahabharat. The paintings are often as old as the building itself and have seldom been restored. If indeed they could. They are made on lime plaster with vegetable dyes. The anonymous painters depicted their subjects in great depth. I often get to see 'restored' paintings – grey-brown cement on portions that have fallen off. Nowhere has there been a serious effort to conserve this priceless open-air gallery.

The road to Alsisar, the first village on our itinerary, is narrow and smooth. I am sitting in front, so have a good view of the surroundings as well as a smoother ride than those at the back. Parshuram doesn't have to guide the driver too much – the driver's used to this route, having ferried numerous visitors. Ganesh is his name, and he's been jeeping over these roads a good long time.

"I used to work in Dubai but returned 10 years ago to drive this taxi. My brother and I own two jeeps and we both drive them. We don't trust drivers," says he. He's a cool driver, not a wild-night-tonight type who tears up the tracks. Makes sense, especially when you aren't sure if you will see a goat, camel or cow around the next bend.

***

Alsisar is a large village about 40 kilometres north of Jhunjhunu. We come upon it suddenly. The road meanders over small hillocks, actually sand dunes, that make for an undulating ride. There aren't any real hills here, just very high sand dunes covered with scrub, a few hardy trees and thorny bushes. Stuff of really hot and arid lands. Human beings are the most abundant life form, followed by the plants and goats. The ship of the desert doesn't walk alone – camels are too valuable to be turned loose to graze, unlike cows in India's cities. They are either tethered to trees in the middle of nowhere or pulling camel carts – their wheels are usually discarded aircraft tyres.

A turn around a sand dune reveals Alsisar. A vast open space, flanked by single storied houses, terminating in a low-walled enclosure, welcomes visitors. The road disappears under sand at this point – sand which is soft and yielding and as yet cool to the touch. At 11 AM, the sun hasn't heated it to baking temperature. All the houses reflect the sun, dazzling me, as they are nearly uniformly white. I see a few old men but little else – those that can work are either in their fields, ploughing for the coming sowing season or in offices. The people of Shekhawati set get store by a government job because there are few industries or other avenues of employment here. Farming is the main occupation here.

A board on a building to my left reads Panchayat Ghar – the local Panchayat office. Parshuram leads me into a small lane next to the Ghar and into a maze of houses beyond. He climbs over a low wall behind the Panchayat Ghar, onto a giant square-shaped saucer with a dome in the centre. The cemented floor, somewhat black with age and lack of maintenance or cleaning, slopes gently down towards the dome. At the base of the dome, where it joins the floor, are little arched openings no higher than a brick each, one to each side of the square saucer. Each side of the saucer, I estimate, will be about 30 metres – that makes for a 30 metre square saucer, or catchment area.

"This Nityaji, is a tank (*tanka* in local parlance). It's about 80 years old. A seth of the village built it and we have recently cleaned and renovated it," says Parshuram, proudly. It was built of stone, bricks and lime mortar but the renovated parts, mainly the dome, are done in cement. The contrast is striking.

The seth remains a nameless benefactor – nobody knows his name and the locals don't remember it. The tank is an underground storage device that holds up to 100,000 litres of drinking water. Atop the central dome is a well with a bucket from where people can draw water; convention has it that *tanka* water is for drinking only. The underground reservoir is lined

103

with lime mortar and bottomed by bricks, so whatever water flows inside is saved from seepage and evaporation for several months even in that hotel climate. Rain falling in the saucer runs into the holes at the bottom of the dome and into the underground tank. I can see the difference between the original structure and the renovated part; the renovated part, which is mostly the dome, is made of concrete while the original structure is made of lime mortar and has turned black over the decades.

Another renovated feature – plastic pipes running from the roof of the Panchayat Ghar and a few other surrounding buildings into the saucer. These augment the rainwater falling into the saucer.

"By adding these pipes, we have doubled the catchment area of this *tanka*," says Parshuram. The pipes bring down the rainwater from the surrounding roofs and fill the tank quickly; less wastage, more water.

"Doesn't the water get dirty?" I ask.

"We clean the saucer before the rainy season starts. We remove all the grass and bushes that have come up, sweep the place and remove any other dirt that's accumulated there. When it rains only the clean water flows into the tank," he says.

In addition, people living around the *tanka* have decided not to let animals into the saucer. There is a high wall around it but even so, they drive away errant goats and dogs.

The *tanka* is a simple yet ingenous system to provide drinking water to people for up to 10 months. The new ones hold between 10,000 and 30,000 litres of water which lasts a family of five for seven or eight months, cost Rs. 25,000 to make and fit into the courtyard of even a modest dwelling. Most new *tankas* have round catchment area with a diameter of 6-8 metres. They can be walled to keep animals and children out, even though it's safe – the holes at the base of the central dome are too small for any child or animal to enter.

Building *tankas* is a joint effort. The community or the owner, as the case may be, chips in with the labour that typically constitutes a quarter of the total cost. *Tanka* water is strictly for human consumption; animals may get a share in drought years but irrigation is a strict no-no. Just a few days' rain are enough to fill a *tanka* because that's how they have been designed. The *tankas* also need little maintenance.

Tanks are either privately owned in this part of Shekhawati or communally owned. The distinguishing feature is the location of a *tanka*. A *tanka* built inside a person's house is individually owned while ones like this are communally owned. There is no restriction, however, on people drawing water even from individually-owned *tankas*, provided the family that owns it feels there is enough water for their needs. Such large *tankas*, as the one in Alsisar, are seldom built any more even though hold over 100,000 litres of water – they would cost upwards of Rs. 400,000 and anyway nobody makes lime mortar any more.

They are ideally suited to the hot dry climate of Shekhawati. Completely covered, the stored water cannot evaporate or seep into the surrounding sandy soil. The concrete ensures it is not contaminated by sub-soil water. *Tankas* the ideal drinking water storage facility that can double up for storing tanker water during droughts.

Visions of falling through rotting concrete into a huge cesspool float before me. I voice my concern and Parshuram assures me that the water tank is only in the centre; I stand on solid ground. Stepping out, I notice a small foot-high 'temple' in a corner. A soot-blackened idol sits inside with a miniature trishul standing guard. It's newly-whitewashed, standing in stark contrast with the blackened top of the saucer.

"At every tank you will see has a temple either inside it or just outside," Parshuram explains. "That's because we don't want people pissing or shitting nearby so that the catchment area remains clean. We also emphasize the close connection between water and religion in India by building a small shrine." The shrine has no deity inside; just a place to light a lamp as if beckoning travelers in the night to water. A reminder to me that giving water to the thirsty is one of the noblest of deeds. It's also an effective deterrent to misuse and water pollution.

The *tankas* have sorted out some of the drinking water problems that people have faced in recent decades but not that of irrigation and water for animals. The groundwater water in this part of Shekhawati is saline; in other parts it has a higher-than-healthy concentration of dissolved fluorides. Drinking water, therefore, has to come mainly from above. Literally from rain, figuratively from the government through taps.

Emerging from the saucer and the surrounding houses, I am surrounded by a bunch of dusty snotty kids. They keep a distance, which is welcome, as I walk to the low-walled structure at the end of the open area. It's a *talaab*, or pond – a square manmade structure also designed to collect and hold rainwater. The difference is, *talaab* water isn't used for drinking but for bathing and washing clothes. The larger *talaabs* cater to animals and irrigation for crops. This is a smallish one, about 15 metres square, with a puddle of water accumulated in the centre.

The walls surrounding it are waist-high and about a foot and a half thick, made of lime and plastered with the same stuff. Hardy, because its withstood over a century of use and, of late, abuse. Some three decades ago, a United Nations agency decided that these *talaabs* were the root cause of malaria in the country and systematically set about destroying them. Never mind the fact that the water in these *talaabs* supports aquatic life that does not let mosquitoes breed. Within the perimeter, along the walls, steps descend to a central square that still holds a little filthy water. People could bathe or wash their clothes on these steps, or simply congregate and spend the time of day.

Talaabs, explains Niranjan, were the cornerstone of traditional village life. People went there to bathe, wash clothes and gossip while their animals had a drink. Large trees usually grew around these *talaabs* and the place was cooler than its surroundings during the day because of the water, making it the hub of communal life. Next to this derelict specimen stands a large peepul tree, the seat of village gatherings in years gone by; now it's a garbage dump and the tree, a refuge for goats and cows.

The *talaab* mechanism is even simpler than the *tanka* one. It's built at a low point where natural gradients meet. Rainwater flows along these gradients, through holes in the wall of the *talaab*, into the square collection area. The *talaab* has a concrete or rock bottom that does not let the water seep into the ground – it can hold water for several months and if the rains have been good, for the entire year till the next rainy season. There is a definite pecking order in the use of *talaabs*, something that was traditionally inviolate. People bathed on the steps along their sides – they didn't use soap back then. They washed clothes, again without soap. This water stayed within the *talaab*. Most *talaabs* were built with an overflow area – when the main tank was full, water flowed over a wall into another sloping tank without steps. Animals – domestic and wild – drank from here. This simple system separated men from animals and kept the water of the *talaab* clean for human use. Lime mortar, that was used to make these *talaabs*, is believed to purify and soften the water.

Sadly though, the catchment area of *talaabs* is much larger than tanks. This leaves them open to encroachment and once encroached, its sewage from houses and not rainwater from the catchment area, that flows into the *talaabs*. In addition to this rot, surrounding houses and the municipality treats abandoned *talaabs* as garbage dumps. A combination of factors, accumulated over the recent decades, has wiped most *talaabs* off the face of Shekhawati.

"It's the alienation of people from their natural habitat. People are concerned more about money, the here and now, rather than the good of the community and the future. They expect the government to provide them water and electricity, roads and education. There is piped water, even though supply is erratic. It's more convenient than drawing water from a well far away. It has made people lazy," philosophizes Parshuram.

It sums up what went wrong and why the people of Shekhawati now face a water crisis, partly of their own making. It's also partly of the government's making – a government that promised grandiose schemes of drinking water on tap and laid pipelines hundreds of kilometres long to bring water from distant lakes and rivers to this region. Like all supply lines, this too is vulnerable as the people discovered; there are frequent disruptions. The resorted to digging tubewells. This solution worked excellently for some years. Then the water table began to sink and the depth of the tubewells increased till strange diseases started happening. Analysis of water samples showed a high concentration of fluorides; the water also tastes salty in the region around Alsisar and right up to Chirawa.

The sarpanch emerges as we prepare to leave. A middle aged man in a white dhoti-kurta, with a white turban and a speckled moustache.

"Where do you get water for your animals?" I ask him.

"We use the tap water for the animals," is the prompt reply. Tank water for humans, taps for the animals. "Not tank water?"

He shakes his head. The conventions still bind people, no matter how much of tradition they have forgotten. Is that enough?

"We save up water for the animals and now the taps supply enough water," he says. "But we don't drink it because we don't know where the water comes from."

***

My eyes have been opened. These circular 'satellite dishes' are actually to catch water from the skies, not signals from outer space. Did an extra-terrestrial intelligence give us the technology to build them, though. Parshuram is unmoved by the question.

We drive north from Alsisar – its hotter now and the road shimmers in the heat. A dust devil beckons us on, past thorny scrub and sandy dunes, to the next village. In the lee of a dune stands another *talaab*, a patch of green against a desolate desert scene. But it's been abandoned as well by all but the stray animal. There is water at the bottom of the *talaab*, presumably from the rains in winter six months before. Its catchment is intact, sort of, as its located miles from any village. As we drive past, I see neither man nor beast near the *talaab*; in a few years it will have become one with the desert it sought to provide succour from.

The animals cannot drink groundwater because its saline. If they do, the heat and salt in the water kills them in a few hours. The salt in the water leaches out the salt from their tissues and the heat completes the dehydration. Human beings cannot drink it for the same reason. And it's useless for agriculture but farmers still use it, desperate to eke one crop from the sandy soil in a year. In a few years, though, their fields turn saline and useless for any production. They have to be left fallow for many years before they can be used again, if at all.

I see a lone house in the middle of what must be fields. The ground is ploughed and there are more trees than normal. Next to the house, I see a smouldering cylindrical structure with a conical shaft below it made of bricks – a lime kiln. Two men tend to the kiln, one feeding coal to the fire in the pit and the other adding stone that will be oxidized to lime. It's a primitive contraption and making lime is a painstaking process. The lime settles at the bottom of the pit and is extracted very gingerly and put in a

107

steel drum to cool. It you touch it, you can burn yourself very badly.

Seeing how lime is made, I understand why people don't use its mortar anymore even though it is believed that structures made of lime mortar are cooler than cement ones and keep water cleaner. They also last a good deal longer, as evidenced by the remains of early Islamic buildings. Nearly all the new tanks are made of cement and bricks.

Traditionally, the seths built the tanks as they were only ones with the money to do so – they gained merit and hopefully and early release from the endless cycle of birth and rebirth in the process. The local people always chipped in with labour, that was counted towards their contribution, so that they could use the water when they needed it. This also gave them a stake in looking after the tanks – they cleaned them before the rains, made sure animals didn't get into the catchment areas to shit or piss, repaired minor damage and generally guarded water with their life. This symbiotic relationship lasted well into the 20th century.

However, the system began to decay in the 1970s with the advent of piped water and handpumps. From a community resource, water entered the private realm. Taps made it possible to get water inside one's home, whereas earlier women had to congregate at the *tankas* to draw their water. This changing focus naturally meant that *tankas* dwindled in importance and slowly fell into disuse. The government also did its part by claiming ownership of all *tankas* that were built on public or common land. Local people who were concerned with their upkeep were told to lay off, the government will provide. The Panchayats were given money for this but assurances were seldom translated into action.

"It's like this," explains Niranjan. "If you take away something that for generations I have regarded as common property and have looked after, and say you will now manage it for me, why will I have a stake in its upkeep. Then you give a local leader money for maintenance which does not happen. How can you expect local people to contribute anything when they know that the money that's come for looking after their common resource has lined the leader's pocket?"

There was, and is, a hierarchy of drawing water, depending on the caste of the person. These were strictly enforced earlier, but with shrinking sources, they became more rigid.

"Upper castes always get preference. If they are bathing, Dalits cannot come close to the water source," says Sunetra Lala, a researcher who's spent several weeks in Rajasthan's villages studying caste, women and water. "And if a Dalit is drawing water, an upper caste person can butt in for his piece of the action at any time. The discrimination varies from village to village but it's there."

It was always the lower castes – sweepers and the like – who cleaned the *tankas* before the rains. But their labour was not always rewarded in kind.

Niranjan is hesitant to talk about this. Like elsewhere in India, the lowest caste have the responsibility to maintain water structures.

"Casteism is always there. I have seen that it has reduced in recent years. In all my work, I have always made sure that people from all castes work together to construct the *tanka*," he says. Maybe it works here, because Niranjan's organization, the Dalmia Trust, makes the financial contribution that is about two-thirds of the total cost while labour constitutes a third. By this, he claims that the distribution of water, and maintenance of the *tankas*, is done equitably.

"Else why would a Dalit chip in alongside a Brahmin," he reasons. I do not see this happening so reluctantly take his word for it.

Around Malsisar, the groundwater is saline. Water levels have been falling by up to five feet a year because of handpumps and tubewells. At 100 metres, there is a thick layer of rock below which there is no water.

Parshuram directs the driver through the by lanes of Malsisar. It's a biggish village, with the drains overflowing onto the lanes. Under the Prime Minister's Rural Roads Scheme, a half kilometre stretch of concrete road has been built in the centre of the village; on both sides, the road is broken. It's a steep climb up to, and off, the concrete section, the only one without sewage flowing on it. Incongruous. A water tank atop a cement tower beckons us – there is a *gaushala* that Parshuram wants me to see where *tankas* have been built to tap rainwater for the cows.

Inside Malsisar, in a clearing, there is a colourful group of women filling pots from a large cylindrical water tank that is filled by the government supply once every two days. It's a 5-metre high concrete cylinder that holds around 20,000 litres. On one side, there is a line of taps and a long sink. The women are brightly clad in pink, orange and red saris that catch the sun in all its splendour. There are a few children too, but water-filling here, as in most of India, is a female chore.

The tank has replaced the *tanka* and the *talaab* as the centre of rural life. It's less of a binder though – women have to queue up to get their quota of water instead of walking to the water's edge and dipping in. The taps are functional and easier to use, no doubt, and women don't have to walk any great distance to get water. But they are a poor substitute for *talaabs* as a means of social cohesion. Nearby, a group of men sit and gossip at the local paan shop.

The *gaushala* is run by a local trust, patronized by a seth of the locality. It's an old place that has been looking after unwanted cattle for several decades. Entering it under the shadow of the concrete water tank, I'm struck by the cleanliness within. It's not like any other cow yard, full of shit and half eaten fodder. The ground is swept, the cows in their sheds (where else) and the bulls in theirs. No unwanted pregnancies here. Plastic pipes run from the roofs of nearly all the buildings into the ground – they flow into two *tankas.*, one on either side of the entrance. These are not the regular satellite-dish *tankas* but just underground water tanks to hold rooftop water. A plaque in front of one proclaims it has been made by the Shekhawati Jal Biradari at a cost of Rs. 25,000 a year before. The plaque in front of the other *tanka* is broken, presumably by a cow backing into it. Peering through the thick steel bars of a cowshed, I see a particularly nervous specimen at the rear, separated from by several steel gates. The reason is soon apparent – the animal snorts, tosses its heads and mock-charges the gate nearest to it. If it had a free run, it would have probably charged the main gate. It's an impressive animals with long sharp horns, standing some five feet at the shoulder.

The *gaushala* system is a departure from the usual rainwater harvesting practice in Shekhawati, where *tankas* are built to store water exclusively for human consumption.

I meet Ram Babu from Jatawa Khurd, a man of around thirty, dark from spending his days in the sun, tells me, "I had sunk a tube well to irrigate my crops several years ago. For some years, things were fine. Then others started sinking tubewells and the water level went down. It doesn't rain much here. Now, I have reached the 100 metre level and the tube-well is useless."

Ram Babu has made a *tanka* in a corner of his field and he has a shared *tanka* in his house. The field *tanka* is essential because it's a long walk – about 4 kilometres – from his village to the field. His labourers need the water when they are working and he lets others draw water. It's not much of a field – ploughed sandy earth sloping fairly steeply up a sand dune on one side, dotted with gnarled Khejri trees. The light brown sand shines almost white in the sunlight. The *tanka* blends with the field. The water code is fairly rigid – *tanka* water is only for drinking.

Agriculture, then, is back to being completely dependent on rains. If it rains, it pours. But otherwise, men from this region migrate in search of work and money. Irrigation with groundwater is risky. It always means the field has to be kept fallow for two or three years after growing a crop water with underground water. Else, the soil will become saline and useless. A couple of rains later, the soil is ready for another crop with the salty groundwater. Its conventional wisdom and no scientist has advised farmers on this. No scientist has advised them on the 'right' amount of water to use for irrigation either – the result, says Niranjan, is that farmers with pump sets flood their fields when they are growing something.

Parshuram says, bouncing up and down in the back of the jeep, "It used to get so bad that people had no water to drink. Those that left in search of work lived to return but those that stayed behind often didn't make it through droughts. These *tankas* have at least solved their problem of drinking water in the summer and through droughts."

Each *tanka* can supply a family of five drinking water for up to eight months if it rains well for even three or four days. The *tanka* fills up and the overflow is let into the fields through a concrete channel. Animals can drink from this channel but are kept out of the 'satellite dish' of the *tanka* by either thorny branches of the desi babul or barbed wire. The thorns are vicious – 5-7 centimetres long – and can puncture my jeep's tires. The driver is wary of them too.

It's hot now and the bottle of water I have is also lukewarm. Not palatable at all. I wonder how the people here manage in the burning sun. The sand that seeps into my sandals when I step out singes my toes. Of course, locals are not made to go out in the midday sun – that's the prerogative of mad dogs and Englishmen and itinerant travelers. Parshuram looks distinctly uncomfortable and hot as well. I offer him some water. He shakes his head, preferring to drink from a nearby *tanka* instead.

It's a small concrete structure in the middle of a field, surrounded by babul branches. I step over them carefully, hard to do because the satellite dish is half a metre about field level. The *tanka* isn't locked, like some others have been. I open the heavy iron lid and peer in – it looks about half full. The water is clean.

"It's about three-fourths full," corrects Parshuram. There's a steel bucket with a rope lying upside-down on the dish. Parshuram drops this into the opening, dips once and draws up half a bucket of water. He closes the cover and pours the water from the bucket into another bottle he is carrying. Then, tilts his head back and pours the water down his throat. I take a little water into my hands and drink it tentatively. Clean or not, it's different from what I am used. But the water is fine and tastes of, well, nothing. It's cooler than my bottle so I top up the bottle, throwing caution to the winds. I see no mosquito larvae or other unidentified floating objects in the water so I decide its fit to drink. Its rainwater anyway so no industrial effluents or pesticides here. And the *tanka*'s well is lined with cement on all sides and the bottom to minimize wastage. Water cannot get in from the sides or the bottom, only from the sky.

"If you had water from an old *tanka* that's made of lime mortar, you would notice the difference," says Parshuram. "That is sweet water. This one tastes a little of cement."

Lime mortar, he says, keeps the water the clean and free of insects. It even gives the water a sweetish taste. Having seen the state of lime mortar *tankas*, I decide to give the trial a miss.

I use a little, as little as possible, maybe two handfuls of the water to wash the salt off my face. Its welcome in the shimmering heat and the water cools me a bit. From behind a wall of shrubbery, a buffalo comes galloping into the field in which the *tanka* is followed in short order by goats and sheep. Then the shepherd, clad in a checked dhoti and light kurta, with the trademark Rajasthani turban – no flaming red here, a sober striped green. He pauses, seeing us. He's a boy, maybe in his mid-teens.

"Where do you graze them?" I ask him. Parshuram translates into the vernacular.

The boy gestures vaguely over the nearby sand dune.

"There is some pasture there," he says. I walk over the crest of the sand dune. It's as barren on that side as it is on this. Maybe the animals can see what I cant.

"He means the Khejri trees and the babul," says Parshuram, coming to stand beside me. There are more Khejri and babul trees ahead but I notice a singular lack of young ones. Khejri, I must explain, is a stunted tree, about 7-8 metres tall, with a head of branches from which sprout little leaves. Those that still have leaves – the locals have cut most green branches for fodder – look luxuriant in the hot sun. They provide fodder, fuel and furniture wood for the people here. Despite their importance and obvious local adaptation, they aren't multiplying.

"It's overgrazing. That and the tractors used to plough the fields kill off saplings. We have tried to protect saplings wherever we have found them but it's not worked."

We stop in front of a house with a large courtyard and a bougainvillea growing in front. Its bright red flowers contrast with the stark whiteness of the courtyard's wall. It's a high wall so I cannot see inside. This is Parshuram's in-laws' house.

"Come and eat," he invites.

"It's too early to eat," I protest.

I enter through an arched doorway. The courtyard is large – its size is proportional to the owner's wealth. This one, like most others, has a dirt floor though a few have stones. Parshuram guides me up five stairs to a building on one side of the courtyard with a large verandah that has several charpoys. It's for guests and generally for the menfolk to hang out. It's made of bricks and cement, the roof of stone slabs placed horizontally on steel rails. Like everything else, it a dazzling white.

In the middle of the courtyard is the main building. A low wall defines an inner courtyard in front of this double-storeyed structure. On one side of the courtyard against the wall of the building is the hearth; on the opposite side is the washing area with pots of water and a brick-high wall. His in-laws sit on the floor in the verandah of this building to eat. Behind the house is where the animals are kept. In one corner of the courtyard stands a spanking new tractor – like with most other vehicle owners, its parked in front for all to see. I don't see any loo – the fields serve this important purpose.

His sister-in-law appears with a *ghunghat* (veil) on her face, steel glasses pushed one inside the other in one hand and a small steel pot of water in the other. She doles them out and then pours water into each.

"Bring tea," says Parshuram.

She re-appears a little later with a steel tray with tiny tea cups and some salty snacks. Then, "Will you have lunch now?" asks Parshuram.

"I don't think we should trouble your in-laws," I say.

The sister-in-law speaks from behind the veil, "No trouble. We just need to make the chapattis."

I give into the temptation of home-cooked food. It's served shortly in the other building.

I wash my hands in courtyard at the base of a tree and sit down on the jute rug to eat. The vegetable is potato curry, red and with a thin oil film. The daal is yellow. The chapattis are smeared with ghee. She sets the plates and bowls before us and then splashes the daal and vegetable into the bowls. The chapattis follow. There is some dry chutney – a mixture of garlic, chilli and salt – and wet chutney made of coriander, mind and chilli.

"It's homemade ghee," the sis-in-law explains. At that point I see the chef – Parshuram's mother-in-law and greet her with a namaskar. I eat like a pig; maybe it's the desert heat that sharpens my hunger.

Later, Niranjan explains the near-dominance of pucca houses. "This region has sent many people to the armed forces. In fact, a man from nearly every house serves in the army or has served in the army. The first thing they do on retirement is build a house with their gratuity and provident fund. They all like to keep their houses clean and orderly. This seeming prosperity is a fairly recent thing though."

Most houses do appear new, maybe less than a decade old. Their functional whitewash is a stark contrast to the painted havelis of the seths, usually pink or fuchsia with colourful hunting scenes on the outside walls. Hardly any of the villagers' houses have paintings as they are usually new, less than 20 years old. It's one way to tell a new house from an old one.

We drive off, rest and refreshed. Parshuram asks the jeep driver to travel further north. The sand from the dunes has washed over the road in many places, completely obscuring it. It's easy for even a heavy vehicle like the jeep to skid off the road and get stuck in the sand on either side. My driver cautiously slows down when he sees the road disappears under sand – he's been through the getting stuck bit before. It's fine sand, white mixed with the brown mud of the plains that becomes clayey and hard with a little water. A little water is enough for people to eke a single crop in a year from the earth.

The sky has acquired a steely hue; it's blazing hot and the road shimmers in the heat. The sand dunes – more low hills than dunes – seem to be so permanent that the road snakes over them rather than around them. Cresting one, I spot a dust devil in the near distance. The whirl of sand rises several hundred feet in the hot still air and dances on and off the road, tempting us to run it over. The landscape is pretty barren with brownish sand stretching away on either side. The slopes of the dunes have sand eddies, where the wind, rather than water, has swept sand and deposited it in a microcosm of the sand dune.

In the shimmering afternoon heat of 3 o'clock, we set out east towards Chirawa, the point of origin of the Dalmias. The Dalmias are cement barons now, but began, like most of the seths of Shekhawati, as traders. The men used to travel to Calcutta and Bombay and return home a few times a year. They had built schools in Chirawa many years ago, one for boys and another for girls; both are very well attended.

Mr. Raghu Hari Dalmia, who heads OCL India Limited, leans forward in this comfortable chair, seated in his small office in Delhi. The wall behind him has a family tree of the Dalmias. He recalls, "Shekhawati used to be a sandy desert when I used to visit it as a child, perhaps once a year. Later I noticed the place had more greenery and when I spoke with farmers, they said they had tapped groundwater for agriculture. However, water levels had been falling for many years. I realized that if this wasn't checked, the place would once again revert to desert.

"My family has been involved in education for many years through the Dalmia Trust. I was asked to take charge of the Trust's affairs. In 2004, I met Rajinder Singh of Tarun Bharat Sangh, a non-profit organization working on soil conservation and water harvesting in Alwar. We met in Delhi where he introduced me to Niranjan Singh."

The first step they all felt was to provide drinking water to people, the second to arrest the falling groundwater levels and the third to restore greenery to the region.

"Rajinder Singh suggested that I build a rooftop rainwater harvesting system in the schools because they have large roofs," says Raghu. This was the low hanging fruit and showed the Dalmias were willing to put money where their mouth was. Both the schools got a system that now meets their toilet-water needs. Pipes from the roof collect at a point, run underground to a tank in the corner of the playground. The tank is essentially a covered concrete well.

In the late afternoon, the Dalmia school stands silent and empty. The elderly chowkidar lets us in and we walk through the high hallway to the playground at the back. Parshuram points to the far corner of the field where a large cylindrical cement structure stands – the storage well. From the well, I see the white and blue plastic pipes leading off the roof and into the ground, and eventually coming up to the well to discharge the water collected on the roof. Exiting, I am fascinated by a large brass statue of Saraswati, the goddess of learning, in the school.

Rainwater harvesting has reduced the amount of groundwater being pumped up; it's also more potable than groundwater in many places in

Shekhawati. The immediate aim, then, is to reduce dependence on groundwater.

Building new *tankas* and *talaabs* is part of Raghu Dalmia's strategy; the other bit is to repair what has been around for centuries. There are literally thousands of *tankas*, *baolis*, *talaabs*, *johads* and *kunds* in Shekhawati. The rule of thumb is – the older, the worse off is the structure. But the fact remains that these could supply a fair percentage of the region's water needs, if they were restored and looked after.

"It would cost many millions to build new *kunds* and *talaabs* but only a few hundreds of thousands to repair and look after the old ones," says Raghu. He has a multi-step approach to making his part of Shekhawati green. The first is providing for drinking water. The second is giving *tanka*-owners saplings of local tree species to plant on their fields. The third is changing agriculture patterns so people grow crops that are locally suitable. The fourth is making an alliance of the Panchayats in Chirawa that will strengthen local efforts. Finally, he wants to make the seasonal Katli river, that flow through three districts in Shekhawati, a perennial river. These are long-term plans, but Raghu is in for the long haul.

The town of Churu lies about 90 kilometres north-west of Jhunjhunu. Its more famous for the pretty painted havelis, or mansions, of the seths of old. Most seths have gone, swallowed by the sands of time. Their descendants live in distant cities and seldom come back. The streets of Churu are broken, covered with a thick layer of sand that has been moistened by water tankers to keep it from flying into houses and shops. Sewers overflow, pigs wallow in the black gutters, cows chew the cud in the middle of narrow streets and cycle rickshaws threaten to drive my jeep off the road. We're actually passing through, looking for a johad outside Churu. I see a beautiful haveli, its façade and paintings in good repair, and we stop.

The caretaker is out but his wife obligingly lets us in. The entrance is through a low door cut in the main wooden gate, studded with brass stakes, to the courtyard. The courtyard has a covering of chicken-wire mesh to keep birds off the priceless paintings. All the walls of the courtyard and the surrounding rooms are covered with hand-drawing of gods and goddesses.

Navneeta Sharma, the caretaker's wife, says, "The house is about 300 years old. The owner had appointed my husband's family as the caretaker. He comes once in a few years. We have been looking after this place. We have lived here for nearly 250 years."

That makes her family the virtual owner of the mansion. Her husband, she says, isn't interested in making it into a hotel to earn money, rather than spending money on looking after the rambling house. Then, she invites us into the inner courtyard that's bigger and even more elaborately painted.

"I've restored some of these panels myself. We cannot do very much because its only my daughter and myself who stay here all the time and it's a large house. It takes me two hours to clean one portion of the house."

It sure is. Three sides of the inner courtyard are surrounded by three-storied buildings, the walls of which are also painted, but the paintings have faded. The soot from years of cooking in the courtyard has obscured many paintings. The plaster has fallen off in other places, to be replaced by cement. The family has locked up all but what is needed for them on the ground floor. Navneeta is around 45 and lacks the energy to run up and down the house, looking after it. The atmosphere is one of splendid decrepitude. Some mansion-owners have had the good sense to cash in on their assets – they have made them into hotels and charge a pretty packet for 'heritage holidays'. I take photos to my heart's content, though Navneeta does say that others charge even for taking pictures.

Rani Ka Talaab, a large pond surrounded by a palace on one side and walls on the other sides, if one of Churu's larger water collection structures. It was built, like all these monuments, several centuries ago. There are five stories inside; the façade is the top floor. When the *talaabs* is full, the two lowest stories are under water. This keeps the palace, and presumably the Sethani, cool in Shekhawati's long hot summer. There are canopied platforms that jut out from the palace – in these, the ladies of the city could bathe in privacy. For the commoners, there are platforms arranged around the other three walls of the *talaabs*. The palace is made of brick, the rest of the *talaabs* from sandstone.

Hanuman Prasad, my guide in the Churu region, says, "The *talaabs* has never dried up. But the water level is low because it's not rained properly for two years."

Not just that, the catchment area of the *talaabs* does not exist anymore. What was open ground from where water would flow into the *talaabs* is now under housing.

Amla Ruia, wife of the owner of Phoenix Mills in Mumbai Ashok Ruia, runs her trust in Ramgarh. It's a few kilometres south of Churu. Ramgarh is an extremely dusty town. We drive through narrow dusty lanes and up a long street, ankle deep in dust. Water tankers have converted the dust to slush. On both sides are double-storied buildings, their top storeys still covered with lovely paintings. The paintings depict life in the 19th century when these buildings were probably made. Sadly, the buildings are overhung with wires. Where the plaster has fallen, because nobody bothers to look after the buildings, not even the owners, ugly graying-brown patches of cement have taken over. Elsewhere along the half kilometre stretch, signboards obscure the paintings. I look at the slush and try to forget the blasphemy.

"I was moved by the plight of the people of Ramgarh during the 1999 drought. I came out of my shell to try and help them. But the people refused. They had become so used to water on tap, that the government supplied from the Indira Gandhi Canal, that they could not understand what I was offering them. I wanted their cooperation," she reminisces, sitting one evening outside the Tarun Bharat Sangh ashram. Dressed in a blue chikan kurta, draped with tasteful costume jewellery, the grey-haired Amla looks every bit the lady of a large house. But she switches roles between that and her work in the dusty lanes of Ramgarh with ease.

Amla returned to Mumbai, disillusioned. She commissioned an expert Sanjeev Bamru to design a project for the region. In due course, Sanjeev produced a plan worth Rs. 10 million but Amla was reluctant to back it without seeing things for herself. Her sister, who had heard of Rajinder Singh, president of TBS, suggested that she have him whet the plan.

"I couriered the plan to him and spoke to him a week later in March 2001. He rejected it out of hand because it said nothing about involving local people. To understand what community participation means, I visited TBS and persuaded Rajinder to visit Ramgarh," says Amla.

After all this, she set up the Ramgarh Vikas Trust and focused on building *tankas* because drinking water was in short supply in villages around Ramgarh. She found the people in villages to be much more responsive than the townspeople. Over the past three years, Amla's trust has made more than 150 *tankas* in these villages. Ramgarh, on the other hand, continues to be the very picture of dereliction.

At one end of the market road is the Ruia haveli; at the other is a splendid painted well. It was part of a complex with a temple, haveli and step well. All that's left now are the remains of the well. Under the cenotaph atop the well are faded frescoes of horses and elephants. The haveli next to the well must have been also richly painted once, but only the ones under the eaves are still visible; the rest have faded in the desert sun. Dust covers everything – even the paintings on the walls of the havelis.

I enter the Ruia haveli through a high iron gate. There is a narrow courtyard to the left; to the right is a verandah with lots of thick mattresses with white cotton covers and bolsters for visitors to recline on. The roof is richly painted. Narender Singh, who I have been referred to, isn't there. I explain what I am doing to another man, who agrees to show the *tankas* after lunch. Lunch time is sacred, even here in the middle of the desert where people eat their first meal at around 11 and the evening one at sundown.

We leave in the jeep for a village outside Ramgarh. What strikes me about the Ramgarh region is that nearly all villages have piped water. The 5 metre-high concrete cylindrical water tanks, into which water is piped every day or every other day from the Indira Gandhi Canal in north Rajasthan, have become part of every village's landscape, as much as wells used to be before. They are the new social centres, where women and children congregate to fill water pitchers. It's still the women who do this, despite the proximity of water sources. Men would not be caught dead filling water pitchers.

At a tank, there is a riot – of colours. Rajasthani women in saris in bright pink, red and orange throng the trough of a tank with their plastic pitchers. To the left, under the eave of a paan shop, the men of the village while away their time. As I train my camera on the women, they too beg to be photographed. At the next village, the pipe feeding the tank has burst; a black rubber hose tied to the burst helps people water and wash their animals while the trickle going into the tank seems to suffice for people.

In the midst of this seeming bounty, is building *tankas* just a way to appease a conscience. After all, getting water out of *tankas* takes effort, something that getting water out of a tank through a tap does not take. The *tankas* that Amla's trust builds are somewhat costlier, at Rs. 32,000 apiece, than those built by Dalmia's trust.

"It's the management," says Niranjan. I leave the issue at that.

Niranjan says building *tankas* even where there is piped water supply is necessary. "The government scheme is erratic. Sometimes, people go for several days without water because of a leak in the main pipe. Then they realize the value of the *tanka* system. We need to mobilize the communities to look after their water sources and not rely on external agencies. Then, restoring or building a *tanka* entails a one-time cost while government water supply schemes have a recurring cost."

Also, he claims that building *tankas* binds the community, while piped water systems divide the people.

But most of the *tankas* seem to be built outside villages, in the fields. It does make life for farmers easy as they don't need to take water with them when they go to the fields. But in the villages, it is piped water that rules, as it does in Ramgarh. Despite that, people are more than willing to participate in building *tankas*. *Tankas* supplied water in villages also in times gone by, as evidenced by two gigantic *tankas* I saw in Bhutia and Devas villages. These incredibly large, but incredibly decrepit *tankas* had circular catchments with a pretty dome in the centre. Both were black with age and neglect.

Parshuram sees them and says, "They were made by the village seth several decades ago. But since piped water came to the village, they have been neglected. Also, they are too large for the village community to maintain on their own. Nobody makes lime mortar anymore so repairing is also difficult."

All in all, a losing proposition. But I think, "Building new *tankas* is more profitable for all concerned than restoring old ones." It seems to be general pattern and Niranjan dodges my question on repairing old *tankas*, saying they don't have the expertise to do so. It's not very convincing because each of these old *tankas* would hold an estimated 100,000 litres of water, so litre for litre, this water would be cheaper than a new one.

Even Dalmia, whose trust Niranjan manages, has no definite answer to restoration of old *tankas* and *johads*, save for a "they must be saved".

Beed Ka Johad stands abandoned about 10 kilometres from Ramgarh. Its walls appear orange in the setting sun. in the centre of the johad is a puddle of greenish water. It's a large, very elaborate johad, some 70 or 80 years old, about 60 metres to a side. But nobody uses it anymore even though there is enough water to support a village's needs for most of the year. There is goat shit on the steps leading down to the water and the reason is not hard to see – a herd of goats drink water from the johad where once only people were allowed. A few thousand rupees would have restored it to pristine condition.

Udaipurvati about 85 kilometres south of Jhujhunu is a hilly region of Shekhawati. There is plenty of greenery en route Udaipurvati and the road is clear of sand, unlike on the drives to Churu and Chirawa. I see a few *tankas* in the fields and near villages; Niranjan says there are more inside villages. However, groundwater is available in plenty. Seeing an abundance of tubewells, I wonder how for long. The fields are lush with crops – vegetables mostly. There are trees of different species and plenty of shrubs. The hardy Khejri is also there, faring much better here than further north. Fortunately there is little keekar and more desi babul.

We get to Godia village, at the foothills of the Khetri hills, that are an offshoot of the Aravallis. We pass through the village and the scenery changes. Its sandy and dry, the familiar feeling of Shekhawati is back. Niranjan tells the driver to take the jeep up the floor of a sandy gully between two very scrubby hills. We reach firmer ground and he parks. The sand is thick and soft underfoot and its bordering on hot. Climbing up the gully, I round a bend and its gets noticeably greener; the greenery gets denser and we stop at wall of stones and mud.

"This is a johad we had built a year ago to recharge the groundwater in this region. There is another further up," says Sitaram, an elderly resident of Godia village. "Before this johad was built, rainwater ran down the gully and flowed away. Now, it seeps into the ground. We have more water in our wells in the village."

This despite scanty rains since the johad was built. The bed of the johad has a little puddle of water from the last rains – the rest is dry and cracked. The trees around it are new growth, not more than a few years old. Their shade is welcome in the midday heat. Sitaram offers to take me up to the other johad, about a kilometre up the gully but I politely refuse his offer; it's too hot and I've seen *johads* before.

Johads mean different things in different parts of India. Here, in the hills of Udaipurvati, they are crescent-shaped or straight walls. A core of stones covered with mud – the stones are the foundation and the mud wall holds the water. They work best in semi-arid areas where rainfall is scanty but

119

intense when it happens. The low walls stop a lot of water but seldom break because they are low, usually less than 3 metres high. The water percolates into the ground over weeks and months, recharging the aquifer. The Khetri hills once had many such *johads* but most have broken. The couple above Godia are part of a new initiative to "catch rainwater where it falls and let it percolate into the ground".

The dust bowl that is Shekhawati has lessons. Its sandy soil has produced a great many of India's industrialists. During the 20th century, all of them left and went to seek fame and fortune in the big cities. They became industrialists from traders. Some returned to plough back profits into social activities – schools, hospitals, temples and recently, water harvesting. Water harvesting was once the main philanthropic activity. The wealthy built *tankas* to store rainwater; they seldom dug wells because the groundwater was saline, and it still is. The wealthy also built *johads* so that people would have enough water to drink, as well as to wash and bathe in. Animals could get what was left. Water followed life and where it dried, life moved on. The myriad pillars of abandoned wells dotting the Shekhawati desert, like upstretched arms asking for rain, are testimony to the amount of work that these people's ancestors put in, and the indifference with which the current generation treats its inheritance. All the wells are dry; the *johads* store water from the last rains. But there aren't humans to drink the water anymore – just the pigeons and crows. A dead eagle, lying belly-up outside the Beed Ka Johad, seems to say "If its old, let it rot".

8 GOA: SUN, SAND AND SEA FOOD ARE BAD FOR ECOLOGY

I am in Goa to see a marvel of engineering that has created a unique eco-system, the Khazaan lands. Using wooden sluice gates, that open and shut with the tide, controlling the flow of water on low-lying fields along estuaries of major rivers in this state of western India, and an intricate system of dykes, Goans have reclaimed land from the sea for farming.

Legend has it that Goa emerged from the ocean. More likely, it was early settlers from inland who reclaimed the land along the major rivers, the Mandovi and Zuari, for farming. They built 3200 kilometres of dykes with local material and allowed mangroves to grow on the outer walls for additional strength. At last count, there were about 18,000 hectares of land classified as Khazaan lands. Put another way, this labour is the equivalent of building eight Egyptian pyramids, says Prakash Paryenkar in the book Fish Curry and Rice.

The Khazaans are the main flatlands in Goa, used for paddy and prawn cultivation, alternately. They are the saline flood plains of the estuaries of two rivers, and some of the smaller ones, that are below high-tide level. The dykes and sluices keep the land from being completely inundated but retain enough water inside to enable prawn and fish cultivation. Water flow between the Khazaans and the river or backwater is regulated by a complex system of sluice gates. These open at low tide and close at high tide.

Physically, Goa is divided into four regions – the Sahyadri escarpment of the Western Ghats, the plateau, the flood plains of the rivers and the coast. The Western Ghats are the range of hills that run from Gujarat to Kerala on the west coast of India a few kilometers inland. They receive extremely heavy and intense rain during the monsoons and are covered with moist deciduous forests – large parts have been decimated by mining and tourism projects. The part of the Ghats in Goa belongs to the Sahyadri range of hills, averaging 800 metres in height. All of Goa's nine rivers originate in these hills.

The plateau region just below the Sahyadris is also densely forested but large parts have been converted to plantations. The government is also developing industrial estates on many plateaus, decimating the environment in the process. Received wisdom has it that the crowns of the plateaus should be covered with trees to handle the rainfall – catch the rainwater, slow its run off into rivers and let it percolate into the ground. The government hasn't heard of this or doesn't care. Buildings are replacing trees, as I saw on many plateaus near the Zuari River.

The flood plains of the major rivers, particularly the Mandovi and Zuari, are where the Khazaan lands lie. All of Goa's rivers are tidal, that is, there is a large difference in water levels between high and low tides. At high tide, sea water from the Arabian Sea travels 15 kilometres or more upstream, while at low tide, fresh water from inland flushes the river of salt water. At high tide, all the rivers flow considerably higher than the Khazaan lands, which is why they need the protection of the dykes and water regulation by the sluice gates. Where erosion is particularly severe, the dykes are reinforced and mangroves allowed to flourish.

I am eager to see the high technology of the Khazaan lands, developed indigenously probably by the Saraswat Brahmins centuries before the Europeans produced a spate of inventions and spawned the industrial revolution. This technology automatically controls the flow of water from the rivers into the low lying lands so that the dual cultivation of paddy and prawns is possible.

The coast is what attracts tourists and has given Goa its place in the sun, literally. The tourism industry is concentrated on these narrow strips of land, as is the fishing industry. Many beaches are over-touristed with an incredible build-up of hotels and shacks and are very dirty. Still, people flock to them. The hunt for clean beaches takes a few people to south Goa, but it's a matter of a time before this part also 'catches up' with the beaches to the north.

Sotter D'Souza, my guide to the Khazaans, meets me in the low balcony of his single-storeyed house on the outskirts of Panjim, Goa's capital city, two-and-a-half year old daughter Priya in his arms. It's a suburb called Porvorim. I introduce myself as we walk down the stairs from the road to him, dodging cacti. It's already warm though its 11 AM on a 'winter' morning in January. This is the best season to be in Goa, after the New Year crowds have departed but the mercury hasn't risen to astronomical heights, nor has humidity reached sticky proportions.

He is a six-foot tall, bearded, ever-smiling man in his forties with hair that is just turning grey. He looks every inch a man of the soil; his family owns several acres of farmland and plantations a few miles from Panjim near the Mapusa river opposite Chorao island. His house is beset with innumerable plants, so much so that it looks like a building in the middle of the tropical rainforest that once covered the state. Standing in his verandah, he completely dwarfs his 2-2/1 year old daughter Priya. It is a modern coastal house built to handle torrential rain, humidity and heat. Sotter used to support the Bharatiya Janata Party 'against the corrupt Congress' but quickly got disillusioned when they came to power – he saw no real difference them and the Congress. He now works with several civil society organizations against the degradation of his state's ecology.

He explains, sitting in the spacious living room with a TV blaring in a corner to entertain Priya, what the Khazaan lands are all about.

"The term Khazaan comes from khar, which means salty. The Khazaan lands are low-lying fields along the estuaries of rivers, owned by Communidades, the unit of village governance in Goa before liberation in 1961. The Communidades own all the land in villages which is not privately owned, and are responsible for maintaining the bunds and distributing and selling produce. Since liberation, the government has systematically undermined the authority and power of the Communidades, that has also affected the viability of the Khazaan lands," he says.

This is a new, social angle to something I thought was purely ecological. It seems logical to assume that the local ecological structures and local social structures were interlinked. A decline in one would affect the other. It is easy to see the decline across Goa.

The Communidades comprise men of different groups of people in a village. One group has all males over the age of 12 of all the land owning families in a village. The other categories include servants of the local ruler who have settled in the village, artisans who are indispensable to village life and men who lives with their wives' families for want of a male heir. All land that isn't privately owned belongs to the Communidade; it is the residuary land owner of the village. They are a unique form of village self-governance that existed in India prior to colonial rule. Unlike in other parts of India, where the British undermined and destroyed the Panchayat system, the Portuguese who ruled in Goa did not dismantle the Communidades.

The Communidades in their own way ensure that everybody has a place to live and enough to eat. It isn't a perfect system and critics say it is chauvinistic and rigidly hierarchical. But as the village committee, the equivalent of the Gram Sabha elsewhere in India, the Communidade ensures the well-being of its constituents. It ensures job security for landless rural labourers, something no individual farmer can do given the uncertainties of the monsoon, when the rains were below average, by employing them in non-farming activities. As an employer, it gives these labourers a choice of employment; in the absence of such a choice, labourers are open to exploitation by a rich individual. If individual farmers want labour, they have to pay market rates and treat them well because Communidades are very influential in the rural labour market.

Communidades used to earn their money by auctioning harvesting rights to the coconut, cashew nut, arecanut and mango plantations on its lands. They also earned from auctions of fishing rights at the sluice gates of the Khazaan lands. These auctions accounted for 90 per cent of their income. From this, they paid taxes, maintained places of worship and community property. This money also paid for the upkeep of the bunds, dykes and sluices of the Khazaans under the Communidade. As much as a quarter of a Communidade's income went towards the last expense.

After liberation, the Indian government set about destroying this system of self-governance, believing it to be a Portuguese legacy. It distributed land to cultivators, usually small and marginal farmers too poor to farm on their own. It enacted the Tenancy Act of 1964 and superceded the Communidades. It deprived the Communidades of their income by setting up parallel structures to represent farmers and fisherfolk – Tenant Associations (TAs) and Water Users Associations (WUAs) – respectively. The plantations were also handed over to private cultivators. Once tillers got ownership of the land they had cultivated for years, they too chose to let it lie fallow since they found that tilling another's land was more profitable than cultivating their own. Only those who wanted to cultivate the land really needed the bunds and sluices of the Khazaans; these were a minority.

Starved of cash, the Communidades can no longer effectively look after the dykes and bunds of the Khazaans. The TAs and WUAs are filled with politicians and thugs interested in fattening their own wallets; they seldom their earning on dyke and bund protection, leave along repairing sluices. The Communidades are dying slowly, but surely, though they still remain a force to be reckoned with in Goa. In the book, Fish Curry and Rice, Jagdish Nazareth writes that 232 Communidades still own 30,000 hectares – eight percent – of land in Goa.

"But come," says Sotter. "Enough of theory. You will understand better when you see the Khazaans. I will show you my village and it's Communidade."

I exit and he locks up. Priya holds my finger as we walk out of the gate. Sotter brings out his bike.

"I have to drop her at my sister's play school, then we can go," he says.

We set off, Priya riding on the tank ahead of her father and holding onto the handlebars for dear life. It's a short journey and we drop her at the school. She enjoys the wind in the face.

Most of Goa's local roads are well maintained, but narrow. Inspite of the heavy rains, they remain in fairly good repair but two vehicles can make for a crowd. The countryside is pretty and undulating in most parts. You seldom travel more than a few kilometres either on a straight line or at the same level – it's always uphill and down dale, twisting and turning. People live in villages or suburbs and commute to towns for work; the network of roads and excellent public transport comprising of buses, taxis, autos and motorcycle riders facilitates this. It makes it easy for outsiders like me to get around at reasonable cost as well. The most I paid for a journey in Goa was from the Railway station to my friend's house at night – Rs. 120, by auto.

The villages are tidy, with whitewashed houses facing the road. Their low verandahs present a menacing look, belying tales of Goan hospitality. The front yards indicate if it's a Hindu or a Christian household. Hindu households have a tulsi in a tall white planter in the front yard. Christian houses have a cross or an angel in white. Nearly all of them have pretty gardens that were in bloom in January. The older houses have sloping, tiled roofs, the better to handle the monsoon deluge, high verandahs and drooping eaves; they also proudly display the year they were built – 1837, 1869, 1932, etc. The newer ones have flat concrete roofs, flat eaves and lower verandahs, not as well suited to handling the heavy seasonal rains. I see moss growing on the walls of most of the newer houses, but not on any of the older ones. Muslim houses are usually painted green and some of them have 786 written in front.

The women's clothes also give the religion away. Christian women wear the archetypical knee length skirt and waist length shirt. Hindus wear salwar-kameezes or saris while Muslims occasionally wear burkhas.

A line of Christian houses suddenly gives way to a few Hindu ones and then the occasional Muslim house. I see more of the first two, and very few of the latter, in most villages. Beyond the first line of two of houses lie the fields or plantations, reaching down the hills in terraces.

It's a Sunday. We pass an enormous church in Sotter's village, part of the Selura Communidade. It was built in the early 17th century, an imposing European structure that dominates the skyline. It's painted a dazzling white. The whiteness contrasts with the black suits that the men wear, and the coloured clothes of the women, emerging from the church after Sunday morning mass. This is an old settlement, predominantly Christian. I can almost smell the old money in the rambling estates on the lower slopes of the hills. Almost everybody is a land-owner and has a steady income from agriculture, a well-paying job or a close relative settled abroad who sends home money to run hearth and home. Many of these families own entire hillsides that are now in great demand by property developers for resorts or housing. They own the cashew, arecanut, coconut, banana or mango plantations on the plateaus. I can see why the institution of the Communidade refuses to die – it is such an old boys club and gives old Goans something to hang onto. It is a sign of good times long gone. Letting go means falling into the abyss of the future.

The Selura Communidade covers three and a half villages. Villages were demarcated along revenue lines, much after the Communidades came into existence. Communidades were demarcated along the lines of the local church parish that extends beyond a single village. Goa's countryside and towns are dotted with churches and shrines, much like north India has temples sprouting from fields and street corner.

The road winds uphill past the church, lined here and there by houses that get further apart as we climb. There is more greenery here of the natural type, less fields and no plantations yet. We reach the top of the hill where the road ends, past some shacks where recently-settled people live. Sotter parks under a spreading peepul tree under which is a garishly-painted temple.

Next to it is a pond called a tollem, created artificially by building a low embankment across the natural flow of water. These are ponds created on the tops or sides of hills to store rain or spring water. This tollem has walls of red laterite rock, the local building material that finds its way into everything from houses to lining fields, that descend in steps to the water's edge. It catches the runoff from the hill behind it. Tollem's can be quite deep. A sluice gate made of wooden slats placed in the grooves of concrete piers controls the flow of water out of the pond. There is a well in a corner of the tollem with some slimy water at the bottom – it's obviously not in use.

Tollems such as these built atop hills catch rain and spring water and store it for some months. They are important for ground water recharge. Typically, a hill will have a cascade of such ponds, each catching the overflow from the one above. In between, people grow crops in fields called ker, watered directly by channels from the ponds or from little springs where the ground water emerges. Either way, there is plenty of water on hills where forests still cover the crown and there are ponds at intervals, such as on this one above the Selura Communidade.

A channel 30 centimetres wide and about 1.5 metres deep runs from the sluice gate of the pond into ker a little downhill. The people living in the shacks – the new settlers, as Sotter calls them – cultivate these fields. The channel is dry at the moment but the farmers take water when they need from the pond. Their overflow feeds another pond further downstream.

"This water channel becomes a nallah that flows through our fields and eventually meets the Mapusa River," says Sotter, waving to the east. "It is fed by other streams from the hills. During the rains, it becomes a torrent."

We ride to the base of the hill and Sotter halts on a small culvert over the nallah. Pointing uphill, where a dry rivulet emerges from the bamboo forests, he says that is the nallah we saw at the top. Up to the road, the nallah is not walled – it's a natural drain. After the road, towards the fields, villagers have lined the gully with blocks of red laterite rock that abounds in this part of the country.

The channel runs along the fields on its way to the river. The red laterite blocks that form the wall have been neatly carved and stacked, held in place by mortar since 1938, or so the keystone of a small footbridge over the channel proclaims. The fields are lower than the channel. The channel's walls are porous so that when there is water in it, it seeps into the adjoining fields. This is usually enough to irrigate an entire paddy crop.

A part of the wall has broken and a group of labourers is mixing cement on Sotter's field. The repaired part of the wall is untidy, made of broken blocks of stone and rock, held together with cement. It contrasts sharply with the older wall, made of neatly stacked rectangular laterite blocks. The cement will prevent water from seeping through, defeating the purpose for which the walls were built. There are no sluices in the sides of the channel to let water into the field; seepage is the only way fields get irrigated. Sotter loses his cool seeing cement in his field.

"Who is the contractor? I want this cleared immediately. Don't you have the sense not to mix cement in the field?" he shouts at the labourers.

The local paddy variety is called konrgut and is grown specially in Khazaan lands. Sotter hasn't cultivated his fields for several years. It simply isn't worthwhile. He spends about Rs. 5000 a year to cultivate the four acres that he owns but gets back only Rs. 3000 – it's a losing game. It's more profitable to leave them fallow or find somebody who is willing to cultivate them for him and pay him a rent. In this part of Goa, farm labour is hard to come by and expensive because of the demand for Indian labour in the Gulf countries.

Sotter's fields still have stalks from a paddy crop of some years ago. His fields are part of a stretch of land that goes from the base of the hills to the sluice gates at the far end, about 3 kilometres away. They are Khazaan lands, though the water from the river does not reach up to his fields – it floods fields further down, beyond a road to the east.

We walk back to the road and ride off towards the distant sluice gates. I am finally going to get a look at this engineering marvel. Sotter's ancestral house appears round a corner. It is enormous, a rambling single storeyed structure set on about an acre of land. A low fence runs along the front, with a gate wide enough for a car to enter in the middle. A few steps lead up to the front verandah from which a single door takes you into the house. All around, teak and coconut trees shade the main building and tropical undergrowth provides a green foil to the whitewash of the house. The inevitable crucifix adorns a corner of the front lawn.

"There is somebody at home," he murmurs, debating whether to treat me to a view of the interior. He decides to go onto the Khazaans and return later, maybe when his brother is back. The road emerges from the trees that surround the dwellings on this side of the field and crosses the Khazaans.

There are lots of little culverts to let water flow easily from one side to the other. If this weren't done, one side of the Khazaans would be permanently water logged by rainwater flowing downhill and the other would be quite dry.

A large tank opens up to our right with steps leading down to its base. There is no water in it and it is quite overgrown with grass. A herd of cows grazes on the bed of the tank. It has no water because the catchment has been built on. Houses, a primary school and a budding restaurant have taken up some of what was the tank. In a few years, the rest will come under buildings as well, unless somebody does something.

The steps in the corner are for the Ganesh immersion ceremony in October, when the tank is full, hopefully after a good monsoon. They are a feature of every tank, but the religious significance has not stopped people with political connections from nibbling away at the tank. A stream gurgles out from under some rocks near the steps and is soon lost in the grass on the bed of the tank. It has cool, clear water, ideal for tapping by a bottled water company. Inspite of the Goans' best efforts, nature still surfaces in the oddest of places. The hill above the stream has houses and plantations, little forest and greenery but there is obviously enough water underground to sustain the little stream. Once, it was a babbling brook which, along with other similar outlets, kept the tank filled through the year. The others have long since dried up and this solo stream bravely keeps one corner moist.

At the far end are a set of sluice gates that controls water from the tank into channels that irrigate fields. We drive up to them and I find the channels are blocked with rubble and garbage. The sluices are frail – in a year of good rainfall, they are likely to break and flood houses downstream.

Sotter says, "The Communidade looked after this tank, kept the catchment free of encroachments and the bed clear of weeds. It repaired the sluices and the channels. Now, the WUA here does nothing. It does not have the money and it's full of political appointees who do not belong here.

"WUAs comprise fishermen who have the rights to fish near the sluice gates. In return, they have to maintain the sluices. TAs are made up of farmers, not just the old timers, but the new ones who have been allotted land to cultivate. Both the associations do not perform well because membership is based mostly on political patronage. The local legislator or strong man tries to fill the associations with his loyalists who have no reason to work. Sometimes, they aren't even locals but migrants from Bihar," Sotter tells me.

This is the other side of the Khazaan crisis, indeed the crisis of Goa's ecology. Sound agriculture is vital to the region's ecology – it balances water availability with need, forest lands with farmland, population with the land's carrying capacity. For centuries, Communidades managed Goa's farming, fishing and plantations as well as natural resources. They allotted the access rights to each natural resource and balanced the two interests, as they were bodies of local governance and knew the carrying capacity of the land. Their decline is reflected by the general decline in Goa's ecology and agricultural output. Sotter's barren fields are just one manifestation of this decline.

We drive along the fields till we reach a tri-junction at a place called Badem. One road heads south-west along the Mapusa River towards Panjim, the other into the interior up along the river. The third is the one we have come on. The road to Panjim passes over a wide embankment that keeps the Mapusa's waters off the Khazaans. There is a small bridge near the junction under which lie the engineering marvel of the sluice gates. I walk over to them eagerly, while Sotter parks his bike in the shade.

The sluices are set under an old arched stone bridge. Concrete steps without railings descend to a platform that stretches out towards the south-west from the bridge into the backwaters of the Mapusa River. Its narrow at this point and I can see through the mangroves to the bird sanctuary on the Chorao island to the south-east. The mangroves, about 50 metres distant, form an outer wall against the full erosive force of the river and protect the inner embankments. Even though the river's mouth is 10 kilometres downstream to the west, at high tide water from the Arabian Sea comes right up to these sluices, and even further upstream. It's a muddy river, flowing slowly to the sea.

There are two shacks on the platform below the bridge with a sign that reads, Serula Shetkari Association office, timing 10 AM to 12 PM. It's after 12, so the office is locked. Bablu, a fisherman who lives in the other shack on the platform, is more helpful. He is arranging his nylon fishing nets, a pretty, delicate tracery in the bright sun, like a woman making folds in her sari. He pulls in the net from a pile on the floor and folds it together – this makes it easy to release from the boat when he goes to spread the net inside the sluice gates in the evening when the sluices are open and water carrying fish enters the Khazaans. There is a wetland inside the embankment that holds the salty water and does not let it flood the fields. This is called a khoi, and it is separated from the fields by a wall made of the ubiquitous red laterite blocks.

Bablu says, "Every evening I spread the nets behind the sluices. I've caught fish as big as my arm."

"Is that all you catch. What about prawns and crabs?" I ask.

As if in answer, a crab frees itself from under a wicker basket where it has been kept since being caught and darts towards me, it's prospective liberator – more like its prospective eater. I jump out of its way and it runs around aimlessly till Bablu puts it back in the basket.

"Crab pots are out there," he says, waving his arm towards the line of mangroves. "They come into this place and it is easy to place the pots because the water is calm. I catch very big crabs too."

"Your Hindi is good, not like a local," I say.

"I am from Varanasi," says Bablu. He's sure come a long way to fish, but likes it here. The pickings are better than in the polluted Ganga back home. Bablu invites me for a ride in his canoe, a dugout made from the bole of a mango tree. I decline.

The bridge has three arches, each with a set of sluice gates. Two are working; the third has been sandbagged and is blocked. Water seeps through the sandbags and into the khoi. Behind me to the south-east, water from the river pushes against the sluice gates that are closed. The khoi and the Khazaans are to the north-west, under the bridge.

I walk along the top beam of the first set of sluices that are in working condition. The entire construction is made of wood – no steel is used anywhere. This increases the life of a sluice gate to around 80 years, if they are maintained, before the wood borers eat through them and weaken them. If they used iron nails to fasten the beams together, they would not last even a year.

The sluice gates are wooden planks, each about 10 centimetres thick in this case, 2 metres long and about 70 centimetres wide. One side has rounded six-inch extensions – the hinges – that are of the same piece of wood. While sawing the gate from the tree trunk, the sluice gate maker cuts the gate section six inches smaller than the hinges, so these protrude along one side of the gate at both ends. The sluices and their frames are made of a local wood called borduim, that is light coloured and comes from a fairly large tree.

To construct the sluice gate, you need to find a suitable site. In Bordem's case, the bridge provided the site. First a thick beam with a cross section of about 15 centimetres by 20 centimetres is placed horizontally across the bottom of the bridge. It is wedged firmly in between the supports of the bridge. This beam has grooves cut into it at both ends and at intervals along its length to accommodate vertical supports.

The sluice doors are fitted into another pair of horizontal wooden beams, called sluice controllers. These are specially cut beams of wood, L-shaped in cross section. One leg of the L has arch-shaped holes cut in it to hold the hinges of the sluice doors. The other is smooth. One control beam is fitted on top of the bottom beam of the sluice gate frame so the arch-shaped holes face upwards. The leg of the L without holes faces the river, from where the water is to flow into the khoi. This leg of the L is the back-stopper of the sluice doors and keeps them from opening in, towards the Khazaans; the sluices can only open outwards to the river.

Vertical beams with ends flattened to fit the rectangular holes of the lower frame beam are pushed through the sluice controller into the lower beam. If the sluices are large, more than one set of vertical beam is needed to give the structure strength. Once the vertical beams are in place, the sluice doors are fixed into the arch-shaped holes in the lower sluice controller. Then, the upper sluice controlled is fitted onto the sluice doors and the vertical beams serve to create a space between the sluice doors and the control beam so the doors don't jam. Finally, the upper frame beam is fixed to complete the sluice gate.

A man is sawing a thick plank of wood behind the Association's office. His name is Shankar Dhule.

"How long do these last?" I ask him.

Shankar says, "Between 75 and 100 years, if they are looked after."

"What do you mean, looked after?"

"Every year, they must be coated with a paint made from the outer kernel of the cashew nut to ward off borers and the effects of salt water," he says. "If that happens, they can last for a century. Otherwise, only a few years."

"How much does it cost to make them and how long do you take?" I ask.

"I take up to two months to completely replace a sluice but the Association's officers take longer to clear the files for payment. I don't know the cost since I don't buy the wood."

These, then, are the high technology of the Khazaans of Goa. Simple wooden sluice doors that open at low tide under pressure of water from the khoi behind them because the water level in the khois is higher than that outside. They shut at high tide when the water from the river pushes them. In the interval, fish and prawn larvae, as well as big fish, enter the khoi and Bablu's waiting nets. When closed, the doors let in a tickle of water but that is deliberately done to reduce the strain on the embankments and the sluice doors. The height of the sluices also ensures that the khois don't run dry, killing the fish in them.

There is another reason for the existence of the khois, a simpler one.

"The khois partly balance the force of the water outside the embankment. If they were there, the embankments would wear down faster and need more frequent maintenance," says Sotter.

They operate quite easily – I try moving one that isn't bearing the weight of the water at high tide. Inspite of its enormous size, it moves lightly. The sluices under the bridge have been there long enough for the borers to get to them. All of them have deep holes where insects have made their homes over the decades and are slowly hollowing them out. Once borers set in, there is nothing that can be done to save the sluices – they have to be replaced sooner or later. The borers also accentuate the effects of salt water on the wood.

The sluices are closed at the moment, under the weight of the Mapusa river at high tide. Water pours through the cracks between the doors and around the frame but it's a slow ingress. The khois will never get so full as to overflow onto the fields beyond. However, the salt water plays a part in organic paddy cultivation. Farmers flood their fields to kill off weeds, but never so long as to raise the salinity of the soil significantly. The water brings in a sort of moss that becomes excellent fertilizer when dry. Paddy is sensitive to salinity and if the farmers miscalculate, the paddy yields fall. The water also brings in fish and prawn larvae that breed in the khois. These act as natural insect controllers.

It takes a while for the doors to close when the tide comes in, which is when the fish come in as well and Bablu makes his catch. Of course, he cheats by keeping the doors open so that he can maximize his catch. This is a violation of the rules that state that the sluices must not be kept open beyond a certain time.

Fishing auctions are big business in Goa. They fetch between Rs. 50,000 and Rs. 2 million, depending on the size of the sluices. This money used to go to the Communidades; now it goes to the WUAs who are full of politicians and businessmen. They aren't interested in caring for the goose that lays the golden eggs, just taking the eggs. It's a lot of money, given that there are about 600 sluices across the Khazaan lands in Goa. The auctions happen at the start of December. The winners are supposed to follow certain rules about regulating water flow, repairing sluices and bunds and fishing. But given the WUAs' composition and the financial muscle of the winners, these rules are seldom followed. If the state government enforces its own rules, it will give the Khazaans a fresh lease of life. But the state's politicians are party to the plunder, so they have no interest in following rules. The income from the auctions is supposed to be spent on caring for the Khazaans but the WUA members distribute it as profit or the office bearers simply pocket the money. The politicians also eye the Khazaans as land to be developed for housing or commercial use and have an interested in ensuring that farming stops.

The bunds, the other component of the Khazaan protection, are also intricate structures. They aren't simply walls of mud and straw. Outer bunds have a core of red laterite blocks. On top of this, bund makers, a specialized breed, lay a mat of bamboo and then cover the whole structure with a mix of mud and straw. Older bunds are further reinforced by mangroves. Communidades appoint professional bund managers called kamats and other people called bous look after the Khazaan lands. Across Goa, about 100,000 people still live off the Khazaans; they can provide jobs to another 125,000 and generate at least Rs. 250 million a year.

Diwar island in the middle of the Mandovi River, a little upstream of Panjim, has vast tracts of Khazaan lands. It is surrounded by a thick wall of mangroves that hides the interiors of this low lying island from across the river. I catch the ferry at Ribander, one of the four ferry points to the island. It's an old tub called Hamzalem that has spent its life grinding from one side of the Mandovi to the other, carting people, cars, bikes and whatever else cares to cross the muddy river. On Diwar, a bus to the centre of the island awaits passengers. I set off on foot.

It's warm and the narrow road run flat and winding through barren fields, strewn with the remains of the last crop. Here and there, puddles of water indicate that ground water is literally skin deep. Kites and the occasional fork-tailed drongo keep me company on the open road – there are no trees. It's a long walk, I realize, once I clear the coastal mangroves, to the next clump of trees in which I can see houses.

A motorcyclist honks at me from behind. It's a narrow road, but not so narrow that a motorcyclist cannot pass. I move off the road, extremely irritated. Instead of driving on, the man stops and nods at me.

"Come I will drop you. Where are you going?" he asks.

"I am researching a book on water and am here to see the Khazaan lands," I give him my well-rehearsed line.

Xavier, his name is, says, "These are all Khazaan lands. I'll drop you near the village."

He points to a shiny shed in the distance. "That is the other end of the island where they do prawn farming."

He is wearing stark black and white, with a bow tie. Xavier is the manager of a resort near the Candolim beach. "I would have shown you around but I have to attend a funeral."

He stops a little inside the clump of trees that is actually at the base of a low hill on Diwar. The village of Piedade lies up the hill at the intersection of the island's four roads. It is surrounded by the Khazaan lands of the Piedade Communidade that stretch up to the mangroves on all sides. They are all barren; it's not crop season yet.

Xavier points me to a path off to the left of the road. "That leads to the Khazaans. Just keep going."

I start off. A couple of women in a barren field are building a wall of laterite bricks around a large plot to keep animals out. It's a vegetable patch, starkly green against the brown fields. On one side, houses peer from under coconut trees. On the other, fields with dried rice stalks stretch to the mangroves, now over a kilometer distant. When they aren't farming, the local folks take up temporary jobs in Goa. The tourism industry is the state's largest employer, agriculture its smallest. The tourism season coincides with the lean agricultural season. The more enterprising open businesses or migrate to the Gulf – Goans are in great demand as they educated and mostly English-speaking.

I round a corner – the fields stretch on endlessly but the shiny shed is closer. I decide to investigate the prawn farm. Prawn farms have sprung up all over the state because of higher returns than paddy. Farmers break the

Khazaan bunds, flood their lands, and those of their neighbours, and create large prawn farms. Prawns need a mix of salty and fresh water to spawn and grow. The Khazaans are ideal places for prawn farms as this exchange of water happens naturally. All they have to do is to inundate farmland with salt water and reverse the water flow, and presto, farmers have a prawn farm.

A family of belligerent cows greets me a third of the way to the prawn farm. I take a wide berth around the closest of them, as I realize I cannot outrun a charging cow on the uneven ground and their sharp horns are best avoided. Children play cricket on more level patches of the fields. Vegetable patches surrounded by barbed wire, stone walls or thorny bush dot the dry fields. It's uncomfortably warm. Each field has its own bund, some a few inches high, others a couple of feet.

From behind a low hill the sound of a train floats across the fields. It's on the Konkan Railway route that runs along the coast from Bombay to Kerala. It came up in the mid-1990s at enormous expense and in the face of bitter opposition by Goans who feared it would destroy their peace, Khazaans and way of life. The peace has certainly gone – smoky diesels pull trains up and down several times a day blowing their sirens. Some of the Khazaans have been affected. But they grudgingly admit it has made it easier for people to work in Bombay, that is only an overnight trip now. The earlier rail link was via Pune and took much longer.

The prawn farm gets closer agonizingly slowly. The dryness of the fields suddenly gives way to a wet patch and my feet sink into gooey mud. I extricate the said foot and shake off the goo as best as I can, and proceed to a pond that has emerged on the periphery of my sight. Foot and sandal cleaned, I find myself alongside a bund about 3 metres high, newly made and covered with the same sticky mud that I just got rid of. I find a corner to climb onto the bund – the top is mercifully dry and slightly spongy underfoot. It leads to the prawn farm.

The farm is unremarkable, after all that. The shiny shed is the roof of a tumbledown shack – only the tin sheets are new. There are two tanks full of extremely still water where prawns are supposedly growing to consumable size. I estimate their size at about 3 hectares. A stiff breeze ruffles the surface of the ponds, welcome in the warmth. Otherwise, there does not appear to be a soul in sight. There are lights at intervals on the bund around the ponds and a mechanism to release water into the fields. I walk around to the shed.

One side of the ponds runs along the far side of Diwar island, along the Mandovi river. It's overgrown with mangroves so dense I cannot see beyond the first few branches. From here, the voices of two men come back to me. I peer into the undergrowth and, unable to see them, walk onto the shed.

It's full of equipment to control the water level in the ponds. There are switches and motors for pumps. Outside, in a recess in the wall, is a small cross blackened by years of burning candles for inspiration by day and illumination by night. The sluices that control the water ingress from the Mandovi are in another shed next to this one. They aren't the hinged variety that I saw at Bordem but wooden slats placed inside the grooves of concrete piers, like the one at the tollem. Nylon ropes to raise or lower them lie scattered on the floor of this shed.

The pond water level is higher than that of the river at the moment – it is low tide. The slats are down, but water gushes between them into the river from the ponds. It's a trickle compared to the volume of water in the ponds and will only lower the level by a foot till the tide turns and the river comes pouring in. There are fishing nets lying around as well – the men who keep the place make a little on the side by catching fish and selling them in the local market. I get to see their catch a little later.

Crossing the sluices carefully – there is a single plank of wood across them – I emerge on the bund once again. It's been recently 'mended'. A misnomer, if there was one. There is wet mud on top, and my foot again sinks into it.

"I just got out of one mess," I say to myself. The choice is to circle all the way back. I choose sticky feet. The stickiness lasts a few steps and then the mud is dry enough to take my weight. The bunds have been repaired in several places, usually where the mangroves protecting them from the river have disappeared. The repairs are shoddy and look like they won't stand the next rains. At the end of the bund, a few steps lead down to the water. I sit on them and rinse off my sandals, yet again and then dry them in the sun.

A path from the prawn ponds leads into the Goltim to one side of Diwar Island. I side step a house with a pair of extremely vicious dogs and reach the road. It's a relief to walk on terra firma again after the muddy field. A group of women look at me curiously – my trousers are muddied and sandals are still gooey despite the wash. I am thirsty and sweaty. One of them directs me to the bus stand, a good kilometer's walk uphill.

I leave Goltim and Xavier materializes out of a house, waving goodbye to me. I wave back. A little further, I spy a coconut vendor and a cold drinks trolley. I have both but, not satisfied, walk into the village – its Piedade now, the name changed somewhere on the way – and have a half-litre bottle of Coke.

"Where do I catch a bus to the ferry?" I ask the shopkeeper.

He vaguely points south, to the center of the island. I walk on and see a large general store, next to which a minibus is idling. I get on and eventually get to the ferry for Rs. 4. A pretty women in a printed floral dress contrasts with the bleakness of the landscape – the brown Khazaans and total lack of trees.

Diwar Island is mostly covered with Khazaan lands and the fields lie below the high-tide level. Houses have been built on higher land on the hill in the center. Unlike Sotter's fields, these are cultivated – I am there in the wrong season. But here again, the paddy-prawn alternation is slowly giving to prawn monoculture. In a few years, the locals would have succumbed to the temptation of quick gains from prawn farming and more or less given up paddy. Most families have at least one member working in the tourism industry and aren't as dependent on farming as they were a few years ago. The decline of the Communidades has seen to that.

Menezes is a case in point. He is from Piedade village and a member of the Goltim TA as well as the Piedade Communidade. Only land-owners are members of TAs; Communidades remain the inclusive village institution that they have always been, but are quite defunct. He runs a wholesale agency for Nestle in Panjim so agriculture is far from his mind. His family owns five fields on Diwar Island but cultivates just one, mostly with vegetables, because paddy and grains have become uneconomical – he loses Rs. 2,000 every year for every field cultivated.

He says, "Some farmers have started prawn farming but it's being done on the quiet because of a Supreme Court ruling against converting paddy land to prawn farmland. But who is to check?"

On 11th December 1996, the Supreme Court directed all district authorities in India's coastal states to demolish prawn and aquaculture farms that violated the Coastal Regulation Zone rules (these broadly state that no commercial activity, including fish processing units, can happen within 500 metres of the high tide line of a coast). It also directed the prawn and aquaculture industry to pay compensation on the 'polluter pays' concept.

Sadly, after the initial euphoria and spate of demolitions, the CRZ rules were diluted. As happens with all rules in India, this one is also observed more in the breach. Prawn farms have mushroomed up and down the Goa countryside in the last few years. Many are owned by the relatives of politicians or large industrial houses, both of which have the clout to force the law to look the other way.

I take a bus to Cortalim, a village on the banks of the Zuari River about 20 kilometres south of Panjim, to meet Antonio Francisco Fernandes. He is a politician-turned-activist, like Sotter, but worked more at the local level. Like Sotter, Antonio is an ever-smiling man and rides a two-wheeler. Unlike Sotter, his is a scooter and considerably more beat up than Sotter's bike. I get off the bus immediately after the Zuari bridge as instructed to do to meet Antonio.

There is a Christian shrine to the west of the bridge which stands empty, the cross a silent sentinel to the barges plying up and down the Zuari, ferrying iron ore from the interiors of Goa to ships in the harbour. On the other side is a small Hindu temple with a flower girl at the head of the stairs. She speaks no English or Hindi and I have obviously disembarked too soon — Antonio told me to get off at the Cortalim circle. A policeman at the shrine to atone for his bribes guides me to the circle. My sandals broke earlier in the day and my friend me his beach sandals. The road right through the highlands of Tiswadi and widens slightly after the Zuari bridge.

Antonio detaches himself from a bus shelter at the roundabout and kicks his scooter to life.

"Nitya Jacob?" he asks me, driving up. I nod and he extends a large, weather-beaten hand. He is nearly 60 but his black hair belies his age.

We ride back to the Zuari bridge. The tide is out and I can see the piers of the Konkan Railway line bridge, running alongside the road. Barges pass under the two bridges, built very high to let them sail under even at high tide. Antonio points east, towards Marcaim, a village surrounded by Khazaans at the junction of the Cumbarjuna canal and the Zuari River.

"Those are Khazaan lands," he says. "They belong to my village and extend all the way up the canal. But very few people grow anything now. It's slowly being taken over by prawn farms in violation of the Supreme Court's order.

"The barges are one of the main reasons why the Khazaans are being destroyed. There is so much mining in the Satari and Sanguem blocks that barge traffic has increased in the last few decades. Nearly 300 of them come downstream every day loaded with iron and manganese ore. Then they return when the tide is low. The bow waves from the barges weaken the bunds and the mangroves. The leak oil and this pollutes the water and also kills off the mangroves. The waves also flood low-lying land."

We hop on his scooter and he very carefully maneuvers into the traffic charging up and down Zuari bridge. The road winds along the Zuari River. Before the bridges came up, the ferry was the only way across — it still runs for the locals who have to get from side to the other. The river is nearly a kilometer wide at this point. Antonio parks on the roadside and leads me into some fields — the first paddy fields I have seen in Goa. This is Goa of the tourism brochures — lush paddy fields of light green set against low hills with a fringe of darker green coconut palms, the hills themselves clothed in the dark remains of tropical rainforest. In a corner of the field stands a well; the fields are protected from the Zuari river by a thin line of mangroves and a wide bund. The bund's condition is not encouraging — the dwindling mangroves have left it open to erosion.

We clamber over bushes and uneven ground as Antonio takes us to see a large prawn farm, tucked away behind fields and bunds and invisible from the road. A bund stretches away to the left. It was a massive outer bund, separating the Khazaans from the river. It has been demolished with dynamite — I can see the stone foundations and the entire cross section of the bund, as well as bits where mangroves still cling to it. The tide is still out so there is no water here but the general muddiness and wetness of the soil shows I am below the high tide level. The owners of the prawn farms up ahead destroyed the bund so they could create their farms. In the process, several acres of paddy fields have been affected by the salt water.

We reach an old sluice gate – a towering structure made of stone and wood. It has slats for gates, not the hinged doors, drawn up and lowered by nylon ropes. The gates are useless, with no walls around them to stop water. When the tide comes in, the fields behind them get flooded inspite of the farmers' best attempts to raise stone walls around their fields.

"When they do, the prawn farm owners destroy the walls. They want to take over the fields here," says Antonio.

From the sluice gates, a path leads to the farms. They are new, possibly less than five years old. They are made of stone with a gravel path on top and are around 5 metres high. I can see two ponds from where I stand; Antonio says there are more towards the north.

Both the ponds are large, each covering around 20 hectares. They have all the trappings of industrial prawn farming – a generator, lights around the perimeter, guards and a pump-house to control water levels. The bunds have been built across fields – the prawn farm owners have evidently taken possession of parts of several fields and built bunds across those they haven't bought, to force owners into selling.

The fields around the prawn farms get fresh water from a little stream that flows down the hills around. It's barely enough to keep the salt water at bay. Paddy sprouts a luminescent green in the fields as we walk back to the scooter. Antonio drops me back to the Cortalim circle from where I take a bus to Porvorim.

The Khazaan lands are under threat from several quarters. The root cause is the need to get-rich-quick, and damn the future. Prawn farming, increased river traffic and pollution, unremunerative farming, the decline of the old social order and the boom in tourism are some of the reasons that these lands, whose creation was a feat of engineering, are slowly disappearing. However, all is not lost and if the remains of the Communidades have their way, a substantial portion of the Khazaans may life to see another millennium.

Kumar Kalanand Mani's organization, Peaceful Society, is in the Ponda block, about 20 minutes by bus from Panjim through Old Goa. I pass the famous church of St. Xavier, where the saint's body lies in state in a glass coffin. Since he died in 1552 in China, his embalmed body has drawn Christians of all denominations and a church of fitting proportions has been built in Old Goa. From here, the bus wends its way to Cundaim, where I get off to find a rider (motorcycle taxi) to take me to Peaceful Society in Madkai village. Instead, I catch another bus that takes me to the

Madkai ferry point on the Cumbarjuna canal where I spend 30 minutes waiting for the bus to fill and return so I can get off.

"You should have told me you were on the bus. I would have stopped it," says Kalanand, when I narrate my travails. "Come, let's see the campus."

It's a pretty campus, sprawled over some 8 hectares. Beyond it lie paddy fields, again cultivated and a pleasing green. Peaceful Society runs courses on sustainable livelihoods with respect to water conservation and researches related stuff in Goa. It is also a rich resource on Goa's ecology. There are residential facilities, a common dining hall and lecture rooms, interspersed with an incredible variety of flora.

Kalanand Mani is just under 60, bright-eyed and of dry wit. He has traveled all over India, he says, studying water systems and collating the best of them into his courses. The two storeyed office building also has a large dining area where the campus cook dishes out delicious Goan fare. We relax upstairs, waiting for lunch.

"I have an intricate water harvesting system on the campus that channelises rain water into troughs, from where it is used to water the plants. We have a large surface tank for water storage, and I have put frogs and fish into it so that mosquitoes don't breed.

"You have seen the Khazaan lands that are important to Goa's plains ecology. I will show you what happens in the plateaus that are crucial. They are the watersheds of the state. The government is just not bothered and is systematically destroying them by making them into industrial estates," he says, switching channels on the TV.

We have a lunch of fried fish, beans, sambar, rice and chapatti followed by desert. It's a real bellyful.

"You expect me to walk around after this?" I ask Kalanand.

"It will digest your food, and then you can have more," he says.

We head for Borim village about 5 kilometres away where Goa's tallest peak Siddhantha hill stands. There are plantations of arecanut, coconuts and pepper with a sprinkling of vanilla that cover most of the hillside. It's radically different from what I have seen on the other side of the country, in the War Khasi hills of Meghalaya. They also grow arecanut but in a completely different manner.

Kalanand parks a little way up the hill, near a colourful temple. A small shrine opposite the main temple building appears to be the reason for the temple – it's old and has a stone carving inside. The spire of the shrine is painted a bright orange. To one side is a tap – the local municipality's water supply – and a handpump – the locals' water supply. The handpump is broken and rusty. A girl fills water from the tap. Strange, considering that the hill has two ponds and plenty of green cover.

We enter the plantations and start our ascent. The arecanut trees are tall and thin, with a small head of leaves dangling the nuts. The nuts look like mini-coconuts, yellow when ripe and in sprays of 30 or so fruit. They have just been harvested so only a few trees actually have nuts on them. The trees are planted on a grid on terraces cut into the hillside. The terraces cover most of the hillside like giant steps. Between rows of trees run the water channels – shallow troughs that run the entire length of a terrace with smaller channels that take water near individual trees, but never to their roots directly. The smaller channels empty into a circular trough around individual trees; the plant itself grows on a small rise in the centre of the trough. Some of the smaller channels end in bowl-shaped depressions where the water stands and slowly percolates into the ground, moistening it.

The water in the main channel flows constantly – excess water simply feeds the fields or runs off to the Zuari River. When a section of the plantation needs watering, the plantation labourers set up a small earthen block on the main channel to divert water to the plants. Once these plants are irrigated, the water is diverted elsewhere. The labourers also use leaves that the arecanut trees shed – these are like large elongated mugs with which they scoop water out of the channel and pour it into the troughs surrounding the plants. The terraces are intersected with an elaborate network of channels, fed by the two ponds higher up.

Water falls from one level of the terrace to the next down stone channels – pretty little waterfalls that gurgle out from behind rocks and trees. There is luxuriant growth at the base of these mini falls, left there deliberately to arrest soil erosion. The hillside is moist – I can see where the myriad streams that feed Goa's nine rivers come from. We climb a steep slope between two terraces, Kalanand finding the going hard. Sotter, who has joined us, makes better time of it. Kalanand helps himself to a fallen branch, using it as a walking stick. The sun is blotted out by a canopy of arecanut trees interspersed with taller hardwoods of the tropical rainforest. Some of the older arecanut trees that have stopped yielding nuts serve as bases for pepper vines, dangling small bunches of green pepper. The terraces descend steeply to a stream – I can hear it but it's invisible in the undergrowth that covers the base of the valley.

We trudge uphill in the humidity. It's not hot but the climb makes us all sweat. A boy across the valley calls out; he is scooping water up in arecanut leaf and throwing it down the valley, where a new terrace has been carved but does not have water channels yet. He waters plants one by one, singing as he does. The sunlight catches the water cascading from the leaf, flashing in the semi-darkness.

We make it to the first pond. It's an artificially created water body, roughly square. Walls of made of red laterite blocks impound rainwater. It is quite deep and; frogs and fish abound. I can hear the frogs and see the fish swimming in small shoals. To one side, from where we emerge from the plantation, are the sluices from where water is released into the plantation. They are some 6 metres deep, made of plastic – a departure from tradition where sluices are wooden slats – and raised or lowered with nylon ropes. They are all closed but water pours out from between the lower sluices and flows into the plantation below.

"If the sluices are so deep, the pond must also be at least this deep," says Kalanand. "They would design the sluices to retain some water even after all has been emptied for irrigation so that the fish don't die and people have some drinking water left."

There are no plantations up here, only forest. It's dense with tall trees and dense shrubbery. Plants that I pay a handsome amount for in Delhi grow wild on Goa's hillsides – a good business proposition is to take them back and sell them, but they would not survive Delhi's dry searing summer. We are on the way to the plantation keeper's house further up.

There is a lovely badh tree outside his house, encased in vines that make a tracery right up the trunk. It's like a giant hand has caught the tree in a vice-like grip for life. The keeper's house is a large, tiled roof, old building, with a tulsi plant in front. I walk around to the back where there are more plantations. These are watered by a pond further uphill – I haven't the stamina to climb further up as it's a long walk. He lives in the middle of the jungle with his family – wife, two sons and a daughter. The man isn't home and the children come out shyly to meet us.

"His mother used to work with me. She would walk all the way from here to my office every day through the forest. There were no roads then, about 20 years ago. She would come alone and work for me," says Kalanand.

This is the other tradition water resource of Goa. Hillside ponds, called tollems, built to impound rainwater, in a cascade so that one feeds the other. The ponds keep the hill streams going in the dry weather and the wells filled so people would have enough water to drink and water their plants and animals. They are multi-purpose ponds unlike what I've seen elsewhere in India where different structures to store water serve different needs. The tollems are linked to the Khazaans though; the water from these ponds eventually reach the Khazaans and are vital to flushing the fields clean of salty water. They are also important for prawn farming as a source of fresh water.

We leave the forests, plantation and tollems behind and emerge on a different landscape. It's an ugly sight with nary a tree to be seen. The crown of a plateau almost directly across the Zuari River from the Zuari Industries chemicals factory has been made into an industrial estate. The state government in its wisdom is converting several plateaus into industrial hubs. This estate has a steel furnace and several rolling mills. A little distance away are giant spheres of a liquefied petroleum gas filling facility owned by Indian Oil. The air is heavy with smoke from the steel furnace. The barren plateau stretches for several square kilometers. I cannot understand why, when converting land for industrial use, old native trees have to be clear felled and replanted, usually with some exotic crap. Trucks by the dozen ply up and down the narrow roads. It's a scene from the orc factory in the Two Towers of the Fellowship of the Ring.

The next plateau is also earmarked for an industrial estate but nothing has come up yet. Shrubbery covers the plateau and a deserted ceremonial hall stands guard at the top.

Goa's abundance of rain concentrated in the four monsoon months of June, July, August and September, is a blessing and a curse. The rain has generated the incredible flora of the state that is vital to preserving its environment. Once cut, the forests seldom regenerate because the torrential rain washes the topsoil away. This is the problem in the Satari and Sanguem talukas where mining has destroyed several thousand hectares of forests. These have been left to their own devices, enormous gaping holes in the landscape. Untreated, they have become artificial lakes that cannot support any life for at least the next several decades.

The protective mangroves do their job well where people have not destroyed them. This is most evident in the condition of bunds around Khazaan lands – the bunds stand where the mangroves do and erode away where there are no trees. Taken together, they make an amazing eco-system created by human beings who understood how to make nature work for them, rather than controlling nature as modernity has taught us to do. Maybe one day soon Goa's rulers will wake up to discover that their golden goose is nearly dead – then they might, just might, try reversing the decline.

8 UTTARAKHAND: WATERY SPIRITS

Tungnath's craggy peak towers some about 4,000 metres above sea level. It's the highest of the five dhams, or places of pilgrimage, in the Himalayas. The others are Kedarnath, Badrinath, Rudranath and Madamaheshwar. It's easy to miss Tungnath, but the view from the peak is to die for. Stretched against the eastern sky are the two better known naths and Neelkanth. On a clear day, says my friend and guide on the Himalaya journey, Ramesh Pahadi, you can see the snow covered hills from Uttarakhand to Himachal. On the other side, towards the plains, lower hills clothed in forest stretch into the blue distance. I am too far into the Himalayas to see the plains.

Ramesh should know as he's been up and down the hills in the two states, documenting water resources, their history and culture, for several years. A Sarvodayee, the 55-ish man lives in a modest rented accommodation with his wife and one daughter. The elder one is married and lives in the plains of Uttarakhand where, presumably, her husband has a job better than what he could get in the hills.

The Himalayas are the origin or India's major rivers that make up the world's most fertile, densely populated plain. The Indo-Gangetic plain, watered exclusively by mountains from the roof of the earth, have nurtured and supported a majority of India's population since the dawn of civilization. The rivers' fragile sources, high in the mountains or glaciers, have been some sort of threat for the past two centuries. And now, the pressure is beginning to tell.

Tungnath has the mandatory temple, a five-storey high stone structure topped by a flattened dome with a golden spire atop it. It looks impressive from a height, but from the entrance, I am less than impressed. It certainly does not look like something I would spend three hours climbing for. The peak is another matter, though. Another 500 metres higher, up a rutted winding path eroded by rushing water from rain or snow melt.

143

Winter snow is still on the ground just above Tungnath in two places. It's a diversion after the hour-long horse ride up the mountain to the temple – Ramesh has a game leg and decided to ride up; I followed, thinking this would be easier than hiking up. I wasn't exactly right as the horses often teetered on the brink of the precipitous path with a steep fall down the valley. Aryaman, my son, takes a break throwing snowballs at me. We decide at the temple to march and make the climb to Chandrasheela, as the peak is called. Ramesh and his wife have made the pilgrimage to pray, so they stay behind.

"I've been up there a few times. You must visit the peak though. It will take you 30 minutes up and 30 minutes down. We will wait for you here," he tells me encouragingly. From the temple, you cannot see the peak – the path up disappears over a rise in the mountain.

I think to myself, "That does not look too bad." And Aryaman and I start climbing.

"Dad, I am tired. I will wait here while you go and come," says Aryaman, half way up. It's an arduous climb for an eight-year-old. But there's no way I can leave my boy on the hillside.

"Look, can you see that flag up there. That's the peak. See how far we have come. It's a shame to come all the way and then go back without reaching the peak. You can tell your friends about your achievement as well," I try to encourage him. The air is too thin and he is too heavy for me to carry him up.

We walk a while, rest a while. There is very short grass and red and yellow wild flowers at this height. Nothing else grows – we are well above the tree line. The green carpeted hillside rolls away from us, smoothly it seems, on all sides to the trees far below. From the hillside along the path, water oozes, trickles down the rocks and disappears into the rubble alongside the path. The snow has just melted and the ground is saturated with water, that is slowly giving up. These tenuous trickles somehow percolate through mud and rock and wind up as the rivers that sustain half of India's people. They are barely enough for animals to lick, not enough to fill a bottle from. But they are drops that make the mighty Ganga.

"See, these little drops of water. You remember the river we drove along to get here. Eventually, they will all merge together to form rivers like those and the Yamuna. This is where we get our water from," I tell Aryaman.

He isn't quite convinced – how many thousands of such oozes will it take to make a river. Of course, not all rivers come from the conglomeration of oozes; the larger ones are from glacier melts. But the water is part of the same cycle and flow. It does take some imagination to link these hillside trickles to the sustenance of life hundreds, even thousands, of kilometres away.

We make the peak eventually and clang the bell above the Chandrasheela temple, another pile of rocks with three idols inside. Behind the temple, on the small plateau atop the peak, earlier climbers have left their mark – little piles of rock signifying their desire for a better life in this material world. I wonder whether the gods will look kindly upon them. We add our pile to the collection there, embellishing it with a stick to indicate our love for forests.

Descending, we pass the Tungnath temple and enter the small settlement below it. It's a collection of small dhabas that dole out fat-grained sticky rice and thin daal or potato-chana. The food tastes divine – blame it on the height and the pure rare air. Water is from a hill spring a few yards away, under a vertical rock face. The water makes the tea taste great. Just behind the dhaba are two small rooms with Rs. 50 written on each door. That is the rent for the room per night. For that, you get a small 4X4 metre room with a cotton mattress and a thick cotton quilt. I peer in, shudder at the prospect of sharing the room and the night with rats, and withdraw.

"It's a great view from Chandrasheela in the morning," says Ramesh. "If you want, you can stay here and return tomorrow."

"No thanks," I decline, hastily.

While Ramesh is finishing his repast, I walk down to the water source at the base of the settlement. A pipe stuck into the hillside is from where these 40-odd people get their water from. Water pours out of the end of the pipe and flows through a small pile of garbage down the hill, where it shortly disappears into the ground to reappear at regular intervals on the way down. But that wasn't the original source.

A couple of yards from the pipe is the *dhara*, the place where water used to collect and be used for various purposes – drinking, bathing and washing, in that order. A *dhara* is a rectangular or square manmade structure usually about 4 metres to a side and about a metre deep, that is built at a place where a stream flows out of a hillside. Usually, they are made of rock and have a solid bottom to prevent the water from seeping into the ground. The stream is channeled into spouts from where it fills the structure – the two spouts in Tungnath's case are made from brass, one of which is a beautifully carved bull's head and the other, an elephant head. Most others are similarly embellished. The water from the *dhara* overflows into another holding area a few feet below and then onto a third one. There is a fairly well-defined pattern of use of water.

Water out of the spout is used exclusively for drinking and pours into the *dhara*, allowing people to fill their pots straight from the hill's mouth. Water collected in the *dhara*, where people bathe or wash clothes. It is only the four varnas, or castes, who are allowed to use this water – no outcastes, animals or women with periods allowed. The overflow from this *dhara* that collects a few feet below in another receptacle where the rest of humanity – outcastes and women with menses – can use the water. Usually, there is a third basin below this from where animals can drink or bathe. The run-off from the *dhara* is usually channeled into the fields.

This traditional system ensures that no living thing is deprived of water, albeit the quality deteriorates with every fall in level. Traditionally, people didn't use soap made from chemicals and there were no detergents – pollution therefore was not an issue. It has become a problem now because of the processed soaps and detergents that are used.

Dharas by their nature provide space for the village community to meet and interact. They are an open construct where people come to the water and use it according to their convenience. Water is plentiful and clean in some parts of Garhwal and still fit to drink as it emerges from the hillside. They are made of local material by local artisans usually at the behest of the local wealthy.

The *dhara* at Tungnath is a small affair – no water flows into it now. The spouts remain as empty mouth in the hillside. The enclosure has become a slimy cesspool, even though people haven't yet start throwing garbage in it. Once, it was used to bathe and wash clothes. Now, it's an abandoned little shed.

"In the 1999 Chamoli earthquake, the source of the water shifted to where it is now, a few yards from the originally *dhara*. The flow also decreased," says Ramesh.

We wend our way down the 3 kilometre path from Tungnath to Chopta, the place on the Kedarnath-Badrinath route where I've parked. The path is about a metre wide and paved strangely enough, with stones placed vertically. This makes walking extremely difficult and despite my thick sandals, the stones seem to poke through the soles. It's a tedious walk at the best of times, and pursued as we are by a storm and high winds, the walk becomes an ordeal. We duck into a rough shelter, made of a pile of stones, by the side of the path. It's the same construct responsible for the deaths of many during the earthquake – the loosely piled stone walls collapsed and the heavy stones that make the roof crushed people inside. The open shelter gives little protection from the biting cold wind, coming at us straight off the snowy hills a little distant.

Soon, the storm blows itself out. We take the path again and trundle down. On the hill side are small flower and short grass. On the valley side, rhododendron bushes adorned with pink, purple and white flowers stretch down the Himalayan meadow to the tree line a few hundred feet below. The trees turn the hillside a darker shade of green and make a continuous carpet up the next hill. Beyond a range rise the snowcapped peaks. It's a continuous panorama. Next to the path, at 500 metre intervals, are taps that drip a steady stream of water. All of them have a jerry can or some such container, left by an owner to collect water over the hours.

We pull up at a small tea stall clinging to a pile of rocks on the hillside, one of half-dozen en route Tungnath. These open seasonally and are run by local villagers. This sample has a floor of wooden planks, walls of jute bags and a roof of tin. The wind blows freely through, making tea boiling difficult. We sit on the path's wall opposite the stall while Rahul makes the tea. He gives us water also, extremely generously. He is one of the owners of the jerry cans we saw further up. He leaves one there at night to fill and brings it down to his stall in the morning, replacing it with another to fill during the day. This way, he gathers his 80 litres of water.

"What are your problems here," I ask.

Rahul says "I don't mind the hardship of sleeping on the hillside in my shack. Nor the loneliness. Nor the lack of customers. Water is the biggest problem. You can see how difficult it is to bring a full jerry can downhill but we have to do it."

A little below the tea stall the path enters the tree line and the forests give a welcome break from the sun, that has shone through and is painfully bright, hot even. The walk downhill is harder than the horse ride uphill even though the horses often teetered on the edge of the path; many times I was staring down the horse's flanks at the steep fall to the tree line far below.

From Chopta to Gopeshwar, the road passes through the dense forests where the Chipko andolan began over three decades ago. Traditionally, people could cut dead wood and use other minor forest produce. They were allowed wood for house building and cooking. But then, the government decided to deny them access to forests, giving contractors the award to cut down and take away trees. Angered, the villagers blocked roads and did not let contractors drive their trucks into the forests. There were skirmishes and a law-and-order problem.

The women then decided that the best way to get what they wanted – stop the contractors – was to hug the trees and force the contractors wood cutters to retreat. Their life before the trees', so to speak. This strategy worked and was actively propagated by the local Sarvodaya activists among other villagers. The movement met with spectacular success and has become a model for anti-logging activists around the world.

Its dense forest, as it has existed for millions of years, unlike the plantation forests in so many other parts of Uttarakhand, where indigenous trees have been cut down and replaced by fast growing varieties, more suited to the timber industry. The oak is one such indigenous tree that has been decimated in large parts of the state. Its leaves are used for goat feed, dead branches for firewood and wood for furniture. Its spreading roots and branches are particularly good at stabilizing the slopes of the fragile hills. Despite its usefulness to local people, the oak has been systematically cut and replaced by commercial species of pine. It was this that the Chipko movement prevented. The dense forest that I drive through between Gopeshwar and Chopta is part of the area afforded protection after the movement.

It's a single lane road, so if I encounter any oncoming traffic, one of us has to find a shoulder and pull over, or back up. Thankfully, I encounter a couple of buses and a few jeeps on the three hour drive. The views of the snow covered hills are breathtaking, peeping through the dense foliage. The narrow winding road emerges from the forests a little above Gopeshwar and then we are into the town.

"This place has been undisturbed for millennia. It's a large area, some 1,300 square kilometres, that we managed to protect during the Chipko movement," says Ramesh. He was one of the early activists and helped mobilize people from villages around to hug trees.

Gopeshwar is a small town halfway between Kedarnath and Badrinath. There are maybe 15,000 people, and it's the largest town in the region. The most respectable place to stay is a hotel run by the Garhwal Mandal Vikas Nigam and at Rs. 200 a night, it is eminently affordable. For that princely sum, you get hot water on call, a smallish room with an attached bath and a dining hall where the basic veggie-daal-rice or roti routine is available. Don't expect any fancy non-vegetarian fare – I got chicken one day with some difficulty, and then it wasn't very edible. It's noisy, because the main parking lot for the town is right in front. Visitors to the town cannot drive into the main market. From 5 AM onwards, people doing the Dham circuit from the plains in their minivans start to leave, having spent the night somewhere in town. There is a cacophony of sounds – horns, diesel engines starting up, shouting and yelling.

The entry to the market is right outside the hotel, under an archway with the words Welcome to Gopeshwar Municipal Corporation written on it. To one side is a garbage dump and on the other are rickety shops. The market itself is nothing to write home about – a line of shops selling cheap plastic stuff, clothes and assorted items for daily use. The Sarvodaya office is half way down, up a few steps in an old but serviceable building. It's quite bare, save for publicity material and books and inhabited by men of great vintage. Ramesh runs a little printing press in town where he turns out calendars, greeting cards, visiting cards and the like in addition to his own newsletter. This and his writing gives him enough to get by. The printing press has a couple of machines but is small – the air is heavy with the acrid smell of printing ink and thinning fluid.

At the far end of town, the road ends in a small square, on one side of which is the Gopeshwar temple. It's again of great antiquity, like those at the five Dhams. Gopeshwar is the summer retreat of the deities from Rudranath and Gopinath – for the six winter months, the idols from these two temples are kept and worshipped at Gopeshwar. It's similar to the Tungnath temple save that its set in a town, not against hills. I enter the temple through a high portal and then a passage leads me directly to the sanctum sanctorum. Myriad candles illuminate the deities. Walking around the courtyard, I see old stone sculptures and an ancient tree, growing atop the ruins of a what was a small stone temple. Ramesh's house is across the wall from the temple. He tells me the temple is rumoured to be 1,500 years old, which probably applies to the small stone temple in the courtyard. Adi Sankaracharya had visited these five dhams and their wintering places in the 6th or 7th century AD, so all the places of worship probably date at least from there.

Ramesh joins me when I leave the temple. We walk to the end of the road, where the Gopeshwar *dhara* is. A large board proclaims Vaitarni/Rait kund – the *dhara* of the temple. Steep steps lead to the *dhara*. It's well kept with a marble platform around it and a covering of wire mesh screens. Beyond lies a hill and the road to Chopta. The *dhara* is a square, about 20 feet to a side. The top level is made of marble and water pours of one of three spouts.

"The *dhara* is still the main source of drinking water for people in town, inspite of piped water supply," says a man, noting my interest. He bends for a drink, cupping his hands under the flow to direct water into his mouth. I follow him into the *dhara* – the water is cool and sweet, filtered in the bowels of the earth.

"It's better than the tap water here," says Ramesh.

The priests of Gopeshwar's temple are the only ones allowed to bathe in the *dhara*. The water from this section flows into a large concrete pool a few feet below the *dhara* where a bunch of boys from town are having their evening bath in the setting sun. In contrast to the water in the *dhara*, that is clear, the water in this concrete tub is murky with soap. The soapy water flows into a drain from where animals drink.

Ramesh shakes his head. "The soap pollutes the water and the animals get sick. This is the problem with partial traditions."

On the way up, we pass a group of small shrines of great antiquity, small carved rocks in the shape of temples. The *dhara* is actually a part of the Gopeshwar temple, not these shrines. Once, they were part of the same complex; now they are separated by a few metres of housing.

Ramesh explains the link. "A temple is not said to be complete until its water source has been built. You will always find a *dhara* or other source of water next to a temple in Uttarakhand. It works the other way around also – where there is a water source, there is a place of worship. This keeps people from defecating around water and polluting it."

Garhwal had hundreds of *dharas* once, all in good repair. These were built by the local rulers or the wealthy to benefit everybody. Since the

1960s, they have slowly gone out of fashion and now, there are only a few still in use. It isn't as it the others have collapsed or don't have water anymore; people have piped water supply and find it tedious to go to a *dhara* to collect water. It does not matter that their piped supply is irregular and sometimes dirty. Water in the house is worth much more than water in a *dhara*.

Seems the logic works the length and breadth of India. In Shekhawati, each of the *tankas* had a cubby hole with an idol. In Chambal, most tanks had a small temple on one side. In south India, nearly all temples have a large water tank, or eri, inside their complex. And *eris* have a shrine on their banks. The link between water and religion is deep and as complex as the people who live in India.

An enormous deodar stands watch next to the *dhara*'s signpost, another monument to the past, when these trees and the majestic oak ruled the forests.

In the neighbouring region of Kumaon, similar structures are called *naulahs*, with one basic difference. *Naulahs* are not necessarily filled through spouts but also from underground streams. Their water is also used for drinking, washing and bathing. Most *naulahs* are made of stone and if the builder fancied, he would make it in the shape of an animal – elephant, cow, buffalo….

Ramesh says, "Almora in Kumaon used to be known for its *naulahs*. When it was founded by the Chand rajas in 1563, *naulahs* were the main source of water. This continued even when the British made it the capital of Kumaon in 1815. There were so many of them that the town was never short of water. Most localities in town are still named after old *naulahs*."

Kumaon, with a share of one-third of Uttarakhand's water, has a crisis each summer driven in part by the tourists from the plains and the hotel industry. It has relied on these traditional structures in the past but now, tankers have taken over. People have become more dependent on tankers since they got tap water; trekking uphill and down-dale for water is simply not their cup of tea anymore.

People use large and small rivers in Uttarakhand for drinking, bathing, washing, etc., and also for energy. Fast-flowing water channeled into what is now called run-of-the-river schemes to turn grinding mills and dynamos. The traditional water mills are called *gharats*.

"I've estimated there are half a million *gharats* in the Himalayas," says Ramesh. These aren't all in Uttarakhand but spread across the entire Himalayan range. For centuries, *gharats* have been an important focal point for hill village communities. Traditional *gharats* were built collectively by everybody in the village, each contributing his or her own expertise. They used local material and craftsmanship to make the mill that was the place for social intercourse, in addition to milling wheat and maize.

The traditional *gharats* are built in a small valley where a fast-flowing stream can drive a water wheel. These *gharats* have two types of water wheels. One is a circular assembly with wooden vanes stuck vertically onto a wooden wheel with a hole in the center. This is mounted horizontally, not vertically, on a wooden rod and immersed in the water – it spins with the force of water. The other kind has a massive central wooden hub into which wooden vanes are hammered at an angle of 45 degrees to the vertical; this maximizes the impact of water. In both cases, water is channeled onto the vanes.

The hut with the grinding stones is built on a small bridge across the stream so the stream's entire force is channeled onto the water wheel under the hut through a hollowed tree trunk; this concentrates the force of water. The rod attached to the water wheel turns one of the two grinding wheels in the hut above. Wheat or maize is poured into a basket-shaped hopper, from where it goes into the hole in the upper wheel. The flour is collected on a jute bag spread under the wheel. The hut itself is a typical stone-mud-thatch affair, cheap to make and repair. During the monsoons, *gharats* sometimes get washed away and the community bands together to rebuild it. The use of local material keeps costs down.

The wood for the water wheel and connecting rod is local, from a hardwood tree. The stones used for grinding are locally sourced and shaped. A carpenter makes the water wheel and connecting rod. A local artisan makes the hut and assembles the *gharat*. Water from the stream is channeled onto the water wheel through a pipe made from a hollowed tree trunk, again available locally. With local labour, a village can assemble its own *gharat* at nominal cost.

The *gharat* operator or *gharati* gets 1/16 of the quantity of wheat ground as payment, seldom in cash, that he estimates and keeps. This is not enough for a family to live on anymore. A traditional *gharat*, with a wooden water wheel and connecting rod, can grind up to 60 KG of wheat and about 50 KG of maize on an average day; the *gharati* gets about 4 KG of wheat and 3 KG of maize, that are worth around Rs. 100 on the market. For a five-member family, that is simply not enough. Compounding their problems is the spread of diesel and electric millers in nearby town of Uttarakhand that can grind up to 400 KG of wheat a day. They make nearly seven times what a traditional *gharati* does, even though their running costs are higher. Diesel and electric flour mills have been recognized as a small-scale industry in Uttarakhand, and so get concessions from the government. The state government granted *gharats* the status of a cottage industry in 1987-88, that allows owners to get loans and other help from the government.

Srinand Prasad Matiyal, is a *gharat* owner in the Gadora village, about 25 kilometres from Chopta, near Pipalkoti. His enterprise is hidden from the road by a thicket. Ramesh, Aryaman and I walk down the path, round a bend that is flooded with water from a stream and abruptly come upon Srinand's *gharat*. The road of running water, muted from the road, becomes louder as we approach his building. The place appears deserted.

Srinand emerges, in a blue kurta and white pajama.

"This is Nitya, from Delhi. He is researching water traditions in the Himalayas. I thought his work would be incomplete without a visit to your *gharat*," says Ramesh, by way of introduction.

Aryaman has run off to the *gharat* hut. I greet Srinand and walk to the hut, eager to see this age-old contraption in operation. There are two buildings, one traditional – stones and thatch – and the other modern – concrete and corrugated iron. The *gharat* is in the traditional one, a dynamo and risk husking attachment in the new one. The *gharat* works, the other equipment does not.

The *gharat*'s hut abuts the hillside. Water from the stream 5 metres above is diverted into an aluminum pipe that channels it onto the water wheel below the hut. The wheel, spinning at about 150 revolutions a minute, turns the grinding apparatus located in a corner of the hut. Wheat or maize is fed into the upper wheel through a metal hopper and the flour collected in a woven plastic sack. Srinand estimates and keeps his payment, and there is seldom any dispute over it.

"We keep every 16th handful of flour for ourselves," he explains.

There is a weighing balance also, dangling from a beam in the roof with the 10 and 15 KG weighing stones scattered around. The air inside the hut is heavy with flour dust that covers everything, even the two women who have been crushing grain there for ah past 20 minutes. They have tied their saris around their mouth and nose to keep the powder out. I take off my sandals and enter but beat a hasty retreat after taking photographs. The wheels produce an unpleasant grating sound that reminds me of fingernails being dragged across a blackboard.

I peer over the edge of the concrete slab. The water rushes out, having expended its energy on spinning the stones. It flows more sedately through a channel into the valley below. The original path of the stream, off to my left, is nearly empty as all the water is being used at the moment to run the *gharat*. across the channel, the small valley is green and tranquil. I can the bridge we has crossed on the road to get to Srinand's *gharat*; beyond that the valley continues uphill.

"Be careful. I'll ask him to turn off the water so you can see the water wheel," says Ramesh.

A few seconds later the water stops rushing from under the hut. The level of the stream rises. I gingerly cross the channel and squat, peering under the hut to see the wheel.

It's a wheel made of cast iron, one of the improved *gharats* that were developed by Prof R P Saini or the Indian Institute of Technology in

Roorkee. A water wheel made of cast iron that does not rust, ball bearings to reduce friction and a steel connecting rod were the improvements he devised in the *gharat* under a government programme to improve *gharats*. The steel connecting rod is sunk in a concrete slab below the hut where it rotates on ball bearings. The shaft goes through the floor of the hut into the grinding room through another set of ball bearings. The grinding stones are better milled.

The improved *gharat* costs Rs. 15,000, quite steep for a local person. It also costs a lot more to maintain than a traditional *gharat*. For example, ball bearings cost Rs. 400 each; once a set wears out, it has to be replaced immediately, else the *gharat* cannot function.

"The owner has to go to Saharanpur to get these. That is a two-day journey by bus. It's the same with the water wheel that is made in a foundry there," says Ramesh.

"It took me over a year to recover the cost and pay off the loan," says Srinand. "The power mills are the main problem now. They make at least two times what I do every day even after paying for diesel and power. Still, my *gharat* has a lower running cost."

He would not even think of reverting to the traditional *gharat*. But then, Srinand is a privileged one.

"What is this equipment in the other building," I ask him.

"That is a dynamo," he says, pointing to a motor-like instrument. "And that a rice dehusker." This is a large metal contraption with a hopper on top and a spout on one side. Both look as if they haven't been used for a while. A large wheel on supports with a shaft running through the wall used to drive either piece of equipment. Water channelised from the stream above to a turbine outside the building drove the wheel, to which either equipment was connected by belts.

Ramesh explains. "The dynamo isn't used because Srinand cannot legally sell power. He can generate it for his own use but cannot distribute it. The dynamo produces 5 KW, that is too much for him to use. There is no distribution mechanism here. The state government has not allowed *gharati*s to sell power."

The rice dehusker is used seasonally and nets Srinand additional income. His bread and butter come from the maize and wheat crushing operations. Srinand, Ramesh estimates, makes about Rs. 250 a day from this work. It's not a huge amount but enough to keep him and his family in clover.

Srinand's son Jayanti Prasad is the treasurer of the Water Millers Association of Chamoli, that helps members get loans and spare parts for *gharats*. It also ensures that non-association members are denied access to money for the improved *gharats* in order to protect its own interests. Even at the micro-level, money dictates politics.

A little further down, I see this in action. There are three other *gharats* downstream of Srinand's but he gets the most business because he is the closest to the road. The others have to be content with the overflow, which is also substantial enough to keep them in business. The last of the *gharats* is a traditional one, made of wood.

The owner of the second *gharat* complains, "The pin that joins the axles has got worn out so I have to run my *gharat* at a slower speed. I cannot crush as much grain. I have asked the Water Millers Association for the pin but they keep saying the part is not in stock. The real reason is that if my *gharat* runs to capacity, it will affect Srinand's business."

And the traditional *gharati*, who aspires for an improved version, has been denied a loan and equipment. The unspoken reason is unwanted competition for Srinand.

This last *gharati*, Diwan, has a ramshackle hut in the shade of an acacia tree. The stream gurgles down to a point about 3 M above his hut from where a hollowed tree trunk channels it to below his hut. The familiar roar of the water sounds from the bowels of the hut and the stream emerges below, flowing sedately. I peer into his hut, that doubles as his dwelling, unlike Srinand's that is only used for the *gharat*.

It's a poor man's quarters. There is a basket hanging from the ceiling, lined with clothes, that is the crib for the man's child. In a far corner, with a window for light, sits his charpoy. In another corner is the hearth. The grinding stones are in the opposite corner, near the door of the hut, in a small depression in the floor. The difference in appearance is palpable. So is the difference in the speed of the *gharat* – this one's stones rotate far more slowly than Srinand's, or even those of the person immediately upstream.

Diwan says, "I've asked the Association every season for an improved *gharat*. They have refused, saying there are already three here so there is no need for a fourth."

"Why don't you go somewhere else?" I ask.

"This is my village also. Why should I go anywhere else?" he retorts. "Let them go somewhere else." He waves upstream.

Diwan barely manages to make ends meet. He supplements his income by working as a daily wage labourer in Chopta and other towns.

"There simply isn't enough work for all these *gharats* any more," says Ramesh. "The population of Uttarakhand isn't large enough to support them, what with power mills and packaged flour. They cannot sell electricity and rice husking is seasonal. Cotton ginning has not caught on because readymade clothes are easily available. Still, the government has done the right thing in giving them the status of a cottage industry."

Gharats can multitask, unlike power mills. They can crush more than wheat and maize – Ramesh extends their utility to powdering spices and oil extraction in addition to what's already been tried.

"The *gharat* flour tastes better than mill flour," he says. True, flour from a small mill tastes better than flour out of a plastic bag. Maybe it's because of the *gharat*'s slow grinding speed that preserves flavour and nutrition better than the mills.

All these make *gharats* suitable for local industries in the hills where accessibility and cost matter. The question remains – how cost-effective are they given mass-produced goods. The further I go into the Himalayas, the costlier these things get. But I don't seek people weaving their own clothes from cotton ginned and spun in their own villages. Sure, there are a few who produce traditional handloom cloth but these aren't enough to support many *gharats*. And most *gharats* aren't equipped to process cotton.

What would help *gharat* owners is if the government allows them to sell electric power in their neighbouring villages. At 5 KW each, *gharats* can light up several homes. They need a power distribution network that can be provided fairly cheaply at the village level – there is no need for a major power grid but a small local grid that connects *gharat*-based dynamos to houses in nearby villages. Given the unreliable power situation, this would definitely help matters in Himalayan villages. It would also go some way in making *gharats* a remunerative proposition in this day and age.

"Uttarakhand is dotted with failed power projects based on *gharats*," says Ramesh, on our way back to Gopeshwar. "Since 1975, the government has tried various schemes to generate power from *gharats* in a viable manner. None has succeeded for a variety of reasons."

The return on investments is small, based on the low firm power output of a *gharat*. There is a question mark over distribution and pricing of power. Then there are legal issues that have never been tackled. Added to this are the state electricity board people who make money providing connections, raising the capacity of existing connections and repairing faults. The final one – locally trained technicians for repairing faults – is surmountable provided there is a demand for the power.

The future of *gharats* doesn't look very bright. However, there are many organizations in the region that haven't given up. If we assume that each *gharat* can generate just 3 KW of firm power, and there are 250,000 in the Indian Himalayas, then they can generate a combined 750,000 KW of power. This can power at least as many households across the mountains. More than the quantity, it's the location that makes this power attractive. It would be generated at the village level where power supply is either non-existent or erratic, and distributed right there.

The beauty of *gharats*, I saw, was that you could string many of them along a single small stream and all of them could run, each supporting a family. The operation of one *gharat* does not interfere with that of the rest. Most *gharatis* are from the lower castes and poor. They are averse to taking risks, preferring instead to let things run as before. If the *gharats* are to get a better deal, their operators will have to be uplifted first by training in both technical and entrepreneurial skills. At the moment, if the *gharat* does not help them to make ends meet, they seek manual work elsewhere.

***

A jacaranda tree is in full bloom in the hot afternoon. It doesn't feel like the Himalayas at all – more like a suburb of Delhi. If it wasn't for the mountains and the pine trees, I'd think I was in the Aravallis on a hot day. A loud double thumb reverberates in the valley as I get out of the car. We near the bottom of a picturesque, forested valley in between Chopta and Pipalkoti. On one side is a semi-finished house, on the other the forested hillside. We had passed the Gadora village a kilometre back. It's a typical Uttarakhand village, huts made of stone and adobe with either tin or stone roofs or some concrete houses. The mandatory telephone booths that seem to be the main occupation of all people in the village – they must do good business because mobile phones do not work in the hills and this is the route to Badrinath. Its yatra time and the road is full of Tata Sumos and Toyota Qualises trying to push one another into the Alaknanda roaring by a few hundred metres below.

Narender Kumar emerges from the semi-finished looking house. Actually, it's finished but rods and other construction material lying around gives me the impression that he left off half-way. At road-level, there is a small shop where he sells squashes and jams made in his house at the level below. The shelves are crammed with plastic jerry cans of squash and large plastic jars of jam. His squashes are of rhododendron or amla and jams of apple and amla. Ramesh does the introductions. To the left of the shop is the roof of his house and steps leading down to the courtyard. From there, a path leads into the fruit orchard in the valley below.

"Have a drink," says Narender. "Then we will go and see the hidrum."

"What's a hidrum?" asks Aryaman.

"You will see. Can you hear it?" says Ramesh.

The steady thumping from the valley seems to be more muted inside the shop and all the harder to hear what with the traffic on the road. We finish our drinks, lukewarm in the warmth of the afternoon, and emerge onto the roof. The stairs have no railing so we hug the wall going down. From the courtyard, Narender leads to the path into the valley. It's wide at the top but quickly disappears into the fields just below his house. We pick our way over newly-ploughed earth to the far side of the first terrace. At the end, there is a narrow cement canal, about 15 centimetres wide and twice as deep. Its half-full with rapidly-flowing water; water that the hidrum has pumped to a tank near this house from where its released into the fields through this canal.

The path and canal run together from here. It's easier to walk on top of the canal even though its steep in places.

Ramesh tell me the history of hidrums as we walk down. "Hidrums were introduced in India in the 1960s. Two non-government organizations modified the European design to suit India and started getting them manufactured here. There are now thousands of these thumpers in the valleys of Himachal Pradesh and Uttarakhand.

"In a village in Himachal, the government installed hidrums to irrigate 75 bighas of land (about 7 bighas make a hectare here) at a cost of Rs. 76,000. In a year, the people managed to grow 2.5 times more wheat then they used to. Each family earned an additional Rs. 10,000 each year from vegetables."

He turns to Narender. "I've seen so many hidrums in the hills. Very few work properly. You are lucky. What is the record of these hidrums?"

"Quite good," says Narender. "They broke down a few days ago but the irrigation department engineer came and fixed it. I was surprised by their prompt response."

Seems like it's not the norm for irrigation department engineers to respond promptly to complaints from people. Ramesh confirms this to me later. Sometimes, they can take a month to act. Larger farmers, and even groups of smaller ones have got together, to build their own maintenance systems for hidrums.

Hidrums are simple devices, developed around 200 years ago in Europe for pumping water. When cheap electricity became available there, their popularity declined. They are ideal for remote hill areas in Uttarakhand where power and diesel are both in short supply or expensive. Essentially, they use the force of flowing water to pump it to a height. Ideally, the ratio of the head of input water to the height that it is pumped is 1:8, that is to say, if the water is channeled to the hidrum from a height of 5 metres, it can pump an eigth of this to a height of 40 metre. But we don't live in an ideal world and the usual ratio achieved is more like 1:4. This ratio is called the lift magnification. The height to which water can be pumped is inversely proportional to the quantity of water pumped.

We reach the bottom of the valley after 15 minutes' clambering down the cultivated hillside. Its overgrown and a fast-flowing stream runs along it. The going gets tough here but the thump-thump of the hidrum beckons us. It's really loud and the sound reverberates off the valley walls. There, in a clearing, is the contraption.

It comprises two large steel cylinders, each around 1.5 metres high, standing in a square concrete enclosure. Their lower portion is submerged in water. The cylinders are fixed to a steel water chamber, also submerged in water. Water from a concrete supply tank, about 10 metre above rushes into the water chamber through a supply pipe. At intervals of about 3 seconds, the hidrums go thump, the water boils around the cylinders and a delivery pipe connected to the cylinders takes the water to the storage tank near Narender's house. It all seems very disorganized and not at all like a system that can pump water anywhere. The enclosure's walls have cracks and threaten to collapse at any time. The cylinders are rusty. I wonder how long they have been down there.

"Since around 1981," says Narender. "But they actually started working much later, in 1995. The irrigation department put up the hidrum but didn't make the channels for us to use the pumped water."

The steel tank under the cylinder has two valves. One is where the cylinder connects to the tank called the delivery valve. The other is an impulse valve that lets water flow through into the concrete enclosure of the hidrum.

The water flowing into the steel tank forces the impulse valve closed. It rapidly fills the tank – once water pressure in the steel tank reaches a critical point, it forces the delivery valve to open with a loud thump that I hear every few seconds. Water rushes into the vertical cylinder. The pressure in the cylinder and the steel tank equalizes and the delivery valve closes; the impulse valve opens. In the meantime, the water in the cylinder has been forced up the delivery pipe to storage tank up the hillside. The process repeats itself and with every cycle, more water is forced up the hillside till it flows continuously to the storage tank. Only a small part of the water that enters the water chamber is actually pumped uphill.

The rate at which the valves open and close determines the quantity of water pumped. This can be easily adjusted by hand; the typical frequency for small pumps is 70 – 90 times a minute. The higher the frequency, the faster the rubber linings wear out. Hidrums come in five different sizes, measured in inches: 1.25" X 0.5", 2" X 1", 4" X 2", 6" X 3" and 8" X 4". These are the ratios between the supply and delivery pipes.

Both the valves have a rubber lining that wears out in a few months because once started, hidrums run continuously. They don't need any electricity or manual intervention to run. They pump water all the time, filling the storage tank and irrigating fields. When the rubber lining wears out, the pump's efficiency drops. This is when the farmers call the irrigation department to repair the hidrum. Given its mechanical simplicity, maintenance is relatively simple and can even be done by a local person, provided he has the tools.

To repair it, the engineer stops the hidrum. There is a pedal at the base of the vertical cylinder that stops the delivery valve from opening. He presses this for a short while and the thumping stops. He puts a piece of wood into the impulse valve to keep that open and let water flow downstream. To change the delivery valve's rubber, the engineer removes a panel on the side of the vertical cylinder, takes out the valve and replaces the rubber lining. The impulse valve is simpler to repair. Repair completed, he kicks the pedal a few times to get the hidrum going again. The entire process of changing the rubber lining for both valves can take a couple of hours.

Hidrums have to be necessarily located on the floor of the valley. Access is difficult and they can also be damaged during the monsoons, when streams turn into raging torrents.

The smallest hidrums lift about 4,000 litres of water to a height of 30 metres while the largest can pump over 100,000 in 24 hours. This means that a large hidrum can irrigate just over an acre of land that is 30 M above but a small one can do just about 1/25th. Smaller hidrums are good for pumping water for human use or watering nurseries. Both, however, are useful for irrigating the slopes of hillsides where water is otherwise hard to find.

Narender has two 6X3 hidrums going 24 hours. He gets around 90,000 litres a day, more than enough for irrigation and his family's needs. However, the excess water flows back down the valley and is used by another set of hidrums further down the valley. He pays nothing. The only other source of water is a pipe that runs along the road and supplies drinking water once a day – it's just not enough for other use. It the hidrums weren't there, Narender's orchard, and business, would not exist.

Of course, Narender could have installed an electric of diesel pump set. Both would cost money to run and would be more expensive to repair. He would have to retrieve them before the monsoons because if they were to be washed away, he would not get any compensation from the government. The hidrums, on the other hand, were installed by the irrigation department, which also looks after them. They are sturdy enough to withstand a fair degree of flooding – even if inundated with water, they don't get damaged.

Hidrums haven't been as successful in Uttarakhand as they could have been. One reason is that the irrigation department, while selecting places to install them, looks only at technical aspects – the quantity of water available, height to which it is to be pumped and therefore the size of hidrum needed, and ease of installation. It doesn't look at the actual water needs and the pattern of land ownership. Very often, many farmers have small plots on the same hillside, causing water-sharing problems. The farmers near the storage tank get more water than those further down – an unusual situation. To keep the peace, they sometimes decide not to use the water at all and the hidrums installed never get used. In other cases, the department puts in the hidrums but not the water distribution network of canals. In most cases, hidrums are simply not repaired when the valve rubber linings wear out. In some villages, there isn't enough farm land that needs to be irrigated so the villagers don't use the hidrums. The department assigns a chowkidar and a mechanic to each village to look after all the hidrums in the area.

"The irrigation department has to meet certain targets. They install hidrums even where people cannot use them," says Narender.

Hidrums do better in places where a single person owns all the land on the hillside and where a local mechanic is available. They cost less than Rs. 100,000 to install, including the cost of water supply channels, and only about Rs. 1200 a year to maintain. A diesel or electric pump of comparable capacity is priced about the same to install but more than 100 times costlier to run – an estimated Rs. 130,000 or so.

It would make sense if the villagers are assisted in installing hidrums where needed, rather than the current top-down approach of the irrigation department. Were this to happen, villagers could decide where to install hidrums and what size would be ideal. They would also sort out water-sharing concerns better than the government can do. In fact, this issue needs to be addressed before any plans are drawn up because it frequently leads to conflict in the village. Another way to ensure that villagers use the water, and take care of the hidrum, is to involve them in building the supply and irrigation channels as well as train one of them to look after the device.

The irrigation department, on their part, says villagers aren't ready to use the facilities they are offered. This sounds like the typical bureaucratic refrain – we give the natives everything but they are too ignorant to use them. Instead, a partnership would go a long way in making sure simple, cheap irrigation methods get widely adopted.

Uttarakhand, the cradle of the large rivers of the sub-continent, has a problem of plenty. There is plenty of water in Garhwal, but a shortage in Kumaon. All Kumaon's towns are parched in summer. Garhwal's towns have a water shortage when the deluge of tourists from the plains ascends to them in summer.

On one hand, there is a shortage. On the other, there is a crisis of quality. For the past 200 years, Uttarakhand's hills have been systematically logged. First by the British to get timber for the Imperial navy and the railway network. Later by the Indian forest department to make money. And still later by timber contractors, protected by the politicians of the plains. Native forests were cleared and replanted with commercially useful species such as pine. In the process, the fragile hills lost their ability to hold, and gradually release, the deluge of monsoon rain that they receive in a few months of the year.

"Kathgodam was the main place in the hills where timber was processed. It means a timber godown. The town developed because of the saw mills set up there to cut the trees. I remember as a child watching the entire river choked with cut trees. The loggers would clear part of a slope and roll the logs down to the river. They would float down to Kathgodam. During the couple of months that they took to reach there, the wood would get nicely seasoned," says Ramesh.

I look down the slopes to the river. It's wide and fast. It's hard to imagine the hills could produce so much timber and yet have any left.

The population has also increased and growing towns and villages, none with any sewage treatment systems whatsoever, pollute the rivers. Driving along the Alaknanda river, from Rishikesh to Chamoli, a distance of about 250 kilometres, I notice the river gets clearer as I move into the hills. I break journey at Srinagar in deference to Aryaman, who is car-sick and quite road weary.

A sign on the highway beckons me to the Ivy Top Resorts hotel. It's a steep climb up an unpaved road to Pine Top hotel. The hotel is at the top of a small hillock. Its run by Mr. B N Ghildyal, whose father bought the land while in the Indian army back in the 1940s. He has an amazing variety of fruit trees, some which are in bloom and there are raw fruits on the others. He's made the main house into a hotel and charges Rs. 1000 a night, exclusive of food. It's well worth it, because the view of the Alaknanda upstream and downstream is great. In the evening, I sat on the lawn with a beer contemplating the river coming downhill. In the morning, I sipped tea on a porch – he's making a restaurant behind the hotel – gazing at the river wending its way down to its confluence with the Bhagirathi river. You can drive from Rishikesh to Gopeshwar in a day, but it's a long drive and Pine Top hotel makes for a pleasant interlude.

In the hills, there is a strict driving code. All hill driver follow this irrespective of what they are driving. It's best to get acquainted with it – though none of them will tell you, you can guess it. If you are on the valley side of the road going up, you have absolute right of way. If you are on the hill side of the road going up, you get right of way only over small vehicles; you need to make way for trucks and buses to pass. This is the same if you are on the valley side going down. If you are on the hill side of the road going down, you have to let everything pass. There is a trump card in all of this – turn on your indicator to signal you are turning right: this tells oncoming traffic to get out of your way! Hill drivers are cool, and usually let you pass if you slow down and move out of their way.

Lunch was at a small dhaba outside Pauri, full of taxi drivers. Their conversation is about accidents, discouraging. The lunch is better. A fixed thali of local fat rice, chapattis, a vegetable and daal for Rs. 20. We quickly eat our food and get on our way – I am keen to leave the dhaba and its scintillating conversation as fast as possible. It a lovely winding and fairly deserted road thereafter to Lansdowne.

Lansdowne in Kumaon typifies the hills, with its problems. It's a pretty cantonment town at a decent height, so it's cool even in the day. But there is no water. The town is entirely supplied by tanker, operated by individuals and the army. Rather odd, I think, for a town that is also the headquarters for the prestigious Garhwal Rifles regiment of the army. I see people queuing up at the few handpumps in town; they can fill one pot and then have to wait a few minutes for the pump to recharge before filling the next.

People use funnels made of plastic bottle halves so that no water is wasted. Strange that a hill town should have no water source. Maybe its founders the British weren't big on baths.

At the GMVN hotel, that has nice cottages for Rs. 1000 a night including breakfast and morning tea, I am told by the manager that water will come by 5 PM. We check in at 3 PM after a longish drive from Gopeshwar, via Srinagar. The road branches off the highway there and heads over the hills from Garhwal into Kumaon. We badly need to bathe but there is absolutely no water, save the small jug of drinking water. I content myself with a wet tissue instead. Uttarakhand as a whole does not seem to have a water crisis yet, given the plethora of rivers. But climate change is slowly changing that. Glaciers are retreating at a faster rate. They, and the myriad streams that ooze all year round from the rocky hills, feed India's major rivers. Melting glaciers are good news in the very short term – there will be more water for all. But once the glaciers are gone – climatologists predict they will be in another 300 years – most of the rivers will dry up too.

Deforestation has reduced the amount of rainfall in the hills, both in terms of the total quantity received and the number of rainy days in the monsoons. This is having an immediate impact on the whole of north India. Power and water shortages have become more acute in summer. Most of the hydro-electric dams do not have enough water to generate power that will meet the every-increasing demand, both from rural and urban areas. The extremely controversial Tehri dam still has not filled, and cannot provide water to Delhi as was promised, nor generate any electricity. The mountains are so fragile that landslides are common and the rocks absorb a lot of the water that the dam is meant to store. It may still work, provided it does not trigger an earthquake – Tehri dam sits right on top of a major tectonic fault. Protecting forests and allowing them to regenerate is a logical solution.

After it became a state, Uttarakhand was spared somewhat from being Uttar Pradesh's politicians' playground. However, its own population is growing fast, straining natural resources. The near-total lack of sewage disposal facilities means that most of the rivers are already quite polluted when they reach the plains. Both the Ganges and the Yamuna are notorious world-wide for being extremely polluted rivers. The only saving grace, if I can call it that, is the absence of polluting industries in most of the state.

The government conjures up ever-grander schemes to 'solve' the drinking water problems of the population. For example, it lays a 50 kilometre-long pipeline to take water from a river high in the hills to Pauri at an astronomical cost. Of course, the pipeline develops leaks or breaks with predictable regularity. So the people who depend on it are left, literally, high and dry. Tapped water never melds people together – it only divides society. Taps are intrusive – the water is thrust into your life. Traditional devices were inclusive – people went to them, they accommodated large numbers of people as they were designed to do and water provided a meeting point for lives.

This is fallout of forgetting one's traditions – the *naulah* and the *dharas* – that kept people adequately supplied in ages past. One of the solutions in Uttarakhand is to revive the hundreds of such water supply and harvesting structures.

Both the feeling of belonging to a cohesive community and quality of water has declined over the years. People lament water, its quality and quantity; you should have tasted the water then, they tell me, it was something else. This, this isn't what we called water. But they do nothing – the government, that distant father, will provide for their needs. Uttarakhand's denizens are a resigned lot.

Uttarakhand does have a crisis of intellect. The average person here, in the abode of the gods, is singularly disinterested in protecting his environment. There seemed to be even less of this than in other parts of India, Rajasthan for example. The people have no feeling for the rivers or forests here. This is the state's paradox – its problem of plenty.

9 BUNDELKHAND: THE HAND THAT BUILT THE KHAJURAHO TEMPLES

A thousand years ago, the Chandela Rajputs ruled this central part of India. It was Bundelkhand's most glorious era, when they built the temples at Khajuraho, forts and palaces – and massive *talaabs* (tanks, some of which are as big as lakes). But over the past 1,000 years, Bundelkhand has been in steady decline and now is one of India's most 'backward' regions, if backwardness is to be measured by the yardsticks of industrialization.

It is also one of India's most dramatic regions. Enormous expanses of forests, interspersed with fields and *talaabs* that spread for hundreds of hectares. The soil is fertile, yielding up to two crops a year. The forests, logged to death during the British colonial rule, are slowly growing back. The *talaabs* are in different stages of (dis)repair.

Bundelkhand lies between the Indo-Gangetic plain to the north, the Vindhya range of hills to the south, and the rivers Yamuna to the east and the Betwa to the west. The land slopes gently from south to north, and most of the rivers flow in this direction to join the Yamuna at various points. The rivers of Bundelkhand, notably the Betwa and the Ken, restore some semblance of life to the Yamuna, that emerges from Agra in the north as a filthy drain.

Bundelkhand gets its name from the Bundelkhand Rajputs who rule this region for two centuries from about 1600 AD. It was probably one kingdom during the rule of Maharaja Chhatrasal, from 1691 to 1731 AD, who challenged the Mughals. Before and after, it was fragmented, and the object of constant attack. It now comprises 13 districts spread over the states of Madhya Pradesh and Uttar Pradesh. Bundelkhand is also the badlands of India – the famous dacoits, Phoolan Devi and Malkhan Singh lent it their notoriety and now, kidnappings, rapes and murders are routine.

Attara is a non-descript dusty town on the eastern fringe of

Bundelkhand, about 150 kilometres west of Allahabad. Go another stop on the train from Delhi and you reach Chitrakut, where Rama is supposed to have spent his exile years, after killing the demons. It's not 'Ram-rajya' anymore, but more 'Rakshas-rajya', the rule of demons. The Attara station has a single, long platform of which only the central area has a roof. The rest is shaded by massive peepul trees and the ground below is white with bird-shit.

I emerge from the station and Suresh Raikwad, my friend and guide for the Bundelkhand sojourn, greets me. He's a short, moon-faced man in his late 20s, always smiling and dressed in a simple shirt and trousers. Suresh is from a nearby village called Tendura, where he has an office, but spends most of his time in Attara and another nearby town called Baandha. The exit of the station is fairly decrepit and crowded. There is a large courtyard outside with ankle-deep dust, in which an assortment of vehicles await passengers – jeeps, autorickshaws and cycle rickshaws – to suit all pockets and distances.

"Namaste, Nityaji. How was your journey?" he smiles as me.

"Fine. I got up early and was anxious to get off at the right station," I say. I didn't want to go onto Chitrakut and battle the demons there.

"Let's go to the guest house and freshen up," says Suresh.

The Lakshmi guest house is just that – a rambling building with a dorm on the ground floor and rooms on the first and second floors. There is no method in the madness – climb the stairs to one room, another few to another, and so on. I get a room with a bathroom. The walls of the bathroom look ready to cave in on me so I use it very sparingly. The mattresses are hard and covered with printed sheets, so it's impossible to make out if they are clean. There is a TV in one corner, resting on an ancient cooler. This room has windows so I can look out on the guest house's dusty yard. The paint is new, though, as is the bed. On the ground floor, just below my room, is another that the local police use for drinking, gambling and whoring.

"Sharmaji, please give us breakfast," Suresh calls to the hotel's owner. "We'll have parathas and daal."

And to me, he says, "This place is famous for its daal."

Suresh has borrowed a bike for running around the place. We leave for Tendura after breakfast. Attara town is a dust-bowl. All the lanes are lined with shops – eating places, clothes outlets, hardware stores, vegetable vendors and most of all, vehicle repair garages. Atarra used to be a major mandi (grain centre) once but has since lost its pre-eminence as others have come up. It's a small town of traders.

The roads don't exist for the most part. They have long since eroded down to their stone foundation and vehicles pitch and yaw over these in first or second gear. There is the inevitable round-about in the centre of town with a hideously painted statue of Dr. B R Ambedkar, arm outstretched, in the middle of it. We bounce over railway tracks and leave town. In fact, the town lies to one side of the railway tracks – on the other is an expanse of marshy land from where Attarra's large, vicious mosquitoes come.

The road to Tendura is no better. Small pieces of tarmac interspersed with gaping potholes. The bike is an ideal machine for this and Suresh zigzags from one stretch of tarmac to the next. I manage to get a look around. The Rabi crop has been planted and the fields are green. It's mostly mustard and gram (chana). Some of the larger farmers grow wheat. The Kharif crop is paddy, jowar, coarse cereals and pulses; paddy is a sown as a monoculture while the others are sown together in the same plots because of widely different water needs.

There are two kinds of soil – one is very clayey, locally called kabar, and retains water. The other is called mar and is easier to work. Small channels with water run along the road, infested with water hyacinth, another unwanted British import.

The road disappears and Tendura appears, rambling off to the left of the road; its fields stretch to the left. Each plot is marked by hedges that also act as wind-breaks and strengthen the low walls around the fields called bunds.

The village is a rambling collection of houses built anyhow with spaces around them that merge to form roads. None of the roads were ever anything other than dirt tracks that, in the rains, become an impassable expanse of slush. Nearly all the houses are brick-and-cement though the older ones have stone walls, plastered with lime and covered with the usual cow dung-straw-soil mixture. It is a large village of around 5,000 people, sub-divided into three localities. Farming is the main occupation though a few of the youth, educated and 'above' farming work in Attara or Banda. Some drive jeeps. It seems education alienates people from their lands because, once educated, people no longer want to farm.

The Raikwads are a fishing community. They used to make their living catching and selling fish from the region's tanks and rivers. Only a few still do so, concentrated in villages around the larger *talaabs* in Bundelkhand. Suresh's family took to farming several generations ago and are well-established in the village.

"Here is my house," he says, stopping under a spreading acacia tree in an open space between two buildings. It's a low-ceilinged, two-storeyed building with a platform outside the front door where people congregate in the evenings. A buffalo sits on a bed of straw, chewing nonchalantly.

There is a well a little down the road, its four masonry towers pointing forlornly skywards. It used to be the only source for drinking water in the village, fed by seepage from the three village tanks.

"Since handpumps were installed in the village some decades ago, it's become the local garbage dump," says Tribhuvan Singh, a red-haired 20-something who works with Suresh. The inside walls have all but collapsed and garbage floats on the water. In a few years, it will be history.

I duck under the low front door of Suresh's house and walk through the passage beyond with head lowered to avoid hitting the thick wooden beams holding up the first floor. It's a simple construction – thick walls with beams set in them. Stone slabs placed on the beams to form the floor of the first floor. The ground floor is for animals, even though it's broomed and clean. The first floor is for human beings. I emerge from the animals' room into the inner courtyard that is paved with flagstones. It's completely enclosed, with double-storeyed rooms on three sides and a wall on the fourth. Suresh's office is to the left and stairs without a railing lead up to it.

His courtyard houses the bathing area and toilet. There is a place for firewood – no cooking gas here – and cow dung cakes. Clotheslines criss-cross the courtyard borne down with the morning's washing. Suresh's father, a white-haired mustachioed man emerges from one of the rooms on the ground floor.

"Don't waste your time going up to his office. Come with me," he says.

Before I can protest, he ducks under the doorway and is out. I follow. He takes me to a *talaab* on the outskirts of the village, about 200 metres from the house. Naya *talaab*, as it's called, is the largest in Tendura. It's not new, as its name implies. It's got a 400 year-old legend behind it. A few months previously I had visited Tendura – Naya *talaab* was covered with water hyacinth and its water stank. Now, it's clean and the water, clean enough to bathe and wash food in before cooking. An ancient peepul tree spreads its roots on the bund at a corner; its roots seem to claw the earth like the fingers of an old emaciated hand. They are great to sit on and contemplate the stillness of the pond in the mid-day heat.

Suresh had led the villagers in a week-long campaign to clean the *talaabs* – about 50 people extracted the hyacinth, dried and burnt it. They deepened the pond and used the excavated mud to repair and raise the embankments. They pretty much set it back a few decades, when people used to look after their *talaabs* and the *talaabs* in turn ensured that villages seldom never faced a shortage of water.

In the fields across the tank, I see two sarus cranes. Tall and graceful, they are looking for small fish and frogs in the fields. Their red heads bob just above the hedges bordering the fields. I stalk them, hoping for a decent photo but they are evasive and eventually fly away. It is good luck here to see the cranes.

A village elder waddles up to me. He is Chedi Lal Prajapati, a former sarpanch and now advisor to everybody on all causes. He was one of Suresh's brigade in the charge against water hyacinth. Chedi Lal gestures to me to sit on the embankment in the shade of a badh tree, spreading its branches across the pond. The breeze coming off the pond is cool. A woman washes a cane basket full of yellow daal in a corner of the *talaab*. She sees me and pulls her sari over her face.

Chedi Lal says, "The water is every good for cooking daal because its rain water. The groundwater here is brackish in places."

He narrates the legend of Naya *talaab*. "Many years ago, some say 400 years, a man passed this way with several bags full of money. He left a few with the villagers who lived here then and disappeared. When he didn't return for many months, the villagers decided to use the money to build this *talaab*."

I walk around the village with Chedi Lal. He circles the *talaab* and on the far side, I find that people have built houses on the banks of the *talaab*. The *talaab* does not have the mandatory temple but a small shrine under the *badh* tree, where we sat.

"This would never have happened in the old days," says Chedi Lal. "In the last few years, things have changed in our village. Because of these changes, these people feel bold enough to make houses on the banks of the *talaab*. Earlier, they would be ostracized if they did this."

We're joined by Ram Snehi Verma, another man of Chedi Lal's vintage. Walking round Naya *talaab*, we reach a small bridge – two wooden planks across a gully – and then another smaller pond called Vijayi *talaab*. This is choked with hyacinth and a few houses protrude onto it. The hyacinth from here occasionally washed over into Naya *talaab* and has to be cleared. A child washes his ass in the water after shitting a little distance away; the rains will carry his production into the water.

Ram Snehi follows my glance. "We used to have very strict rules about shitting and pissing around *talaabs*. You can see they aren't followed any more. It was forbidden to use the embankments as toilets. People would fill their pots and go to the fields to shit. If they were caught shitting on the embankments, they were fined or even thrown out of the village."

Chedi Lal takes up the story. "Every year, before the rains come in June, there is a village mela (fair) around the *talaabs*. All the families who used the *talaab*'s water assemble to cook and have a good time. This reinforces our bond with the *talaabs*. During the mela, one member from each family helps to excavate the pond and strengthen the embankments.

"After the rains, in September, we have another festival. The village deity is put on a float and towed around the pond, which is full of water after the rains. There is fun and feasting for a week. We thank the gods for their bounty."

Village life, then, is intimately wound up with the life of its *talaabs*.

Going further around the village, we come upon the Baba *talaab*, named after a sadhu. The story goes that Sadhu Baba used to live here, and had a small pond to himself. A cholera epidemic struck the village and its people went to Sadhu Baba for advice. He told them to deepen and widen the pond and the epidemic would go away. One person from every household chipped in and sure enough, once the work was complete, the epidemic vanished.

"It's very deep – nobody knows how deep. There are large fish here too, but we do not eat them. It is said that people who eat them, die like fish out of water," says Chedi Lal.

There are as many legends as there are *talaabs*. There are as many *talaabs* as there are villages in Bundelkhand. There are an average of 14 wells to each village, some in the villages and others in the fields. There is a plethora of rivers, drains and gullies that water and drain Bundelkhand. It gets an average of 1,000 MM of rain a year. Bundelkhand should be rich – in water, agriculture and natural resources.

Just how rich it is comes home to me in the next few days. There are no industries in Bundelkhand – some says it's too remote; others blame the high crime rate. Precisely because of this, the water is clean in almost all parts and safe to drink from wells, handpumps and even some rivers without treatment. Farmers use very little pesticide or fertilizer so toxic run-off from fields is low. Most *talaabs*, even those whose beds are cultivated, are reasonably uncontaminated. I become a guinea pig of sorts, trying out water from tanks whose bottoms I can see – no, I am straight. And you are reading this book, right?

Farming is largely traditional and land-holdings are small across Bundelkhand. Professor Bhartendu Prakash, who runs the Vigyan Shiksha Kendra in a village near Attara called Tindwari, has studied the farming patterns in the region and its water resources. He is a short, white haired man with a white bandana on his head. His eyes smile all the time. He lives in the family mansion, a sprawling single storeyed house on the outskirts of Tindwari. A chemical engineer by training from IIT Kanpur, he has been experimenting with organic farming since 1965 and training farmers in the region to do so as well.

He's published a book, 'Problems and Potential of Bundelkhand with Special Reference to Water Resource Base'. In this, he says, "Because of the uncertainty of water availability, people depend mostly on dryland farming."

In practice, this means that people maximize the use of rainwater in the absence of assured irrigation. They build bunds on their fields, the height varying from one to two metres, depending on the size of the field. They repair these every year, just before the monsoons. They use the kabar soil for the bunds because it holds water better than mar and makes stronger bunds. It rains heavily in July and August and the fields fill up water. This serves two purposes. One is to kill off weeds that cannot survive prolonged inundation. The other is to saturate the soil with water and recharge the groundwater tables.

Come October, farmers let out water from the fields in a very controlled way, field by field, so as not wash away the top soil or damage the fields. The bunds are broken in places so that the water drains away slowly. They plough and plant towards the end of the rains as the soil, otherwise hard and difficult to work, has softened. If they delay, the soil hardens and becomes impossible to work. As the fields empty of water, they plant their crops – paddy, coarse cereals and pulses. Paddy needs stagnant water, so this is grown while water is still standing in the fields. The others need less water, so are planted after the fields are drained.

"Traditionally, there was no Kharif crop, only a Rabi crop of wheat, gram or mustard, which used only the moisture in the soil. Later, people started growing rice and irrigating their fields with tanks or wells. In the last century, the British built a network of canals to encourage agriculture and generate more revenue. They were fine for a while but after independence, have slowly decayed. Now, they are every unreliable," says Professor Prakash.

Farmers are changing their cropping pattern. They are growing cash crops like soya. In the process, the bunding system is going the way of the region's economy. This will affect the water table, water quality and ultimately, the farmers because theirs is a subsistence economy where people grow enough for their own needs and a little more. Very few have large marketable surpluses.

The road from Attara to Panna, a town 75 kilometres east-south-east famous for its diamond mines, barely exists. You could call it a road for the first 30 kilometres while in Uttar Pradesh; once we cross into Madhya Pradesh, the road becomes a dirt track. Our jeep pitches and yaws as it growls past picturesque villages dotted with *talaabs*. We briefly hit the civilized national highway that connects Baandha to Satna further south, but all-too-soon turn off onto a 'state highway'.

The natural richness of Bundelkhand comes alive, in contrast to the poor condition of the road. The villages are smaller, usually a few huts scattered around a larger house. Nearly all houses here are wood or bamboo structures, topped with thatch. Most are small, single room dwellings though the larger families have managed to add rooms so the huts look large. A corner of the front room serves as the kitchen and the far corner, as the bedroom. A two-room dwelling would have the bedroom in the rear. The villages are as unstructured as Tendura. Nearly all have a source of water – well, tank or stream – that lets them grow at least a crop a year. People are out tending their fields, bent double in the mid-day sun. It's not hot, being December, but the sun is bright and manual labour is tough in any weather.

Landholdings are small, with two-thirds of the people owning less than two hectares of land. This is just about enough for a family of five to survive on, provided the rain gods smile. The people here are poor by any standards, rural or urban, clinging on to their land. Their poverty contrasts with the wealth with which nature has endowed the region. The more fortunate or educated leave for the nearest town or larger village in the hope of finding something better.

From the plains of Attara, the countryside gets rockier and hillier. We reach the ancient Bundelkhand capital of Kalinjar, now just a dusty town on the broken road, on the border between the two states. The Chandelas probably built the fortress atop the 300-metre high hill that dominates the town. After the Chandelas, no ruler held the fortress very long. The Afghan king Sher Shah Suri died here. Finally, the British managed to annex and hold Kalinjar.

My driver Ram Babu Sharma doubles as a guide. Pointing up the hill, he says, "There is an ambience about the place that lends itself to prayer. You must see the Neelkanth temple – it is beautiful."

The fortress is quite derelict, that I can see from the road. We press on, keen to get to our destination, the Gangau weir, before nightfall. I don't fancy being out there at night with dacoits and wild animals.

A little later, we pass Ajaigarh, another dusty fortress town. After that, the road starts a gentle climb. We rock from side to side as Ram Babu tries to find patches of tarmac. Eventually, he gives up and contents himself with driving on one side of the road. Two wheels are in a deep muddy rut that is smoother than the road and the other two wheels find the occasional patches of tarmac. Thus, sitting in a jeep inclined at 30 degrees to the vertical, we plod up the western end of the Vindyachal hills. In places, the Baandha canal runs along the road, carrying water to that town 100 kilometres to the north from the Gangau weir on the Ken river. Luckily for us, it hasn't rained or these 'roads' would be impassable. The dust swirls up behind us and settles on everything inside the jeep. Suresh in the back seat looks at home in these surroundings so I try to blend in too.

We enter the forests of Panna. These were the hunting grounds of the local raja of Panna, but he converted it into a reserve. It is now part of the Panna Tiger Reserve. The forests are all new-growth. Till the mid-18th century there were dense forests, according to district gazetteers. Then the British, who needed wood for their navy, railway network and industrial revolution, arrived and stripped the land of what they could find. The forests are dry deciduous, comprising of teak, saal, mahua, kahri, karaunda and bamboo, among other plants. Palash, or flame of the forest, is not in bloom so I don't get to see its startling reddish orange against the green of the trees.

One thing becomes clear very quickly. Where there are settlements, there are no forests. Where there are forests, there are no people. These are people who 'have lived for centuries in communion with nature' and 'depend on forests for their very livelihood'. I see little evidence that they look after the forests – there is more evidence that they decimate forests to meet their needs. True, the forest department and government policies are the reason these people feel they don't own forests anymore, and therefore need to plunder them. However, that does not justify their continued decimation of already scarce resources. It is like cutting the branch you're sitting on.

We climb a range of low hills, leaving the little villages and farms behind. The forests are denser here but again, new growth. These are the outskirts of the Panna National Park. The road is slightly better and we pick up a little speed. In the 60 kilometres so far, we have passed only a handful of vehicles. In the hills, we pass a couple of cyclists. From a few hundred feet up, the valley with the wooden huts, green farms and forests climbing up the hills looks picture-perfect. It's cool, despite the late afternoon sun's best attempts.

A clearing appears to the right and presents another pretty sight. There is an archway just off the road with the builder's name on top – an obscure seth from a bygone age. To the left is a small temple with a massive shivling inside; a banyan tree spreads its branches over it. Directly behind the archway is a square *kund*, lined with stones but not cemented, about 15 metres to a side. To the left of the *kund* is a well for drinking water; to the right is a tank that catches the overflow of the kund for animals. The underground water flows from the hill behind to the well, then to the *kund* and then into the animal-drinking area. There is a small building behind the *kund*.

Three armed policemen sit around the *kund*, making their evening meal. They are on duty in the middle of the forest in an operation to catch a dacoit who had kidnapped two men a couple of days before. It's reassuring to have the policemen around, disturbing to know we are in the lair of the bad guys. It wasn't for the bandits, the place would be serenity itself. This was obviously a sarai, or place for travelers to rest, as the crumbling walls around the kund and the well show. There were other buildings around where people could spend the night. All that's gone now, and just three policemen remain to guard an ancient monument.

Opposite the *kund* is a waterfall with a stone fence. It's blackened by years of water flowing over it. From there, the water runs into a ditch and thence into the river at the bottom of the valley. All this is seasonal – it's bone dry now. Even so, the high water level in the *kund* indicates an abundance of groundwater, even though there is little on the surface. We see no animals during the three hours we spend in the Panna National Park, even though it is supposed to have a healthy population of tigers, deer and larger mammals. I am disappointed and vow to return for a visit someday.

The access from Khajuraho is better than this.

Panna is the headquarters of the district. We come upon it suddenly, over a hill. It's a crowded small town, the distinction being that it was the centre of a princely state. We drive through town to the main *talaab* – Dharam *talaab*. This is pretty and large, covering around 40 hectares. Hills make up two sides, and the catchment, of the *talaab*. A wall, up which we climb to reach the *talaab*, makes up the third and fourth sides. Essentially, the wall impounds rainwater flowing down the hills and has created the *talaab*. It was built by the local raja who now lives in a splendidly decadent bungalow in town. The *talaab*'s benefits go almost exclusively to the new royalty, the district collector, who inherited the British-built house on the hill overlooking the *talaabs*.

The collector's house is to the east, in a small grove of trees. To its south is an old and decrepit palace similar to the funeral houses of the Bundelas that I have seen at Orchha. On the west bank, along the wall the created the *talaab*, is a small ugly modern temple. East of this is a tumbledown palace that might have the Panna king's pleasure palace; he could chill on the banks of the *talaab* with his favourite consort. In the middle of the *talaabs* is a building where, I am sure, the queen and her attendants would go to bathe. There is the inevitable tale of an underground tunnel from there to the palace in town.

A few swan-shaped paddle boats float on the *talaabs*. On the wall, where we stand, lie the remains of a mundan – a hair-shaving ceremony that is done on special occasions or when you lose a close relative. The graying hair probably belonged to somebody who has lost a dear one late in life. There are two stones facing each other, one where the barber sat and the other where the shaved one sat. The somber scene contrasts with the revelers on the boats, who paddle close on seeing me taking pictures, and shout 'photo, photo'.

I drive up to speak to her highness about the local water systems, but she is indisposed. Her house has an awesome collection of plants and ancient trees; the forests here must have been like this before the white man came.

"How can one be indisposed in such a beautiful place?" I ask the guard. Suresh pulls me away.

"Let's find the raja," he suggests.

Sharma has meanwhile found out where true royalty abides and we are soon honking rickshaws and cows out of the way in Panna. The main palace is a school that even at 4 PM has children. We walk through the royal cowsheds, full of healthy buffaloes and cows contentedly chewing the cud. The raja's descendant's bungalow appears beyond this.

It's nice, and bespeaks of glorious times long gone. An old Mercedes shares a four-car garage with a Maruti Esteem. Hollowed tree trunks double as pots with large hedges in them. We go through the gate mindless of the 'Beware of Dog' sign on it. An old woman is watering the garden – she is the housekeeper and must have been a sight when younger. Age and care have worn her down.

"We want to meet raja sahib," I tell her, introducing ourselves.

"He isn't here. You can speak to him on the phone," she says, looking at me steadily, inscrutably.

She takes us inside the bungalow. The verandah is separated from the garden by a series of low archways and its wall is decorated by another series of deer heads, again crumbling with age. The phone is an old dial-type – she slowly dials the man's number.

"What's raja sahib's name?" I ask.

"Lokendra Singh," she replies. "He was the MP from here till the last elections."

Seems his majesty is a lot of former things but a current nature-lover. A faded newspaper clipping on a pin board shows him being felicitated for making *talaabs*. He made five of them between 1977 and 1979 – the Virshingpur, Bhapatpur, Paddha, Mutwa and Katra *talaabs* in town. The Dharam *talaabs* predates Lokendra Singh's dynasty and is now looked after the public works department. Just shows what 'royal' patronage can achieve.

The road – it's actually a road now with more tarmac than potholes because it connects Khajuraho to Panna – leads us past the village of Rajgarh, with its accompanying *talaabs*, to our day's destination. This is the Gangau weir, built in 1906 by the British to divert the Ken river waters into a canal system. They did this to encourage farmers to grow cotton for their mills in Lancashire. They also did this to control this basic resource – once the weir was built, the quantity of water in the river fell and only certain crops were possible, at the behest of our imperial rulers. Farmers had to pay for water, where once they got it free. There wasn't enough in the river to satisfy their needs so they needed canal water to irrigate their fields. This situation remains persists till today.

The farmers I met en route, with fields along the canal, had one complaint.

"We never get water when we need it, only when the irrigation department feels like releasing it," said Manush Ram, a farmer in a village near Ajaigarh. "We grow one crop a year, usually paddy or sugarcane. If the rains have been good, we manage a second crop."

The cropping pattern in irrigated and non-irrigated areas seems to be the same. What is the point of irrigation then? It appears to be a backup for rain failure, but then, there will be less water in the river and consequently, less available for irrigation.

A board on the highway nearly opposite the turnoff to Khajuraho proclaims the Gangau weir. More ominously, it says, 'Site for proposed Dodhan dam'. Then there is another weir mentioned, the Rangawa bund. Gangau and Rangawa are about a century old. Dodhan is yet to be built – it's part of the Indian government's hair-brained scheme to link the country's rivers in order to solve the annual flood-drought problem. Through this fanciful and enormously expensive scheme, it hopes to transfer surplus water from one river to another via a network of canals. The first link is to come up in Bundelkhand between the Ken and the Betwa rivers, transferring water from the former to the latter. Only, the Ken is a smaller river and almost runs dry during the summer while the Betwa has plenty of water year round.

The road is narrow and hedges cover half of it, their thorns grazing the sides of the jeep and setting my teeth on edge. There is a barrier just before the Gangau weir and Sharma veers off to the right into the Panna forest – we were supposed to go straight to reach the dam. We return to the barrier and the man lets us through after a brief look inside. The road after this point becomes a stony track – it's all weather but narrow and bumpy. We ascend the plateau that lies on one side of the Gangau weir. The woods are lovely and deep and we have almost reached our destination, as evidenced by the distant sound of a water fall.

Cresting the hill, we see the weir. It's unimpressive. I thought it would be a high dam but it's actually a low, long wall built to divert water rather than hold it. It stretches in a broken line from one bank of the Ken to the other, topped by massive steel plates to regulate the flow of water. We drive down to a hut on the side of the weir and walk down to the top of the weir.

A group of men is repairing a breach caused in 2004 when flash floods washed away a part of the weir. They pour concrete to rebuild the wall, and then they will have to put the steel plates back up. The man in-charge, the junior engineer, is a young graduate called Rajiv Kumar.

"We haven't got enough money to fix all the damage," he says, pointing to another, lower wall downstream of the weir. "That also got damaged but we cannot fix it. We also cannot complete repairs on the main structure. This is a condemned structure as the irrigation department feels it has completed its service life."

"What do you mean, condemned? It looks fine." I say. The weir does look OK, minus the breach we are standing on.

"It's silted up," he says. "The original life was supposed to be a 100 years."

Sounds familiar. A weir built with our money by the British to serve their interests is declared extinct by our government to justify the construction of another monstrosity upstream. That Dodhan dam will inundate several villages and a part of the Panna National Park.

The Gangau weir is in UP, but controlled by the MP irrigation department. In 2002, there was a fight over release of water from the weir. Farmers from Baandha commandeered the weir and forced the people in-charge to release water to their fields, when they discovered that the MP irrigation department was diverting water to farmers in that state.

Rajiv yells to a man on the far side of the weir, "Send Bhajan Singh here."

That's the chowkidar. He is an unlikely chowkidar, at four-and-a-half feet, wizened and white. The thin man wouldn't be able to fight off a pet dog, let alone a bunch of irate farmers. He walks slowly towards us along the top of the weir.

Rajiv says, "He retired some years ago but my predecessor kept him on because he has no family and nowhere to go. He stays in the house above the weir all alone."

"Must be spooky," I ask Bhajan.

He doesn't hear me. Instead, he narrates the incident. "I got my orders from the office to release water to MP so I opened the gate. The farmers came at night and tied me up inside the house. Then they changed the flow themselves and went away. They didn't harm me but warned me not to change the flow of water.

"The night the weir broke, it was raining very heavily. I came out here to check that everything was OK. When I was walking back, I heard a loud noise and felt the weir shake. I ran and right behind me, the water washed the wall away."

Bhajan points to the place where we are standing. "I was there when I heard the noise and ran till that turn."

The turn is about 70 metres away and the wall looks safe enough there. About 30 metres below, water gushes out of a series of small outlets at the foot of the weir. Seems all the excitement in Bhajan's life happens at night in the middle of the desolation – there is no habitation for miles around. The nearest village is Dodhan, where the new dam is to come up, about 5 kilometres away. The barrier is further still.

Our side of the weir is thinly forested and extremely rocky. There are farms upstream, along the banks of the Ken, and forests on the far side. At this point, the river looks substantial but downstream of the weir, its flow is less. The river is clean enough to drink from here, and people in Dodhan draw water for their needs directly from the river. It's a small, harijan village, most houses made of adobe and stone and thatched. The lanes are swept and clean and the front courtyards, where social life is conducted, are neat. Two pretty women sift wheat from chaff and promptly cover their faces when I approach. Another one carries her load of water back from the river – two pots on the head and a bucket in one hand. The water probably weighs more than she does. A girl of nine or 10 follows her, baby on hip. A few cows graze inside a thorny enclosure. The village temple is a small, white dome, where children play. The bell is polished and occasionally, someone rings it loudly, more in play than prayer.

The people here aren't interested in standing and fighting. It's their ancestral land but if they get compensation, they will go. The village headman, Satish, says so emphatically.

"If we get adequate compensation, we will leave. Otherwise, we will stand and oppose the project."

It's surreal to imagine that this place could be under water in a few years. The forests, the farmland and the houses, under several feet of water for the next century.

None of the Chandela *talaabs* were built to inundate farmland, far less houses. They were always built by blocking a rivulet or drain, where they would be no habitation anyway and farming was strictly seasonal and controlled. The submerged land belonged to nobody. *Talaabs* were sited keeping villagers' needs and opinions in mind because they were to look after them. The ruler, or whoever paid to build the *talaabs*, ensured that the villagers contributed labour, for which they were paid, towards constructing the *talaabs*. The ruler laid down rules for sharing water, keeping the *talaabs* clean and the sort of agriculture permitted. He also decided how the *talaab*'s maintenance work and cost would be shared. These were inscribed on rocks that were built into the wall of the *talaabs*.

Typically, the process went like this. Villagers would approach their headman for a *talaabs* who would take it up with the local chief, either the king or his serf. Eventually, it would reach the king who would ask the chief engineer of the realm, or Vishwakarma, to survey and select the site. He would design the *talaab* walls in a way that would minimize submergence of farmland, in consultation with the villagers.

The king would pay for construction because many *talaabs* were built as part of drought- or famine-relief. In this way, people would get an assured source of water for the future and money so they would not starve.

The Chandela *talaabs* follow a typical style. The wall built to store water is made of stone and the black clayey soil of the region of is used to seal the cracks. This makes the wall fairly water-proof, though water seeps through a full *talaab*'s walls. Nobody minds this because it raises the underground water table and keeps fields around the *talaabs* moist.

The catchment area usually slopes towards the wall and used to be forested or hilly, so as to fill the *talaabs* quickly after rains. The *talaab*'s wall is faced with rock, not mud, where it faces the maximum impact of water, such as at the bottom of the rivulet. Some of the larger *talaabs* have walls that are entirely faced with rock – this solid construction ensured that the wall would withstand even torrential rainfall. Most of the walls are extremely thick, between 6 and 12 metres, and look like a low hill than a *talaab*'s wall, because they have become part of the landscape with large trees and other vegetation growing on them. These seem to strengthen, rather than weaken, the walls.

The stone facing of the walls serve a practical purpose. They are built in steps, albeit extremely steep and irregular, with platforms extending like Moses' hand onto the water. The daring can walk down to the water' edge to fish, wash clothes and bathe. All *talaabs* have shallower steps near the point of exit for the water so that people can easily get to the water for their needs.

These stone steps often have inscriptions such as found in temples, and religious figures. Nearly all the *talaabs* have at least one temple on their banks, and the larger ones have several. Traditionally, this meant that their water was pure but with migration and the population explosion, people increasingly use the *talaabs* are open air toilets – they shit and wash their asses in the same water, temple or no temple. Maybe the stone faced gods don't mind anymore – they have seen it all during the past millennia.

The Chandelas were voracious builders – temples, fortresses, palaces, and *talaabs*. The Madhya Pradesh irrigation department, under whose jurisdiction *talaabs* fall, lists 1094 of them in just two districts of Chatarpur and Tikamgarh. These are the two districts with the most tanks. Khajuraho is also in Chatarpur, and is another, more famous, tribute to the Chandela's building prowess.

The Chandelas built them, and dynasties down the ages including the British maintained them. But our government has forgotten about the Chandeli *talaabs*. It thinks they have outlived their utility. In just 10 years, *talaabs* that have been around for a 1,000 have gone from a valuable asset to a liability. In August 1988, the MP irrigation department drew up a Rs. 1,000 million plan to rehabilitate these tanks. That meant repairing the walls, deepening them and ensuring that the catchment areas were cleared or encroachments. It also included rebuilding irrigation canals in the *talaabs'* command areas.

R K Rawat, sub-engineer with the water resources department in Nowgong, a small town 23 kilometres from Chatarpur, says, "These tanks are all extinct. Their walls were made of stone and filled with clay that has washed away during the years. They cannot be repaired unless the walls are pulled down and rebuilt. It is simpler to build new structures."

That is really strange, coming from a man whose department just eight years ago prepared a project proposal to rehabilitate *talaabs*. How have 1,000 year old entities gone from being viable to extinct so soon. Maybe the Ken-Betwa link project holds answers to the Water Resources department's change of heart.

The project proposal says, "For tanks under control of the Water Resources Department, the improvement cost is Rs. 25,000 per hectare of irrigation capacity of the tank. For tanks under control of other agencies like Panchayats, Blocks and Zila Panchayats, the cost of restoration has been considered as Rs. 48,000 per hectare of irrigation potential. For the rest of the tanks which are to be considered for nistar (human) and water conservation purposes, the cost per tank is Rs. 600,000 per tank."

It goes on. In Tikamgarh, it would cost just Rs. 31,077 per hectare to restore 300 Chandela tanks. This would improve their utility for irrigation, water conservation and groundwater recharge. It is considerably less than the cost of new irrigation projects, that the department puts at Rs. 80,000 per hectare.

Clearly, looking after what we already have is a cheaper option. It doesn't suit the powers-that-be because there is much less money to be made here. Consider the cost of the Ken-Betwa link, that is Rs. 4.5 billion (at 1994 prices) and you get the picture. Restoring tanks would be a decentralized activity with lots of people making small pots of money. Building the link would be a centralized endeavour with few people making big bucks.

Bhagwan Singh Parmar used to work with the Rajiv Gandhi Drinking Water Mission as the officer in-charge of the Chatarpur district. He says he quit because he was an upright officer and could not handle the constant pressure for bribes by seniors. Bhagwan Singh now has his own NGO with an interesting agenda – to see how much farmland a family should have in order to meet all its needs. He owns about 5 acres of land on which he grows food, herbs and vegetables. He is just off the highway outside Nowgong. Any talk with him on any subject veers round to his uprightness in less than 10 minutes.

He has a different take for the decline of *talaabs*. "The rulers handed over care of the *talaabs* to the local *zamindar*. It stayed like this for generations and as long as the dynasty survived, the *talaabs* also did. Once their power waned, the *zamindar*s appropriated the *talaabs* and usually demolished them to take over the land, which was fertile. In those days nobody could challenge the *zamindar*. Many tanks were destroyed like this."

If *zamindar*s destroyed some *talaabs*, the Chandelas must have built many more than survive around today. Bhagwan Singh takes me to the Jagat Sagar, an enormous *talaab* outside Mau Ranipur, about 40 kilometres from Nowgong on the road to Jhansi. It is a good road, because it connects to Khajuraho. The land is flat, so the *talaab*'s catchment is vast and open, with fields on the farthest southern fringe. It spreads over 103 hectares but hasn't got much water because of poor rains since 2004. The wall, running about 2 kilometres from east to west, built to create Jagat Sagar, has several temples and palaces along its length. At the western end are new, garish temples dedicated to Ram, Hanuman and Shiva. In the middle stands one to Shani, or Saturn. Behind the wall to the north is a sun temple – one of the few in India.

Bhagwan Singh narrates the legend of Jagat Sagar. "The king who renovated the *talaab* was so proud of his work that he decided to make temples to all the gods. This created such a commotion that they descended to earth to dissuade him. The king contented himself with just these two temples – to Shani and Surya. The rest have been built later."

Chatarpur is named after Maharaj Chatrasal, whose descendant Maharaj Jagat Raj ordered the *talaab* deepened and widened. The *talaab* is probably many centuries old, what with Jain inscriptions on its stone steps. The Jain monks who lived here then must have made themselves a small pond. The Chandelas enlarged it and later rulers kept adding to it. Going east on the *talaab*'s wall, I see temples to several deities, including a hall of 64 pillars. The history of the *talaab* is there for see, in bits and pieces, along its length and embedded in its walls.

An old and somewhat demented baba stays there now, living off whatever people choose to leave him and firewood from the many trees in the place. He is a sight, with a flowing white beard and mane, and a g-string that would make Rakhi Sawant blush.

Just opposite this place are shallow steps with engravings that lead down to the water. A few women and children bathe and wash their clothes in the relatively clean water. On the top of the wall here, a small whitewashed temple with a very black shivling stands guard. Next to it is a large stone carved with apsaras in erotic poses. It is completely out of place, as it somebody has placed it there.

Suresh says, "There are supposed to be many more stones like these in the water. Nobody knows how old these are or how they got there."

They are probably the remains of an old Jain temple, parts of which were used to make the *talaabs*.

Beyond the temple, the stone facing of the *talaabs*, built in steps, leads steeply down to the water to the west and east. The entire wall, up to the palace, has this surface so that it can withstand the sudden rush of rainwater and all of it is in intact. The wall itself is massive, about 12 metres thick, and looks more like a ridge – a centuries-old banyan tree is proof of its age. Just to build another of this size would cost hundreds of millions of rupees. Excavating it would cost a few hundreds of thousands.

We walk eastwards. Bhagwan Singh says, "This is a hanuman temple, about 2,000 years old."

It certainly looks old, but his figure is incredible. Beyond this are the remains of a palace.

"That is the maharani's palace. She used to come here to bathe," he says. A full building just for bathing. It made of thin bricks, heavily weathered by the centuries.

At the moment, a poor woman is using the facilities, such as they are, to bathe and wash her clothes. Her parrot green cotton sari, draped over the bushes that lead from the palace to the water's edge, flutters in the breeze. Just beyond the remains of the palace stands a majestic banyan tree family – parents and children 'walk' in all directions just beyond the exit of the palace. A cool breeze comes off the *talaab* seducing me to sleep in the shade of the banyan tree.

Jagat Sagar can hold enough water to irrigate fields up to 10 kilometres away through its canals for three consecutive years without any rainfall. At the moment, it has only a few feet of water – a fisherman walks behind his boat, trailing a net, to catch what he can while another paddles some distance away. The *talaab* is vital to the hydrology of the area as it maintains the water tables in the region. It keeps the wells and handpumps full. If it runs dry, the entire Mau region will face a water problem.

This *talaab* is part of a larger system of *talaabs* in the Mau Ranipur region. It collects water from its own catchment as well as the overflow from the Sahaniya and Gora *talaabs*. Gora *talaab* is about 8 kilometres west of Jagat Sagar. Between the Sahaniya *talaab* and Jagat sagar, on a hill, is a palace that belonged to Mastani, one of the mistresses of Baji Rao Peshwa. It was probably a later ruler who built the wall that created the Sahaniya *talaab* because a palace – now a museum, abuts it. The palace is to the east of the *talaab* and its main catchment, a forested hill, is to the north-west. Across the *talaab* to the west are other palaces that Chatrasal supposedly built. One is an imposing multi-storeyed building atop a mound commanding a view of the entire countryside for miles around.

Entering it, I see a beautifully painted chamber with a raised platform. The place is a maze.

Bhagwan Singh says, "There is a labyrinth. If you go up one way, you cannot come down the same way."

Sure enough, the upper floors – I cannot figure what number it is – have stairs and passages going every which way. The way to the dome is through a door that leads into an open space, then a sharp left and up some stairs. I decide to pass but the others venture up. There is enough inside to keep me occupied. Next to this building is a small domed structure painted startlingly white against the blue-green background, its dome embedded with coloured tiles: The place where King Chatrasal supposedly disappeared, or attained Samadhi.

Outside the multi-storeyed palace, a group of labourers mix lime mortar in the old-fashioned way. A huge millstone stands in a circular depression in the ground, with a thick wooden rod through a hole in its middle. One end of the rod is tied to a post and the other to the back of a tractor. Lime bubbles in a tub nearby and is gingerly poured into the depression by a man without any protection. Others add gravel and stone in a ratio of 1:4:4. The tractor starts up and drives around in circles, grinding the mortar together. When done, they shovel it onto a wooden basket and cart it off to the palace, which they are fixing.

We drive to Gora talaab, a short distance away. The road does the usual disappearing act as we approach a Raikwad-dominated village called Todna. They still pursue their traditional vocation as the *talaabs* holds plenty of water. Half-way through the village, a high concrete road appears, and disappears before the end of the village. A group of pretty women do their evening washing by one of the village handpumps. They quickly retreat as the jeep approaches, and return when we are past – most were topless. Todna is more organized than others I have seen with houses along straight lanes. The houses are better built even though they are not brick and mortar constructions.

Gora *talaab* is the largest of the three. It has the Chandela stamp – stone-faced walls built between two hills to block a large rivulet. The wall is massive, at least 30 metres high. In the middle of the wall is a sluice gate, a later addition, that controls the exit of water into a 25-kilometre long canal system to irrigate many hundred hectares of land. The stone facing admittedly looks like steps, but only goats venture down in search of the odd plant and water. Near the gate, the stones are too steep for human beings to walk down – they are more negotiable further out.

From a vantage point to the north of gate, next to the inevitable temple, I get a panoramic view of the *talaab*. On the far side, there are yellow fields of mustard, grown on the bed of the *talaab* as the water level dips. Trees way beyond the fields indicate the far bank – they are almost too far to see. It is nearly 500 metres across the water to the other side and the *talaab* is about 2½ kilometres long from Todna village to the hills at the other end. The *talaab* is only about a quarter full because the rains haven't been good since 2004.

"When this is full, you cannot see the far side," says Suresh.

A platform halfway down the steps lets me stand over the water and gaze down into its blue depths. In a year of good rainfall, the water reaches the platform but now it's about 3 metres above the water. Here again, I see stones with religious figures carved into them – apsaras, serpents and bulls. The water is amazingly clear and I can see the plants growing on the bottom. A few youth fish, unsuccessfully.

Their village is up the hill a little way and their fields over the embankment. I return to the top of the embankment and cross to the other side. Water gushes from an opening at the bottom, controlled by the sluice gate, into a cemented canal that runs straight as far as I can see.

Right outside the gate, people have set up fishing nets. These are triangular, with one side under water and the other two propped up like a tent. The lower side is weighed with stones. The nets are arranged in V-formation behind each other so that no fish can swim through. They are all empty – Suresh says they may catch something by morning.

The canal is flanked by lush fields, green with newly-sown crops. There are orchards here as well. The Gora talaab ensures that farmers in the command area do not want for water. The thump of tubewells irrigating the fields from groundwater, kept high by the *talaab*, reverberates off the hill behind me.

The irrigation department is supposed to look after Gora talaab while the Mau municipality has charge for Jagat Sagar and Sahaniya talaabs. Jagat Sagar is the best kept of the lot though the other two aren't badly off either. However, siltation remains a problem with all three, as indeed with all the *talaabs* in Bundelkhand. This is because rainfall is torrential and rainwater carries a lot of topsoil away with it. This usually washes up into a *talaabs* and has to be dredged every few years, else they will silt up. The agencies that are supposed to maintain the *talaabs* don't do so, pleading a shortage of funds.

We return to the museum on Sahaniya talaab. It has a magnificent collection of sculptures gathered from the bed of the various ponds around. There are stone carvings of gods and goddesses dating to the Chandelas and some even further back. The more recent exhibits have to do with the guns, clothes and armour of Chatrasal.

Dr. A. L. Pathak is the curator in-charge of this treasure trove at the Majaraja Chatrasal museum, Dhubela, Chatarpur. He has been there for years and loves 'his sculptures' as he calls these priceless items. The museum is basic and has a Rs. 2 entry fee. Sadly, I think, it's so inaccessible and unmarked that even tourists en route Khajuraho, for whom this falls on the way, won't stop to see these incredible pieces of our heritage.

Sitting in the lawn, he says, "Most of the Chandeli *talaabs*, as these are called, were made in the Khajuraho-Mahoba-Bandha region between 900 and 1200 AD. The rulers kept a ratio of one *talaabs* for every village though local people built their own so the ratio was higher. Some of the *talaabs* date even further back, and were probably built by the Jain monks who lived here so that they could meditate in peace. The Chandelas renovated and enlarged most of them."

This part of India was densely forested till a few centuries ago. It must have made an ideal getaway for monks and other seeking spiritual peace, and who didn't want to do all the way to the Himalayas.

Dr. Pathak continues. "Now, they have mostly silted up. This has reduced their capacity to store water to the extent that they overflow after just two or three days of heavy rain. They dry up much faster as well."

The crying need is to desilt them. It's impossible to build new *talaabs* because there isn't any land left and anyhow, making new ones will be very expensive. Even the water resources department's proposal says so.

Urmil is a small river that rises in the Bijawar hills and joins the Ken after about a 100 kilometres. It has been dammed about 20 kilometres from

Nowgong on the road north-east to Mahoba. The dam is low built on a flat plain. It takes advantage of the slope of the land and encircles a large tract of water with its two arms. It's like a lake, the far end shrouded in the haze that rises from the water. People mine sand and farm on the bed of the lake. The dam's gates are closed. The control room is locked. A sign on the side says "Urmil dam is Mahoba's largest source of water". It's a new dam, completed in 1993 at a cost of about Rs. 360 million. Water flows from two canals, one on either side of the dam, to Mahoba town about 30 kilometres to the north-east.

Mahoba would not have needed this dam's water. It has a few *talaabs* of its own – Khetri talaab and Madan sagar. Mahoba was part of Chatrasal's kingdom and a part of the earlier Chandela empire as well. It is said to have been founded then and the remains of Khajuraho-style temple in the middle of Madan sagar testifies to this. It was well-endowed with water resources, till a few decades ago. The usual drama of neglect, decline and greed played out here. They neglected their ancient resources, that decayed. Rather than reviving these *talaabs*, the government opted to build the Urmil dam and channel water from there because there was more money to be made. The situation is worse for people in Mahoba because farmers along the way extract water from the open canals that pass by their fields; the town's water supply suffers.

Khetri taal, as it's called, is a dead pond. In its heyday, it would have covered an impressive 150 hectares. It now smells of sewage and water covers less than 20 hectares. It's an open air toilet, temples and idols notwithstanding. Khetri taal is silted up right to the top of its wall. The headless torso of a polished black granite figurine sits guard under a small peepul tree on the wall. There is the shrine to the taal under a Banyan tree but it's not been potent enough to halt Khetri taal's decline.

The other one has fared better, but only just. Madan sagar is a serpentine body of water. It's impossible to tell where it starts and ends because there are houses all over it. It seems that settlements have come up on the *talaab*'s drying bed and divided it into small stretches of water. The largest one still meets part of Mahoba's water needs; the smaller ones breed mosquitoes under a thick carpet of water hyacinth. They are convenient toilets for the houses that have sprung up along their sides.

The most impressive of the *talaabs* near Mahoba, and the best kept, is Vijay sagar. This bears the marks of Chandeli architecture. Vijay talaab is in good shape because it's a bird sanctuary with a tourist complex inside. It's 4 kilometres outside Mahoba on the road to Baandha. The wall that created the *talaab* stretches between two hills across a ravine. The water is clean and the *talaab* covers about 250 hectares. A few migratory birds float on the water but otherwise, all is calm.

In the forest nearby is an old Chandela fort, re-affirming those ancient's affinity for water. A nursery with saplings of local trees completes the scene. A few families lounge around and couples find secluded places on Vijay sagar's wall to cuddle up.

I find a remarkable sketch on the toilet's wall. It's a diagram of the panchwati tree plan. The translation is roughly – 'Peepul, Bel, Bargad, Amla and Ashok are the five trees of panchwati. They need to be grown in five directions (as indicated in the diagram). The Peepul should be planted to the west, the Bel to the north, Bargad to the east and Amla to the south. The Ashok should be to the south-west. All trees should be 10 metre from the centre. In this manner, if a man plants Peepul, Pomegranate, Mango, Chameli and Bargad trees, he is assured of a place in heaven'.

This just underlines the status of trees, water and earth in our culture. A lot of this has sadly fallen by the way.

The Chandelas were the main *talaab* builders, but not the only ones. Much later, in the 16th century, Baji Rao Peshwa from Pune came to the aid of Chatrasal against the Mughals. They defeated the Mughals and Chatrasal gave Peshwa a large part of his kingdom as tribute. Baji Rao's eye fell on Mastani, the comely daughter of one of Chatrasal's servants and he took her for his mistress. In return, the Peshwa ordered the construction of tanks at Baandha, one of which still thrives today. It's variously called the Nawab tank or Shankar tank. It is deep and covers about 6 hectares. Nawab tank is fed by the Ken River and it's never dried up in its history. The surroundings have been designed for different purposes – one side towards the forest has a slope where horses can drink; next to that is a place for washing clothes; there are steps for bathing where some privacy is assured; and finally, there is the inevitable temple.

My driver Sharma entertains me on the drive back to Attara from Baandha. The jeep's tape recorder runs fast, so the male singer sounds feminine. In the local Bundeli dialect, the pedestrian poetry sounds sweet. As we hurtle down the highway dodging rickshaws, the tape recorder belts out an ode from a rickshaw puller to a city girl – urban butterfly – taking a ride with him.

The water from most *talaabs* Bundelkhand was used for human consumption, mainly bathing and washing. Wells provided drinking water. Agriculture was entirely rain fed because of the effort involved in lifting *talaabs* water to the fields. The *talaabs* started to be used for irrigation only after Bundelkhand became part of the British Empire in the early 19th century. Water became a source of revenue and the Crown appropriated all water sources and its distribution. They did look after the *talaabs* but community involvement in *talaabs* maintenance dwindled, till in the 1970s, it faded away altogether.

Suresh attributes this to the advent of the handpump. "Individual sources of water replaced communal ones such as *talaabs*. Families or communities can own handpumps. Only communities own *talaabs*. Handpumps have made it easier to extract water. They have taken people away from *talaabs*. Even though *talaabs* are vital to the handpumps' success, by maintaining the water table, people seldom make the connection and let the *talaabs* go to seed."

The result is dry handpumps and wells. Then people sink tubewells to tap deeper aquifers. That works for a while till the water table falls and tubewells have to be re-bored. This has been happening across the region, as indeed across India. The Green Revolution is partly to blame because all the so-called high yielding varieties need large amounts of water, pesticides and fertilizers to deliver.

Revolutions have passed Bundelkhand by, maybe because of poverty and maybe because it is such a backwaters. After the last round of wars with the Mughals, the place has been passed over by successive governments.

Bundelkhand maybe a poor region, measured by modern standards. It is a crime-infested, dacoit-ridden region that development has overlooked. If it was not for Khajuraho, it would not exist in India's consciousness. Murders, rapes and kidnappings do not even make news here anymore. People attribute this 'jungle raj' to UP Chief minister Mulayam Singh's penchant for appointing Yadavs to every conceivable post – state civil service, the constabulary and in local governance. They thrive on crime, doing nothing to rid the place of it. The people are resigned to it.

There aren't any big dams to raise the green lobby's hackles. The national media goes as far as Allahabad but not into the badlands of western UP or eastern MP.

But Bundelkhand has lessons on local resource management for everybody. A case in point is the Urmil dam. Mahoba had its own rich and diverse sources of water – tanks and a seasonal river. These went to seed, under the greed of colonizers, migrants who needed accommodation and the familiar apathetic bureaucracy. The one tank that survives and still does its job, though rather poorly, is on the verge of disappearing under buildings. In their place, a modern dam on the Urmil river conveys a precarious supply of water to the town. Farmers downstream of the dam who used to irrigate crops from the river, now suck water from canals.

The result is that neither gets enough. Urmil is a small river and can barely meet the needs of people living along it, far less those of a town.

The answer would have been to desilt and rehabilitate Mahoba's tanks that together can supply enough water to the town even if the rains fail for a year or two. The groundwater situation is iffy but tanks store a known amount of water, that is available year round.

Then there is the question of cost. The Urmil dam cost Rs. 360 million. It would have cost a tenth of that to desilt and restore Mahoba's two tanks.

This folly is the result of bureaucratic and political greed. Government officials and politicians make money off large projects such as dams. Small projects such as rehabilitating tanks do not yield as much even though there are thousands of tanks in the region and reviving them could become a project worth thousands of millions of rupees.

Now, the government looks set magnify compound this stupidity by building the Ken-Betwa link canal. Instead of spending Rs. 1,000 million to renovate *talaabs*, it will spend Rs. 4.5 billion or 4.5 times the amount in order to create additional irrigation that the region does not need. It will displace 8,500 people and submerge a part of the Panna Reserve Forest, as well as fertile fields. The project will transfer 'surplus' water from the Ken to the Betwa River.

There are several problems with this. There is no surplus water in the Ken. The project is based on the premise that people grow a single crop in the Ken's catchment. That is true because traditional agriculture here involved growing just the single rain fed crop; farmers grew a second one only if they had good rains or were near a source of water. If, as Bharti, a former Zila Panchayat member from Baandha, says, "Farmers here start growing a second crop, there will not be any surplus water in the Ken".

Standing on a bridge outside Baandha, over the Ken River, it is easy to see where the surplus lies. Donkeys cross the river in summer laden with stones. A man crossing the river at the same goes down into the water to his hips.

"Where is the surplus?" asks Bharti.

Some 230 kilometres to the west, the swollen Betwa slides past the silent funeral palaces of the Bundela Rajputs near Orchha. The river is full of water, impossible to cross on foot. It is one of the major rivers of Bundelkhand. Where is the surplus, where the deficit, I wonder, standing on a sandy bank of the Betwa looking across at the Orchha palaces.

The project will not reduce floods or droughts. Both the rivers rise in the same range of hills and flow through the same part of the country. They both join the Yamuna at different points; the Betwa joins upstream of the Ken. When there are floods in one, there are floods in the other. So also with drought. What will happen after the link is built, explains Dr. Prakash, is that there will be perennial floods in the Yamuna between the mouths of the Betwa and the Ken and water shortages downstream. The Betwa will always have excess water and the Ken will be always short of it. The excess water will flood the plains between the rivers, and flow back up the Ken for a short distance. Downstream of the Ken on the Yamuna, villages will face water problems.

That is not considering what people in Chatarpur, Mahoba, Baandha and other towns will face. The Ken is their lifeline. Diverting water from this already deficient river will deprive them of an already tenuous source of water. In addition, the land slopes from south to north. The canal connecting the two rivers will go from east to west, intersecting the land and cutting the natural flow of water.

Land to the south will be waterlogged and to the north will be short of water. The canal is to be a large affair, like a small river. It will disrupt the natural drainage of the entire region.

In short, the Ken-Betwa Link project will be a social and ecological disaster larger than the Narmada or Tehri dams.

The solution to Bundelkhand's water problems is simple. Renovate the *talaabs*, clear their catchments and enhance their command areas. Remove the encroachments from around the *talaabs* in cities and towns. Deepen them and strengthen their walls – without having to rebuild them – so they can hold more water. It is unlikely, the predictions of the Mr. Pathak notwithstanding, that the walls will break if the tanks are dredged. As Dhan Foundation has done in Madurai, create water users associations that map onto the gram sabhas of yore. These associations should be handed charge of looking after their *talaabs*.

Just for a few rupees more, Bundelkhand can change from a crime-infested backwaters into a region that truly reflects the glory of Khajuraho. It won't be empty talk of India's glorious heritage then, it will be talk backed by full *talaabs*.

10 CONCLUSION: LITTLE DROPS DO INDEED MAKE A MIGHTY OCEAN

It's come home to me from the length and breadth of India that traditional wisdom is indeed, well, wise. Our farmers, yes those we 'literate urban Indians' call ignorant peasants, know a lot more about living with nature than any of us in cities ever could. The tragedy of traditional wisdom is that it's not taught in schools. Rather, we are taught that modern science holds the key to all of humankind's problems, from disease to water shortages, and traditional wisdom is all old women's tales.

While not belittling the contributions of science – we do live longer than a few decades ago, but whether we are healthier is debatable – to our lives, traditional wisdom needs to get back its place. For too long, the western paradigm of education has taught to forget ourselves and place too great an emphasis on science and technology. Most of what we have got are rejects from overseas – their polluting chemical factories, construction industry that insists big dams are an omnibus solution for power and water, nuclear industry that claims it will reduce global warming and the problem of waste disposal, private water utilities that claim to deliver quality services at a fraction of current costs. The list is long and keeps getting longer.

Home truths aren't comfortable. For a bureaucrat or politician, the lure of an Rs. 10,000 million contract to build a big dam is more attractive than that of 10,000 contracts of Rs. 1 million each to reconstruct old tanks. It's easier to extort from one source than from 10,000. Because people will be more vigilant in this case, the projects being closer to home. A large project's financials are seldom scrutinized closely to monitor bribes because they are built to satisfy the needs of a distant populace. Smaller projects are scanned more carefully because local people assume they are for their good and want to know how the money is being spent – it is money for their development that goes into these projects and they are beginning to

189

demand accountability.

Education is one reason, interest by the international community is another. Too many times in my travels, I came across the term "Water Users Associations". It's a term coined by the World Bank and works like this. The Bank gives a loan to a state government to improve water supply. In return, the state irrigation department, not the elected local government entities such as Panchayats mind you, sets up WUAs to manage these 'improved' water resources. A WUA comprises selected people from a village who form a trust or society. They are responsible for collecting water charges from users in their village and maintaining the water distribution network there. The WUA gets a little money from the government, that ultimately comes from the World Bank, for maintenance. The WUA's charges also partly cover the cost of maintenance. So far, so good.

In reality, WUAs are an exclusionary structure. Just as any non-government organization has a core group of members, so does a WUA. The rest of the villagers are simply excluded. It is not representative of the village. WUA members are not accountable to the rest, only to the government. It is an exclusive parallel power structure controlling an important community resource; WUAs can disconnect water supply to a part of the village that is not paying its dues. Far from encouraging people's participation in water supply, WUAs pushes the poor, Dalits and Tribals further into a corner.

The Bank-funded water supply scheme brings water up the village through a pipeline, usually built at enormous expense, from some distant river or lake. Again, this is built with a World Bank loan. The project dispossesses the locals of their land and water, to satisfy people elsewhere – it is inequitable and unsustainable. Inequitable because it encourages recipients to waste water, and denies people at the source of their local resource. Unsustainable because the transport of a basic resource such as water over a long distance entails large costs and people living along the pipeline tap into it at will. This defeats the basic purpose of making the pipeline, increases 'transmission losses' and further encourages wastage. The water supply becomes iffy and contaminated. It becomes a political issue and the government seldom takes action against the line tappers.

WUAs have become the new buzzword for people-centred water resource management. But that's clearly not the case.

People-centred water resource management has to start from local water resource development, not with building a project a long distance away, supplying water to people through pipes at the cost of safeguarding and rehabilitating local water resources. In Rajasthan, the Swajal Yojna under which all this is being done has nothing to do with restoring *tankas* and *johads*. It has everything to do laying pipes along roads from where WUAs take over. All the villages I saw this operating had slushy streets where water overflows from the storage tanks. A new source of filth and disease. The ease of getting water out of a tap dispels native caution over wasting a precious thing.

It also commodifies water. It's hard to price the water in a *johad*, tank or *tanka* that is owned and used by a few hundred people. It's much easier to price water coming out of a tap – so many rupees for so many litres. This is vital in cities so that the urban rich, who have water connections and pay shit-all for the water they use, appreciate its cost. They use water exclusively for domestic consumption – bathing, cooking, washing, watering lawns and washing cars – and industrial use. They can afford to pay several times what they are doing now, an absurd amount of a maximum of Rs. 4.50 for 1,000 litres. In any case a lot of this water goes to flush loos and indulgent showers. In any case, the urban rich has to learn how to use a precious, sacred resource with some respect – the only thing they respect is money so charging 1,000 times more for urban water supply may be the only way they will learn.

From commodification flows privatization. WUAs are at the vanguard of this movement to transfer control of water resources from communities and the government to private enterprise. This is another reason why traditional wisdom is equated with old wives tales, and our wealth of water conservation techniques is being squandered by the government and the very people it has served for millennia. It is impossible for a single private entity to control the myriad lakes and ponds built and looked after by communities. It is simpler to get the World Bank to loan money to the Indian government for laying pipelines to villages. Then to say that water supply and irrigation departments are inefficient and corrupt. Then put the control of these pipelines in private hands in the interests of efficiency, transparency and good governance – the private company was after all chosen after an open bidding process (who promised the most slush money).

Our own irrigation and water supply departments, under pressure to reform (a euphemism for structural adjustment) have stopped recruiting. Their response to complaints, glacial at the best of times, is now all but frozen. Save for a few pockets here and there, both have become synonymous with sloth and sleaze. The government has deliberately driven both into the ground in order to justify privatization of water. Once, these departments were charged with looking after traditional water harvesting structures. They never got the manpower or funds needed to do a good job but at least occasionally got around to doing their working. When they are gone, who will maintain the *tankas*, tanks, *johads*, *shyngiar*, *bunds*, *eris*, *dharas*, *talais*, *baolis*, *gharats*, *wavs* …. It's a long list. I don't see any private company evincing interest in maintaining these diverse water harvesting structures.

For one, each needs its own technique, not technology or science. They are low-tech, but scientific, systems. Only, they haven't been studied as such because they span several scientific disciplines – geology, hydrology, soil science, meteorology, geography and above all, social sciences. A johad is invariably built where villagers have observed rainwater flows and accumulates. It is built with the minimum of material, locally available, and minimal submergence of land. A *tanka* needs more specialized skills and building material. But communities do not view their water harvesting structures as bits and pieces of a puzzle – is it a geological question, a meteorological problem, or what. They view them as a composite, an entity whose form, structure and siting depends on observation and experience of what has worked, and what hasn't. In many cases, communities have asked for a structure to be built a particular location. When it's failed to deliver, they have accepted their failure and constructed another at a more suitable location without fuss. Unlike the government that, when faced with popular opposition and solid evidence of future environmental disasters, persists with its idiotic projects.

We accumulated a vast wealth of knowledge on water harvesting and with it, the skills to maintain this amazing variety of techniques and structures. Using local technology had tremendous advantages in that whatever was built using it could be repaired locally. The *gharats* in Uttarakhand, for example, were built entirely of wood and stone. The huts they were housed in were stone and thatch. Carpenters made the parts of the water wheel and another expert craftsman assembled the *gharat*. If the contraption was destroyed in a flood, as they often were during the rains, the entire village got together and made a new one. The community saw value in the structure – it was used for grinding grain and ginning – and chipped in when needed to renew it. They knew how to and had the materials at hand to do so. The improved *gharats* do not have this advantage – their steel parts have to be sourced from hundreds of kilometers away and are much more expensive.

It isn't just water harvesting and storage, it is an entire way or life. Traditional water structures have engendered communal togetherness. They are open, welcoming structures – compare a tranquil pond to the almost phallic thrust of a tap that pokes out of the earth. People gather around one to relax and swap tales of the day. They gather around the other merely to collect water. One promotes social intercourse, the other functional assembly. Going further, one becomes the centre of social life. The other remains a source of water, nothing more.

The fact that villagers have built and maintained their own structures means that they have a stake in keeping them for posterity. The water is there, they know where it comes from and how safe it is to drink or use for other purposes. Water out of a tap or handpump is more mysterious and while people assume it's safe because if comes out of something – it's not open to contamination, as 'experts' would have them believe – it is seldom the case. I am not making out that all water from traditional water systems is safe to drink – they are not. But traditional water systems were governed by norms that ensured that people didn't shit or piss near them, or animals didn't contaminate the water. Water for human and animal consumption was kept separate meticulously, as in the *johads* of Shekhawati or the *dharas* of Uttarakhand. This ensured that drinking water was reasonably clean.

On the other hand, pipes for water supply run for hundreds of kilometers from a source to consumers. En route, they are broken to be tapped, and pass through dirty drains and sewers. This is one mystery of piped water supply in India – all pipes run along or inside drains and sewers. Given the skills of our public health engineering department engineers, the water in the pipe leaks and suction draws in the muck from the drain or sewer. This contaminates water supply and causes diseases – from a supposedly safe water supply. The modern systems are no safer than traditional ones. In fact, they are less so because maintenance of the mains is nobody's baby. A distant donor least interested in safety once the system has been installed is the least effective guarantee that piped water supply will be safe. Time and again, newspapers report the coliform count in municipal water is above safe limits. Because the pipes pass through filth to reach consumers.

Traditional water systems were equitable, by and large. We have all read stories of how Harijans were denied water from wells owned by *zamindars*. The *zamindars* exploited Harijans and everybody else in the village and grew fat. They were despots, and none too benevolent. But even in those trying times, everybody had access to water and natural resources. There were more forests before the British logged them for their industrial revolution and railways. There were more water sources as well. Villages typically had more than one well and everybody got their share of water, even if they had to wait. Things haven't improved in recent decades – women have to walk longer distances for water and firewood, which they didn't have to do earlier. The poorer she is, the longer she walks. In the earlier scheme of things, the poorer she was, she longer she waited for water – till the upper castes finished their business.

The larger structures were less divisive as their size allowed many people to use them at once. It was also possible to sink wells around them for different castes so that everybody had their own source of drinking water – this avoided conflict.

Our colonial masters played the divide and rule game to perfection. It wasn't enough to divide communities and castes. They separated people from their natural resources. They separated natural resources into sections that could be commodified. Then they separated the natural resources from the country.

The British appropriated water, forests and land and made all three charges of the crown, where they had been under control of communities since civilization began. Then they allotted one resource to a department – irrigation, forest or revenue – to extract money. The sole motive was profit, not maintenance. Each department was run to make money. The only way they had to make money was to price the resources in their control. Forests were auctioned. Villagers were charged for water. Individuals were taxed on their produce. In the process, cohesive village republics fell apart.

After independence, our very own government did nothing to alter this state of affairs. Rather, it perfected the art of doing nothing, not even discharging obligatory maintenance functions. The decline of natural resources that started under the white masters accelerated under the brown ones.

Ironically, this process goes hand in hand with the increasing expectation of people that 'the government will provide'. For everything, 'the government will provide' has become the excuse for sitting back and waiting. Deprived of their resources, and rights over forests and water, people too have stepped back and expect their new masters to provide. Forests, water and land – all three have gone to seed extremely quickly. The government doesn't provide for the people. The alienation between land, water and people is complete.

People see this and say, "Well, this money is for our development, so let it do its job", quite forgetting that they have a role to play as vigilantes to ensure that the money for their development does indeed do its job. Between development, illiteracy and popular sloth, the politician-bureaucrat-contractor nexus makes hay. Where illiterate people have demanded accountability, things have happened. Where literate people have been vigilant, development has taken place. That is why our rulers do not like to be questioned – literacy and an active public question them. They get answers that are inconvenient to politicians. But they are an important step forward towards saving what little natural resources are left in India.

The government plays the cat between two monkeys all the time. It gives a fat cake to the businessmen-politician-bureaucrat monkey in the shape of large projects. It then gives another cake, admittedly smaller, to NGOs and community-based organizations in the shape of small projects. Then it nibbles first at one and then at the other till there isn't much left in the public cake, but a substantial amount in the large project cake. Too late, the public realizes that small projects are just an eyewash.

The government also plays the game of withdrawal in the guise of inefficiency. It makes its departments so inefficient, short-staffed and starved of funds that it cannot function. Take any government department – education, water, police. They are all so short of funds and manpower that none can perform what it is supposed to. Each has become inefficient and the staff left feel it's more worth their while to make money while they can, rather than work. This gives the government's consultants and donors ample reason to yell, 'privatise'.

First it throttles, then withdraws, and finally, privatizes. The state is slowly and surely abdicating responsibility on one front after another in favour of private enterprise. We don't need 'East India Companies' – that great bogey of those opposed to privatization. We have enough powerful Indian companies, thank you. The river in Chhattisgarh was leased to an Indian company, not a foreign one. However, the water supply systems in Delhi and Chennai have been partly handed over to multinationals. Maybe they will do a better job of making people appreciate the true value of water, even though the urban poor will be collateral casualties in their 'education campaign'.

India's cities have become enormous water sinks. They require ever-increasing quantities of water and do nothing to produce their own. Expensive projects like the Tehri dam in Uttarakhand come up to cater to urban India's needs. People living a few kilometers from the dam continue to depend on streams and an increasingly uncertain piped water supply. They get no benefits from the dam. Riparian states play spoilsport – Uttar Pradesh arbitrarily decides that farmers in the already heavily irrigated region between Delhi and the dam need more water, so it will not release water for Delhi. Haryana routinely overdraws its quota of water from the Yamuna so Delhi's water treatment plants wont function. Large builders in Delhi, who decide the fate of hundreds of acres of land, say rooftop water harvesting will not work – it's not a solution to the city's water problems. Who wants ugly pipes running up and down pretty architect-designed massive flatted complexes? They can instead dig a tubewell and draw water from underground. That is a surer solution, perhaps.

The average urbanite wastes 40 percent of water he or she uses. Cars are washed, when they could be wiped. Taps are left running while brushing teeth, when they could be turned off. Washing machines run with a fraction of their rated loads. Plants need watering, coolers need filling, courtyards need washing. Then water is needed for construction, malls and hotels. In all of these, urbanites use far more than they need. After all, another dam can be built and its 'those' people who will have to pay.

It's not just end-users who are wasteful. Leaky pipes, tapped pipes and public taps that don't close are equally responsible for wastage in all of India's towns and cities. Tankers that supply water spills hundreds of litres while filling and transporting water – they still remain a profitable business.

All this prompts the World Bank and Asian Development Bank to say that improved (read private) water supply in cities will bring down the cost of supply while providing better and more reliable service. They quote studies in their defence where Mrs. X, mother of 5 living in a Mexico city slum, used to pay $ Y for Z litres of water a day. Then water supply was privatized and presto, she now pays $ Y/10 for Z litres of water. She saves time that goes into earning more money. Sure thing, but what happens to a whole lot of others who used to get water free. They also pay for the same service level. And the water utility that has raised charges many times in the past two years to increase its profits – that is after all why private enterprise exists. Maybe private water utilities in cities are the only way to force people to appreciate the true value of water.

The government continues with its idiotic obsession with large projects. River Inter Linking and big dams remain high on its agenda, now underwritten by fatter World Bank and ADB budgets – almost as if to say that they endorse what the government of India is doing. It is easier for them to support large projects than many small ones, purely because they are high-cost inefficient lending structures of a bygone age. They are jacking up lending to the water sector to remain relevant in today's world. In an increasingly private sector dominated economy, WB and ADB feel their funds can help leverage larger kitties for big projects. This, they hope, will keep them in business because, after all, they have to lend to credible government to make their balance sheets look good.

They are cold blooded about it. "We find ourselves irrelevant and have decided therefore to jack up lending to the water sector," is how a senior ADB official put it. It was an ego problem for the man to come to the negotiating table with less money than the government could put up. "The government told us they don't need us," he choked.

What the people need is a proactive policy to revive and maintain water harvesting structures. This isn't possible without government support as the government has replaced the rulers who made most of these structures possible. Occasional meetings of surface water harvesting councils, a pittance in the budget towards reviving water harvesting structures and a moribund irrigation department won't do. A better though out, integrated set of policies – and replacing the current water policy – is needed to pull our traditions out of the mud.

The government can do it. It has shown the rare drop of compassion and understanding that indicates that everything isn't lost. But that drop has to break the mould in which bureaucrats, politicians and their pet contractors have set themselves in. It also has to break down the self-imposed separation and defeatist attitude of people. One side has to blink first – I would suspect this has to be the government because the problems began from there.

There are isolated instances across the country where good work is happening to restore our heritage. The Dhan Foundation in Madurai, Peaceful Society in Goa, Tarun Bharat Sangh in Rajasthan. But these are proverbial drops in the ocean. NGOs too need to set aside their egos to cooperate effectively; otherwise they become pawns in the power games the bureaucracy plays so well.

If they do link together, and link with the people, and the government wakes up even in fits and starts, there is no reason to suspect that the wisdom of ages will die away. It may live to see another millennium. India may be able to harvest 40 percent of the rainwater that falls on its surface, instead of barely 15 percent it manages now. Then, and not when large project are pursued, will floods and droughts become a thing of the past. Then we will have ensured our food security and the future of our people.

ABOUT NITYA JACOB

I am the programme director for water with the Centre for Science and Environment. My job involves advocacy and research work of the Centre on water, sanitation and waste water to improve water-sewage service delivery and equity.

Earlier, I worked as the Resource person of the Water Community, the UN's knowledge management (KM) programme that helps individuals and institutions expand their activities and horizons. My work informed policy and programs of the government, NGOs and donors. I brought out publications that reflected state-of-the-sector knowledge on water management, governance and conflicts. For example, I facilitated e-consultations to seek provide the government inputs for the development of India's five year plan.

I have written extensively on India's traditional water wisdom, rural governance and trends in rural development. I have been writing on environment, health and social trends as well as on business topics for nearly 25 years. My essay was published in an UN-sponsored publication Water Voices From Around The World.

I have a Bachelor's degree in Sociology and a master's degree in mass communication. I have an advanced certificate in integrated water resources management.

Made in the USA
Middletown, DE
28 October 2023